RIDER

The Vision of Dhamma
Buddhist Writings of Nyanaponika Thera

Edited, with an introduction
by Bhikkhu Bodhi

Foreword by Erich Fromm

RIDER
London Melbourne Auckland Johannesburg

First published in 1986 by Rider & Co. Ltd,
an imprint of Century Hutchinson Ltd, Brookmount House,
62–65 Chandos Place,
Covent Garden, London WC2N 4NW

Century Hutchinson Publishing Group Australia Pty Ltd
PO Box 496, 16–22 Church Street, Hawthorn, Melbourne, Victoria 3122

Century Hutchinson Group (NZ) Ltd
PO Box 40–086, Glenfield, Auckland 10, New Zealand

Century Hutchinson Group South Africa (Pty) Ltd
PO Box 337, Bergvlei 2012, South Africa

Set by Deltatype, Ellesmere Port
Printed and bound in Great Britain by
Anchor Brendon Ltd, Tiptree, Essex

British Library Cataloguing in Publication Data

Nyanaponika, Thera
The vision of Dhamma. Buddist writings of
Nyanaponika Thera.
1. Theravada Buddhism
I. Title   II. Bodhi, Bikku
294.3'91 BQ7185

ISBN 0–7126–9537–0

Contents

Foreword

That in a world in which there are no values except success, no norms except the commandment to increase production and consumption endlessly, a society in which men change themselves completely to manipulated tastes and to public opinion – that in such a world a need arises to find again a meaning to life and a longing becomes felt for some kind of religious renaissance, this is only too understandable. Christianity and Judaism today have little attraction for the young generation, perhaps because of their authoritarian and anti-rational elements. The attraction of Far Eastern religions, especially of Buddhism and Zen Buddhism, and of Far Eastern techniques like Yoga and Meditation is considerably greater.

Unfortunately, but not surprisingly, this interest is misused by cults which are not serious and partly even sheer swindle. These cults appeal to the same weaknesses that they promise to 'cure'; instead of furthering a new development through insight and activity, they influence the average man by mass suggestion, by dependence on so-called masters, by stultifying methods of contemporary industrial and political propaganda. To 'cure' becomes big business. Often it is enough to come from India in order to establish oneself as a guru and to gain influence over hundreds or thousands of people.

It is against this background that one has to understand the significance of the person and the work of Nyanaponika Thera. He is a scholar, a teacher, a helper – no guru, no 'leader' and no seducer. As a scholar he is one of the most outstanding members of the Theravāda school in Sri Lanka, and his translations of classic works of Buddhism into German and English are a cultural achievement of great significance. He himself has the traits of all great scholars in all cultures: he is objective, unfanatical, reliable to the smallest detail and modest. Important as his transmission of Buddhist texts into Western languages is, of even greater importance is his role as teacher and helper. I know of no other book about Buddhism comparable to *The Heart of Buddhist Meditation* in presenting with such lucidity the essential thoughts of this 'atheistic religion' which appears so paradoxical to the Westerner. His style is always simple, but it is that simplicity which emanates only from a person who has mastered a complex subject so thoroughly that he can express it simply. The reader will do well if, as I have, he reads and rereads many paragraphs and passages again and again in order to understand the author fully. His style corresponds to another trait of his personality; he wants to convince without overpowering – his person disappears behind the logic of his argument. Those who want to subject themselves to a guru, who find the truth in mystification, will soon put aside his writings.

Nyanaponika Thera – in this respect also a true pupil of the Buddha – does not only want to teach; he wants to help, to cure and to show the disciple the way to cure himself. Perhaps he would not have fulfilled this task as adequately as he has done had he not – as a European born at the beginning of the twentieth century – acquired a deep knowledge of the psychological problems of contemporary man. So-called 'religious problems' as such do not exist for him. They are the expression of human problems and on this level Nyanaponika Thera shows that he is a first class psychologist or, to put it perhaps better, philosophical anthropologist. He understands man – the basic condition of his existence, his passions and anxieties – so deeply, that he can present Buddism as the answer to the spiritual needs of men of today – or perhaps even of tomorrow.

Indeed, the writings of Nyanaponika Thera are a 'Guide for the Perplexed' in the last quarter of this century. They are exactly the opposite of the popular cults. In his book on Buddhist meditation mentioned above, he has succeeded in describing the method of genuine meditation so clearly that it is accessible to anyone who is serious and does not shy away from the effort. But far beyond meditation, Nyanaponika Thera has emphasized those elements in Buddhism that appeal to the best qualities of contemporary sober, critical and yet longing man: rationality, independence, the giving up of illusions and submission to authorities and the full grasp of inner reality. (Here is a point where Buddhists' self-examination and psychoanalysis as I understand it, touch each other.) Nyanaponika

Thera, in contrast to so many false interpretations, has emphasized that peace and joy, not destruction and nihilism, are essential for the 'feeling-world'. He has emphasized especially that Buddhism does not only want to help those who strive for the absolute goal – Nirvāṇa – (and even few of those reach it), but also those who (in his own words) strive to 'know themselves, if but temporarily and partially, to be free from the slavery of passions and the blindness of self-deception; to be masters of themselves and to live and think in the light of knowledge'.

This is not the place to present the picture of Buddhism as Nyanaponika Thera has given it. I also cannot pursue the thought to show on which points I differ from Buddhist doctrine in its totality. Such a task would require a detailed analysis of the difference between the position of radical humanism and Buddhist teaching, a task which could only be solved in the frame of reference of a special book. I can only report that acquaintance with Nyanaponika Thera's work has given me many significant insights and that, of the people to whom I have recommended his books for study, quite a few have reported to me that these works were the beginning of a new orientation and a new practice. I am convinced that Nyanaponika Thera's work may become one of the most important contributions to the spiritual renewal of the West, if it can only reach the knowledge of a sufficient number of people.

Erich Fromm

This essay was originally published in German under the title 'Die Bedeutung des Ehrwürdigen Nyanaponika Mahāthera für die westliche Welt' ('The Significance of Nyanaponika Mahāthera for the West') in *Des Geistes Gleichmass. Festschrift zum 75. Geburtstag des Ehrwürdigen Nyanaponika Mahāthera.* (Verlag Christiani, Konstanz, 1976.)

A Note on Sources

The record of the Buddha's teachings upon which the Ven. Nyanaponika's writings are based is the Pāli Canon, the primary scriptural authority for Theravāda Buddhism. Preserved in the ancient Pāli language, which many Theravādins regard as the tongue used by the Buddha himself, this Canon comprises three divisions, the *Tipiṭaka* or 'Three Baskets' of the doctrine: (I) the *Vinaya Piṭaka*, the Division of Discipline, containing the rules of conduct governing the monastic order; (II) the *Sutta Piṭaka*, the Division of Discourses, containing the Buddha's sermons and dialogues; and (III) the *Abhidhamma Piṭaka*, the Division of Higher Doctrine, which presents the teachings from a strictly systematic philosophical point of view.

Though the Ven. Nyanaponika has been a keen student of the Abhidhamma, as evidenced by his German translations of several Abhidhamma texts and his *Abhidhamma Studies*, his primary inspiration in the works collected here comes from the Sutta Piṭaka. This division consists of five collections: (1) the *Dīgha Nikāya*, the Collection of Long Discourses; (2) the *Majjhima Nikāya*, the Collection of Middle Length Discourses; (3) the *Saṁyutta Nikāya*, the Collection of Grouped Discourses, comprising shorter discourses arranged according to subject matter; (4) the *Aṅguttara Nikāya*, the Collection of Numerical Discourses, comprising shorter discourses arranged according to a numerical pattern ranging from one to eleven; and (5) the *Khuddaka Nikāya*, the Miscellaneous Collection, containing minor anthologies of verse, stories, treatises and other texts. In this last collection four works figure prominently in the Ven. Nyanaponika's writings: the well-known *Dhammapada*; the *Sutta Nipāta*, an anthology of verse with a distinct emphasis on the ancient ascetic ideal; and the *Udāna* and the *Itivuttaka*, two books of short discourses each ending with an inspirational verse.

In the writings included here, references to the Dīgha Nikāya, the Majjhima Nikāya, the Udāna and the Itivuttaka indicate the number of the sutta within the collection; to the Saṁyutta Nikāya, the chapter followed by the number of the sutta within the chapter; to the Aṅguttara Nikāya, the numerical division followed by the number of the sutta within that division; and to the Dhammapada and the Sutta Nipāta, the number of the verse. Unless otherwise indicated, all translations are the Ven. Nyanaponika's own.

The Ven. Nyanaponika's work also draws heavily upon the commentaries to the Pāli Canon, most of which were composed by the great Theravāda Buddhist scholiast, Ācariya Buddhaghosa, on the basis of the ancient exegetical texts he found in Sri Lanka when he arrived there from India in the fifth century CE. The most important commentarial work, both for the Theravāda tradition as a whole and for the Ven. Nyanaponika, is the *Visuddhimagga*, a virtual encyclopedia of Theravāda doctrine and meditation. This has been published by the Buddhist Publication Society in an excellent translation by the late English scholar-monk, the Ven. Bhikkhu Ñāṇamoli, under the title *The Path of Purification* (1975). With one exception – a passage in 'The Threefold Refuge' written even before the Ven. Ñāṇamoli's work appeared – all the citations from the *Visuddhimagga* incorporated here are taken from this edition.

Although in the West several Buddhist doctrinal terms are better known in their Sanskrit forms than in the Pāli, it was felt that, because the Theravāda tradition assigns them very specific meanings not always matched with the same precision by the Sanskrit, the Pāli should be consistently retained throughout. The most important of these, followed by their Sanskrit equivalents, are: Dhamma-Dharma, kamma-karma and Nibbāna-Nirvāṇa.

Introduction

Buddhism is essentially a path to inner freedom which centres upon the discipline of seeing. What lies at its core, beneath its sometimes bewildering profusion of forms and doctrines, is a liberative vision to be cultivated by an arduous yet meticulously methodical course of training. This vision, which gradually alters one's most basic conceptions and attitudes, runs through every stage of the genuine Buddhist path, from the first glimmer of understanding which induces a person to enter the path right through to the indubitable knowledge of deliverance which consummates it. In the special terminology of the tradition it is called the vision of Dhamma: a penetrating insight into the nature of things as they really are independently of our grasping, wishful thinking and manipulative activity governed by self-serving ends.

The transmission of Buddhism from generation to generation, and from one geographical region to another, ultimately depends upon the transmission of this vision, without which there will be only the passing on of lifeless forms, not the communication of living Dhamma – the truth which quickens, elevates and liberates. Particularly at the present critical juncture of Buddhist history, when the future of Buddhism in its Asian homelands is seriously jeopardized both from within and from without, and thirst for a knowledge of its teachings becomes increasingly more acute in the West, the revitalization of the Buddhist vision and its articulation in a language relevant to the pressing existential problems of our age has become an urgent necessity. But unlike institutes and temples, the vision of Dhamma cannot be moulded and managed by organized bodies for collective purposes. By its very nature it is unavoidably personal and thus can only be transmitted by those individuals, specially endowed, who have opened to it and made it the vital centre of their lives.

One such individual in our own time, and one of the major bridge-builders in the Western encounter with Buddhism, is the German-born Buddhist monk, the Venerable Nyanaponika Thera.[1] A distinguished member of the Theravāda Buddhist Saṅgha (monastic order) in Sri Lanka for almost fifty years, the Ven. Nyanaponika is best known among general readers of Buddhist literature in the West as the author of *The Heart of Buddhist Meditation*, a work which has already acquired the status of a modern classic and is widely regarded as the most lucid and reliable exposition in English on Satipaṭṭhāna, the meditative practice of right mindfulness. Westerners with a specific interest in Theravāda Buddhism often know of the Ven. Nyanaponika by way of his other accomplishments as well: his numerous tracts and essays on Theravāda Buddhist doctrine and practice, his limpid translations into English and German of scriptures from the Pāli Canon and his prodigious labours in establishing and directing the Buddhist Publication Society (BPS) in Kandy, Sri Lanka, which he has served continuously as President and Editor-in-Chief since its founding in 1958. But all these concrete manifest achievements of the Ven. Nyanaponika spring from another achievement, indiscernible in itself, which infuses and animates them from within. This other achievement is his own accession to the Buddhist vision of Dhamma: the thoroughness with which he has absorbed it, internalized it and brought it into accord with a highly astute Western mind, and then given expression to it in works which touch contemporary man in the depths of his spiritual crisis, inviting, inspiring and gently yet confidently leading him to share that vision and to experience its healing, liberating efficacy.

The Ven. Nyanaponika's vision of Dhamma, as revealed in his writings, has all the qualities of good ocular vision. In its lucidity it has the quality of clarity; in its exactness and fidelity to fact, the quality of accuracy; in its penetration to the fundamental truths of existence, the quality of depth; in its discernment of long-term consequences and goals, the quality of distance; and in its encompassment of a wide range of human concerns, the quality of breadth. Moreover, somewhat analogously to the brain's capacity to fuse into one the dual images conveyed to it by the two optic nerves, the Ven. Nyanaponika displays a remarkable ability, in his thought and literary work as much as in his person, to harmonize antitheses and turn them into complements; it is this, in fact, which makes him so versatile as an interpreter of Buddhism to the West. He brings together the rational, analytical and critical faculties of the European mind with the concrete and intuitive faculties of the Asian mind; the detachment and objectivity of a scholar with the devoted commitment of a practising monk; the capacity for cool, unsentimental inquiry with a warm, heartfelt concern for the well-being of his fellow men; a clear perception of man's predicament in its private depths with a comprehensive view of the social, political and historical dimensions of the human condition. And throughout his writings, no matter how intellectual and scholarly he may at times become, he never allows the theoretical investigations and textual analysis to dominate as ends in themselves, but always keeps them subordinate to the controlling aim of the Dhamma: the understanding of the way to deliverance from suffering.

Over the years, while serving as Editor-in-Chief for the Buddhist Publication Society, the Ven. Nyanaponika has continued to expound and interpret the Dhamma through his writings published by the Society in its two series of booklets, The WHEEL and BODHI LEAVES. To date these works have remained separate and scattered – as individual booklets, introductions to compilations of Buddhist texts or contributions to anthologies. When viewed in their totality, however, they present us with one of the most mature, comprehensive and authoritative contemporary expressions of Buddhism, a vision of Dhamma at once distinctly personal yet representative of the authentic Buddhist tradition at its best.

It is the purpose of the present book to bring together, between the covers of a single volume, the works of the Ven. Nyanaponika that have appeared in the BPS's WHEEL and BODHI LEAVES series. The book includes all his original writings published in these two series except some biographical tracts on eminent disciples of the Buddha, an allegorical essay ('The City of the Mind') and his introductions to translations of individual Buddhist suttas; the latter, though often illuminating, remain too closely tied to the texts they explicate to stand by themselves as independent essays. As can be seen, the Ven. Nyanaponika is not a prolific writer, but what he lacks in verbosity is more than compensated for by other features of his work: by its depth and concentration of thought, its clear and clarifying insights and its wise, sympathetic counsel. Coming from a Westerner with a full life's experience in the Buddhist monastic order, the value of his writing is further enhanced for the growing number of Westerners seeking to understand the Buddhist experience on its own terms and to assimilate it to their more familiar frame of reference. It is a small but telling indication of the effect his writing has had that after the publication of *The Heart of Buddhist Meditation* several readers of the book, having no prior acquaintance with the author but moved to write to him, spontaneously and independently began their letters with the address 'Dear Teacher'.

The remainder of this Introduction will provide the reader with a brief biographical sketch of the Ven. Nyanaponika, an overview of the Theravāda Buddhist teaching which inspires and informs his vision of Dhamma, and some background information on the works included in this anthology.

LIFE SKETCH

The person who was to become the Great Elder Nyanaponika was born in 1901 in Hanau, Germany, with the name Siegmund Feniger. His Jewish parents gave him a traditional religious upbringing and even at a young age he evinced a keen personal interest in religion. In his late teens, soon after he started work in the book trade, disturbing religious doubts stirred him to an intense spiritual search, in the course of which he came across books on Buddhism. The new discovery had an immediate appeal, and his confidence in the teaching grew stronger the more he read until by his twentieth year he already considered himself a convinced Buddhist.

For the first few years his Buddhist interest had to be pursued alone, without a teacher or even a sympathetic friend. But a family move to Berlin in 1921 brought him into contact with other German Buddhists and several years later, in Königsberg, he himself helped form a Buddhist study circle with a lending library quartered at his father's shop.

During the early days of his reading on Buddhism Siegmund had come across the works of a German monk named Nyanatiloka, who had entered the Order in Burma in 1903, achieved an astonishingly rapid mastery over the canonical Pāli language and risen to eminence as a Buddhist scholar and teacher. His reputation as an authoritative exponent of the Dhamma, enhanced in Europe by his published writings and translations, drew to him a small but steady trickle of earnest

Westerners eager to enter the Order, and to provide for their training he had established a centre for Western monks called Island Hermitage on an island in a lake in southwest Sri Lanka (then a British colony known as Ceylon). Favourable reports about the Ven. Nyanatiloka and his hermitage passed through the German Buddhist circles, and when they reached Siegmund they implanted in his mind an idea which gradually grew into a compelling urge: to go to Asia and become a monk himself.

For several years his plans were delayed by his father's death and by the darkening political conditions in Germany. Thus it was not until early 1936 that he could leave Europe for Sri Lanka, where he joined the Ven. Nyanatiloka at Island Hermitage. After several months of preparatory training, in June 1936 he received the lower ordination (*pabbajjā*) as a novice and the following year the higher ordination (*upasampadā*) as a bhikkhu, a full monk, with the name Nyanaponika, meaning 'flowing towards wisdom'. Under his teacher's guidance he took up the study of Pāli and Theravāda Buddhist doctrine, and on his own studied English, which he had not learned before. Within a short time after completing his basic studies he moved to the temperate upcountry for a period of contemplative living and his first sustained attempts at translating Pāli texts into German.

With the outbreak of war between Germany and England in 1939, the Vens. Nyanatiloka and Nyanaponika, like all German males resident in British colonies, were consigned to internment camps – first in Sri Lanka itself and later at Dehra Dun, in northern India. But undeterred by the difficult circumstances of internment, the scholar-monks pressed on with their work, the Ven. Nyanaponika completing German translations of the Sutta Nipāta, several Abhidhamma treatises and an anthology of texts on Satipaṭṭhāna. Following their release and return to Sri Lanka in 1946, he pursued the lines of inquiry stimulated by his research into the Abhidhamma, the fruits of which came to light in his *Abhidhamma Studies*, a boldly exploratory attempt to uncover the philosophical and psychological implications of this complex systemization of the Buddha's teaching.

The early 1950s brought the Vens. Nyanatiloka and Nyanaponika to Burma for consultations concerning a Great Buddhist Council, the sixth in Theravāda Buddhist history, which the Burmese government was planning to convene in 1954 to review, re-edit and reprint the entire Pāli Canon and its commentaries. When the consultations were over, the Ven. Nyanaponika stayed on in Burma for an extended period of training in insight meditation under the famous meditation master, the Ven. Mahāsi Sayadaw. This experience, which impressed him profoundly, moved him to write *The Heart of Buddhist Meditation* to make available to others the benefits of Buddhist mental training. In 1954 teacher and pupil returned to Burma for the opening ceremonies of the council, and in 1956 the Ven. Nyanaponika went back alone for the closing ceremonies. Unless there were Greek monks at the Third Council in India, the two German elders were the first Westerners ever to participate in a major convocation of Theravāda Buddhism.

The most significant turn in the Ven. Nyanaponika's career as an exponent of the Buddha's teaching came in 1958, shortly after the passing away of his teacher, when together with two lay friends from Kandy, he founded the Buddhist Publication Society. Originally the founders formed the Society with the idea of issuing only a limited number of booklets on the basic principles of Buddhism, but the response to their first publications was enthusiastic beyond their expectations and encouraged them to continue. Thus the BPS lived on and steadily grew.

In his earlier works written before the BPS was formed, the Ven. Nyanaponika had been developing a vision of the Buddha's teaching as the most viable solution to the crisis and confusion faced by modern man: an experiential, practicable way for man to rediscover a genuine meaning to his existence and to restrain the hatred, cruelty and violence so rampant in the modern world. Now, as President and Editor-in-Chief of the new Society, the Ven. Nyanaponika found himself presented with the opportunity to transform this vision from the personal guideline of his own expository writing into the governing philosophy of an entire publishing enterprise aimed at an incipient worldwide interest in Buddhism. To meet the occasion, the Ven. Nyanaponika applied himself so completely to his work for the BPS that his own personal biography almost disappears in its larger history. He wrote tracts himself, commissioned works from other Buddhist writers, collected and translated suttas, compiled anthologies relating Buddhism to issues of contemporary concern, reissued old Buddhist classics long out of print and scouted fledgling authors whom he encouraged to mature their talent and contribute to the Society. The measure of his success in accomplishing his aim is indicated by the success of the BPS itself which today, after twenty-six years of development under his leadership, has become the world's most prolific publisher of Theravāda Buddhist literature in English. Its vast range of publications, highly esteemed for their authenticity, high literary standard and instructional value, constitute a voluminous library covering virtually all aspects of Theravāda Buddhism.

THE THERAVĀDA TEACHING

The Ven. Nyanaponika writes as a Theravāda Buddhist monk, and though his essays are all fully intelligible in themselves, a short summary of the Theravāda Buddhist teaching will enrich their meaning for the reader by showing the background out of which they emerge and the body of doctrine they are intended to expound and explore. Theravāda Buddhism, the 'Doctrine of the Elders', is the oldest continuous Buddhist tradition and the one which has preserved most carefully the original teachings of the historical Buddha. Prevalent today with a striking uniformity of observance in Sri Lanka, Burma and Thailand, the Theravāda is distinguished from the schools of its northern and Far Eastern counterpart, Mahāyāna Buddhism, by its conservative doctrinal stand, realistic world view, anti-speculative empiricism and consistent stress on individual responsibility. But though from one angle the Theravāda may be considered only one school of Buddhism among others, as the preserver of the Buddha's original teachings it may also be regarded as the fountainhead of the entire Buddhist heritage from which all other forms of Buddhism emerge.

In its conception of the Buddha, the salient feature of the Theravāda is its emphasis on his humanity and full historicity. For the Theravādin, the Buddha who lived and taught in northern India in the fifth century BC was not a god, divine incarnation or cosmic principle made manifest in flesh. He was first and foremost a man who found the way to release from suffering, and his attainment of Enlightenment beneath the Bodhi Tree was a human attainment accomplished by his own exertion, rigorous self-discipline and probing intellectual analysis. In relation to the world his function is not that of a saviour but of a teacher. Out of compassion for others he makes known the path that leads to the end of suffering, and it is left to each individual who seeks that goal to walk the path himself, in reliance upon his own strength and wisdom and, of course, the guidance given by the Buddha.

The Buddha's teaching, called the Dhamma, is the doctrine of deliverance which he himself discovered through his Enlightenment and proclaimed on the basis of his own clear comprehension of reality. The most concise expression of the Dhamma, its unifying framework, is the teaching of the Four Noble Truths: suffering, its origin, its cessation and the way leading to its cessation. This was the great realization that broke upon the Buddha's mind as he sat in meditation under the Bodhi Tree after six hard years of striving. It is not only the formulated content of his Enlightenment, but the ongoing significance of his message to the world, setting forth the crucial undeceptive truths upon which the whole prospect of man's deliverance depends.

The four truths all revolve around the recognition of suffering (*dukkha*) as the central problem of human existence, and in the first truth the Buddha enumerates its diverse forms:

> What now is the noble truth of suffering? Birth is suffering; decay is suffering; death is suffering; sorrow, lamentation, pain, grief and despair are suffering; not to get what one wants is suffering; in short, the five aggregates of clinging are suffering.

This last clause – referring to a fivefold grouping of all the factors of existence – implies a deeper dimension to suffering than is covered by our ordinary ideas of pain, sorrow and despondancy. What it points to, as the fundamental meaning of the first noble truth, is the unsatisfactoriness and radical inadequacy of everything conditioned, owing to the fact that whatever is conditioned is impermanent and ultimately bound to perish. This aspect of suffering comes to light most clearly in the most comprehensive manifestation of impermanence and peril: the beginningless round of rebirths in which all living beings revolve, *saṁsāra*. Thus, to appreciate the first noble truth in its full depth and range, it is not enough to consider merely the sufferings of a single lifetime. One must take into account the entire round of becoming with its ever-repeated phases of birth, ageing, sickness and death.

In the second noble truth the Buddha traces suffering to its origin or cause, which he identifies as craving (*taṇhā*):

> What now is the noble truth of the origin of suffering? It is craving, which gives rise to repeated existence, is bound up with pleasure and lust, and always seeks fresh enjoyment here and there; that is, sensual craving, craving for existence and craving for non-existence.

Itself the product of ignorance, an unawareness of the true nature of things, craving springs up wherever there is the prospect of pleasure and enjoyment, bringing along with it the multitude of mental defilements responsible for so much human misery: greed and ambition, hatred and anger, selfishness and envy, conceit, vanity and pride.

Craving gives rise to suffering, not only by engendering the immediate pain of want, the sense of lack, but more specifically in the context of the four truths by generating rebirth and thus maintaining bondage to saṁsāra. But the process of rebirth, in the Buddhist view, does not involve the transmigration of a self or soul, for the thesis that everything is in flux precludes a durable entity passing from life to life. Continuity through the sequence of rebirths is maintained, not by a self-identical ego subsisting through the change, but by the transmission of impressions and tendencies along the individual 'mental continuum' or stream of consciousness in which they arise. The direction the continuum takes from life to life is governed by a force called *kamma*, a word meaning volitional action. According to the teaching on kamma, it is our own willed actions, bodily, verbal and mental, that determine the forms of existence we assume in each of our successive sojourns through saṁsāra. The law connecting the two is essentially moral in its mode of operation: good actions lead to happiness and higher forms of rebirth, bad actions to misery and lower forms of rebirth. But whether one's destiny moves upwards or downwards, as long as craving and ignorance persist in the deep recesses of the mind, the cycle of birth and death, the great round of suffering, will continue to turn.

This cycle, however, does not have to go on forever, and in the third noble truth the Buddha announces the key to stopping it:

> What now is the noble truth of the cessation of suffering? It is the complete fading away and cessation of craving, its

forsaking and abandonment, liberation and detachment from it.

Since suffering arises through craving, with the destruction of craving suffering too must cease: a relationship as tight and inevitable as logical law. The state that then supervenes, the goal of all striving for Theravāda Buddhism, is *Nibbāna*, the Unconditioned, the Deathless, the imperishable peace beyond the round of birth and death. The attainment of Nibbāna takes place in two stages. The first is the 'Nibbāna element with a residue remaining', the liberation of mind achieved when all defilements have been extinguished but the mind-body combination brought into being at birth continues to live on until the end of the lifespan. The second is the 'Nibbāna element with no residue remaining', the liberation from existence itself, the cessation of becoming attained with the Liberated One's final passing away.

In the fourth noble truth the Buddha teaches the way to Nibbāna, 'the way leading to the cessation of suffering'. This is the Noble Eightfold Path with its eight factors arranged into three groups thus:

1. Right understanding ⎫
2. Right thought ⎭ III. Wisdom (*paññā*)

3. Right speech ⎫
4. Right action ⎬ I. Morality (*sīla*)
5. Right livelihood ⎭

6. Right effort ⎫
7. Right mindfulness ⎬ II. Concentration (*samādhi*)
8. Right concentration ⎭

The path begins with the minimal degree of right understanding and right thought needed to take up the training, and then unfolds through its three groups as a systematic strategy designed to uproot the defilements that generate suffering. Morality restrains the defilements in their coarsest form, their outflow in unwholesome actions; concentration removes their more refined manifestations as distractive and restless thoughts; and wisdom eradicates their subtle latent tendencies by penetrating with direct insight the three basic facts of existence, summed up by the Buddha in the three characteristics of impermanence, suffering and egolessness.

To each of the four truths the Buddha assigns a specific function, a task to be mastered by the disciple in training. The truth of suffering is to be fully understood, the craving and defilements which originate it are to be abandoned, Nibbāna as deliverance from suffering is to be realized and the Noble Eightfold Path that leads to deliverance is to be developed. The individual who has completed these four functions is the ideal figure of Theravāda Buddhism. This is the *Arahat*, the Liberated One, who has broken all bonds binding to the round of becoming and lives in the experienced freedom of Nibbāna.

THE PRESENT ANTHOLOGY

It only remains for us to add some background information on the pieces to follow and to relate them briefly to the framework we have just sketched of Theravāda Buddhist teaching.

'The Worn-out Skin' is a series of contemplations on the Uraga Sutta, an ancient Buddhist poem from the Sutta Nipāta, which, as we noted above, the Ven. Nyanaponika translated into German in its entirety during the war years. The poem describes the striving of a monk intent on discarding all defilements and delusions to win deliverance from the dualities of conditioned existence. The Ven. Nyanaponika's commentary on the poem is a powerful expression of his understanding of Dhamma which shows the richness, depth and psychological acuity of his thought, and his endeavour to relate Buddhist insights to the Western intellectual tradition as well as to everyday experience.

'The Power of Mindfulness', like *The Heart of Buddhist Meditation*, is concerned with the practice of right mindfulness, seventh factor of the Noble Eightfold Path. It differs from the larger work in its more specialized scope: whereas *The Heart of Buddhist Meditation* explores mindfulness in a comprehensive manner, treating the specific factor of right mindfulness in conjunction with the other components of the path and covering the full range of its application, 'The Power of Mindfulness' aims at investigating its potential in its own right, as the single faculty of bare attention, and at demonstrating the reasons for its subdued but momentous efficacy in promoting mental purification.

'The Roots of Good and Evil' consists of a selection of texts from the Buddha's discourses and their commentaries, introduced and translated by the Ven. Nyanaponika and interlaced with his own comments and elucidations. Throughout his writings the Ven. Nyanaponika has always placed great stress on the Buddha's teaching on the roots as affording a highly direct psychological and ethical perspective on the same basic doctrinal material covered by the Four Noble Truths. He was particularly troubled by the absence of any detailed treatment of this subject in Western books on Buddhism, including large works on Buddhist ethics, and to fill the void prepared this collection himself. The original WHEEL booklet contains forty-five texts, of which only the thirty-five the Ven. Nyanaponika felt were most important have been retained here.

The next selection, 'The Four Nutriments of Life', was included only after some hesitation. At first we were apprehensive that the essay, and the Buddha's discourse which it explicates, might be medicine just too powerful for a Western readership with little prior exposure to the Dhamma. But after some deliberation it was decided that the very reason we considered excluding it – its stark revelation of the tremendous danger inherent in the apparently innocuous and enjoyable routine functions of life – was an even better reason for including it, serving as it does to shake the unthinking complacency with which we go about our usual business in the world and to point to the abyss of suffering over which we perpetually hover. The original WHEEL included a selection of suttas along with copious extracts from the commentaries, of which only the 'Discourse on Son's Flesh', directly connected with the essay, has been kept.

Having pursued the truth of suffering downwards to its darkest and most chastening depths, with the next three pieces we enter the upwards swing of the teaching, corresponding to the latter two noble truths: the path and the goal. The essay 'The Threefold Refuge' deals with the first step to be taken at the very entry to the Buddhist path, the going for refuge to the Triple Gem – the Buddha, Dhamma and Sangha; its inspiring presentation calls attention to the often overlooked devotional side of Theravāda and helps correct the widespread misconception that Theravāda Buddhism is a predominately intellectual, ascetic system lacking emotional fervour. This corrective continues with the next selection, 'The Four Sublime States', a series of contemplations – almost prose poems – on the elevated, expansive states of consciousness attainable when the confining barriers of egocentric grasping fall away and a capacity develops to participate in and share, intensely yet detachedly, the happiness and suffering of others. The last full-length essay, 'Anattā and Nibbāna', marshals the author's masterly knowledge of the Theravāda tradition to tackle the difficult and often perplexing problem of the relation between these two cardinal Buddhist tenets: the doctrine of egolessness as the basic philosophical standpoint and the conception of Nibbāna as the final goal of striving.

Of the shorter essays, 'Seeing Things As They Are' is a slightly expanded version of the author's preface to a three-volume anthology he edited entitled *The Three Basic Facts of Existence*. 'Buddhism and the God-Idea' and 'Contemplation of Feeling' were introductions to anthologies of suttas; 'Devotion in Buddhism' and 'Kamma and its Fruit' contributions to anthologies of essays concerned with those themes. 'Courageous Faith' and 'Why End Suffering?' appeared in the WHEEL *The City of the Mind and Other Writings*, and 'Protection through Right Mindfulness' as a BODHI LEAF.

In concluding, the editor wishes to express his gratitude to the two people whose unfailing help facilitated the preparation of this volume. One is the Ven. Nyanaponika Thera himself, his own chief *kalyāṇa mitta* (noble friend) for the past decade, who even when pressed with other duties was always ready to lay them aside to review material being compiled and to offer his advice and suggestions so that the resulting book would turn out exactly in accordance with his wishes. The other is Mrs. Helen Wilder, a devoted friend and helper of the Ven. Nyanaponika and an editorial reader for the BPS. It was she who first suggested to the editor the idea of collecting the Ven. Nyanaponika's writings, and her capable and dedicated assistance from start to finish enabled the undertaking to proceed far more smoothly than would have otherwise been possible.

The editor's thanks are also due to Liepman AG, Zürich, the literary agents for the Estate of Erich Fromm, for their permission to use the late Dr. Fromm's essay, 'Die Bedeutung des Ehrwürdigen Nyanaponika Mahāthera für die westliche Welt' ('The Significance of Nyanaponika Mahāthera for the West'), as a foreword to the present volume.

Bhikkhu Bodhi

Notes

1. The monastic name proper is Nyanaponika. The word 'Thera' is a title meaning Elder, given to a monk who has attained ten years' standing in the Order. Strictly speaking, as one with more than twenty years' standing, the Ven. Nyanaponika is a Mahāthera, a Great Elder. But to maintain consistency with his name as it appears in earlier writings he has himself retained the title 'Thera' through the years and his own usage is followed here.

The Worn-Out Skin

Introduction

The Sutta Nipāta, in its oldest and most characteristic parts, is a deeply stirring 'Song of Freedom'. The verses of this ancient book are a challenging call to us to leave behind the narrow confines of our imprisoned existence with its ever-growing walls of accumulated habits of life and thought. They beckon us to free ourselves from the enslavement to our passions and to our thousand little whims and wishes.

A call to freedom is always timely because in our lives we constantly bind ourselves to this and that, or let ourselves be bound in various ways by others and by circumstances. To some extent, normal life cannot entirely escape from such a situation. In fact, 'binding' oneself to a worthy task and duty or to an ennobling human relationship is an indispensable antidote to the opposite tendency: the dissipation of our energies. The physical act of walking consists not only in the 'freeing' action of lifting and stretching the foot, but also in the 'binding' function of lowering it and placing it firmly on the ground. Analagously, in mental movement, there is the same need for support as well as for uplift and forward advancement.

But, having the comfort of a 'secure footing' in life, we too easily forget to walk on. Instead, we prefer to 'strengthen our position', to improve and embellish the little cage we build for ourselves out of habits, ideas and beliefs. Once we have settled down in our habitual ways of living and thinking, we feel less and less inclined to give them up for the sake of risky ventures into a freedom of life and thought full of dangers and uncertainties. True freedom places on us the uncomfortable burden of ever-fresh responsible decisions, which have to be guided by mindfulness, wisdom and human sympathy. Few are willing to accept the full weight of such a burden. Instead, they prefer to be led and bound by the rules given by others, and by habits mainly dominated by self-interest and social conventions. With the habituation to a life of inner and outer bondage, there grows what Erich Fromm calls a 'fear of freedom'. Such fear, if allowed to persist and take root, inevitably leads to a stagnation of our inner growth and creativeness as well as to a stagnant society and culture. In a state of stagnation, toxic elements will endanger mankind's healthy progress – physical and mental, social and spiritual. Then William Blake's words will prove true: 'Expect poison from stagnant water.'

Those too who say 'Yes' to life and wish to protect mankind from decline by its self-produced toxins – biological and psychological – will also have to shed that 'fear of freedom' and enter freedom's arduous way. It is an arduous way because it demands of us that we break the self-forged fetters of our lusts and hates, our prejudices and dogmas – fetters we foolishly cherish as ornaments. But once we see them for what they really are, obstacles to true freedom, the hard task of discarding them will become at the same time a joyous experience.

The Sutta Nipāta, however, warns repeatedly of *false* ideas of freedom. He is not truly free who only follows his self-willed whims and desires (*chandagu*) (v. 913), who is carried along by them (*chandānunīto*) (v. 731). Nor can true freedom be found by those who only seek to exchange one bondage for another:

Leaving the old through craving for the new –
Pursuit of longings never from bondage frees;
It is but letting go to grasp afresh
As monkeys reach from branch to branch of trees.

(v. 791)

Mankind is always in need of both lawgivers and liberators. It is for echoing the voice of that great liberator, the Buddha, that the following pages have been written as a humble tribute.

What follows are free musings on the first poem of the Sutta Nipāta, the Uraga Sutta, interspersed with gleanings from the Buddhist texts, which may help to illuminate the verses.

4

Uraga Sutta: The Serpent

1. He who can curb his wrath
    as soon as it arises,
    as a timely antidote will check
    snake's venom that so quickly spreads,
    – such a monk gives up the here and the beyond,
    just as a serpent sheds its worn-out skin.

2. He who entirely cuts off his lust
    as entering a pond one uproots lotus plants,
    – such a monk gives up the here and the beyond,
    just as a serpent sheds its worn-out skin.

3. He who entirely cuts off his craving
    by drying up its fierce and rapid flow,
    – such a monk gives up the here and the beyond,
    just as a serpent sheds its worn-out skin,

4. He who entirely blots out conceit
    as the wind demolishes a fragile bamboo bridge,
    – such a monk gives up the here and the beyond,
    just as a serpent sheds its worn-out skin.

5. He who does not find core or substance
    in any of the realms of being,
    like flowers which are vainly sought
    in fig trees that bear none,
    – such a monk gives up the here and the beyond,
    just as a serpent sheds its worn-out skin.

6. He who bears no grudges in his heart,
    transcending all this 'thus' and 'otherwise',
    – such a monk gives up the here and the beyond,
    just as a serpent sheds its worn-out skin.

7. He who has burned out his evil thoughts,
    entirely cut them off within his heart,
    – such a monk gives up the here and the beyond,
    just as a serpent sheds its worn-out skin.

8. He who neither goes too far nor lags behind,
   entirely transcending the diffuseness of the world,
   – such a monk gives up the here and the beyond,
   just as a serpent sheds its worn-out skin.

9. He who neither goes too far nor lags behind
   and knows about the world: 'This is all unreal',
   – such a monk gives up the here and the beyond,
   just as a serpent sheds its worn-out skin.

10. He who neither goes too far nor lags behind,
    greedless he knows: 'This is all unreal',
    – such a monk gives up the here and the beyond,
    just as a serpent sheds its worn-out skin.

11. He who neither goes too far nor lags behind,
    lust-free he knows: 'This is all unreal',
    – such a monk gives up the here and the beyond,
    just as a serpent sheds its worn-out skin.

12. He who neither goes too far nor lags behind,
    hate-free he knows: 'This is all unreal',
    – such a monk gives up the here and the beyond,
    just as a serpent sheds its worn-out skin.

13. He who neither goes too far nor lags behind,
    delusion-free he knows: 'This is all unreal',
    – such a monk gives up the here and the beyond,
    just as a serpent sheds its worn-out skin.

14. He who has no dormant tendencies whatever,
    whose unwholesome roots have been expunged,
    – such a monk gives up the here and the beyond,
    just as a serpent sheds its worn-out skin.

15. States born of anxiety he harbours none,
    which may condition his return to earth,
    – such a monk gives up the here and the beyond,
    just as a serpent sheds its worn-out skin.

16. States born of attachment he harbours none,
    which cause his bondage to existence,
    – such a monk gives up the here and the beyond,
    just as a serpent sheds its worn-out skin.

17. He who has the five hindrances discarded,
    is doubt-free and serene, and free of inner barbs,
    – such a monk gives up the here and the beyond,
    just as a serpent sheds its worn-out skin.

I   *Reflections on the Refrain*

The refrain:

– such a monk gives up the here and the beyond,
just as a serpent sheds its worn-out skin.

THE SIMILE OF THE SERPENT

The ancient masters of the Theravāda Buddhist tradition
explain the simile of the serpent's worn-out skin, occurring in
the last line of each of the poem's verses, as follows:

The shedding of the serpent's old skin is done in four ways:

(1) in following the law of its own species,
(2) through disgust,
(3) with the help of a support, and
(4) with effort.

(1) 'Its own species' is that of those long-bodied animals,
the snakes. Snakes do not transgress these five characteristics
of their species: in regard to their birth, their death, their
surrendering to a long and deep sleep, their mating with their
own kind only and the shedding of the old worn-out skin.
Hence, in shedding the skin, a snake follows the law of its
kind.

(2) But in doing so, it sheds the old skin also out of disgust.
When only half the body has been freed of the old skin and the
other half is still attached, the snake will feel disgust.

(3) In such disgust, the snake will support its body on a
piece of wood, a root or a stone, and

(4) making an effort, using all its strength, it will wind its
tail around the supporting object, exhale forcefully, expand
its hood and shed the old skin fully. Then it will freely go
wherever it likes.

It is similar with a monk. The 'law of his own species' is
virtue (*sīla*). Standing firm in his own law of virtue, and
seeing the misery involved, he becomes disgusted with the
'old worn-out skin' of 'the here and the beyond', comprising
(such pairs of opposites) as his own and others' personalized
existence, etc., which are productive of suffering. Thus he

becomes disgusted and, seeking the support of a noble friend (a wise teacher and meditation master), he summons his utmost strength by way of the path factor, right effort. Dividing day and night into six periods, during daytime, while walking up and down or sitting, he purifies his mind from obstructive things; doing so also in the first and last watch of the night, he lies down for rest only in the night's middle watch. Thus he strives and struggles. Just as the serpent bends its tail, so he bends his legs to a crosslegged posture. As the serpent exhales forcefully, so the monk musters all his unremitting strength. As the serpent expands its hood, so the monk works for an expansion of his insight. And just as the serpent sheds its old skin, so the monk abandons the here and the beyond, and being now freed of the burden, he goes forth to the Nibbāna-element that is without a residue of the groups of existence (*anupādisesa-nibbānadhātu*).

Commentary to the Sutta Nipāta

Conforming to the 'law of its own species', the serpent discards what has become only a burden. It is worn-out, outgrown skin which the snake gladly sheds. And thus it will finally be with him who earnestly walks the path to the freedom from all burdens (*yogakkhema*). Daily practice of alienation from what has been understood to be actually alien will wear thin the bondage to 'self' and the world, loosen more and more clinging's tight grip, until, like the serpent's worn-out skin, it falls away most effortlessly. Just as, according to similes given by the Buddha, the handle of a hatchet is wasted away by constant use; just as the strongest ship-ropes will become brittle by constant exposure to wind, sun and rain and finally fall asunder – so will constant acts of giving up, of letting go, wear thin and fragile the once so stout and unbreakable fetters of craving and ignorance, until one day they drop off completely.

By such an act of 'shedding the old skin', no 'violence against nature' is done; it is a lawful process of growing, of *out*growing, that which is no longer an object of attachment – just as the old skin is no longer attached to the snake's body. Only in such a way can a person vanquish those passionate urges and deceptive notions of his, which are so powerful and so deeply rooted. In the act of ultimate liberation, nothing is violently broken which was not already detached from the living tissues of mind and body or only quite loosely joined with them. Only a last effort of the powerful muscles will be needed to shake off the empty sheath – this hollow concept of an imaginary self which had hidden for so long the true nature of body and mind. Here it lies before the meditator's feet – like the serpent's worn-out skin – a lifeless heap of thin and wrinkled thought tissue. Once it had seemed to be so full of alluring beauty – this proud and deceptive idea of 'I' and 'mine'. Now this illusion is no more, and a new 'conceptual skin' has grown which, though likewise made of imperfect words, has no longer the deceptive colourings of conceit, craving and false ideas. Mind-and-body are now seen as they truly are. Now one no longer misconceives them for what they are *not* and no longer expects of them what they cannot give: lasting happiness. How big a burden of anxiety, fear, frustration and insatiate craving will have been discarded! How light and free the heart can become if one sheds attachment to what is not one's own!

What actually has to be shed is this attachment rooted in the ego-illusion. But until discarded entirely, this ego-illusion will still cling to mind-and-body by the force of three powerful strands, which are also its feeders: conceit, craving and false ideas. Even if false ideas about a self have been given up intellectually, the other two 'feeders', conceit and craving, are strong enough to cause an identification of mind-and-body (or of some of their features) with the imaginary self.

This identification has to be dissolved on all three levels until mind-and-body are seen to be as alien as those dry leaves of the Jeta Grove which the Buddha once picked up, asking the monks whether these leaves are their self or their self's property. And the monks replied: 'They are surely not our self or anything belonging to our self.' Then the Master said: 'Therefore, monks, give up what is not yours! Give up all clinging to body, feelings, perceptions, volitions and consciousness'[1] (Majjhima Nikāya 22).

It is certainly not difficult to give up what is so obviously foreign or worthless to us, like those dry leaves or any other insignificant trifles we encounter in our lives. It is harder to give up a cherished material object or a beloved human being. It is hardest, however, to detach ourselves from the body and its pleasures, from our likes and dislikes, from the intellectual enjoyment of our thoughts, from deep-rooted tendencies and habits; in short, from all that we instinctively and without question identify with as 'ourselves'. All these constituents of our supposed 'self' are visibly changing, sometimes rapidly and radically; sometimes the changes of our likes and dislikes, habits and ideas, turn them into their very opposite. Yet we still continue to identify ourselves whole-heartedly with those new states of mind as if they were the old ego; so tenacious is the ego-illusion and therefore so hard to break.

Yet it is to that hardest task that the Master summons us: 'Give up what is not yours! And what is not yours? The body is not yours: give it up! Giving it up will be for your weal and happiness. Feelings, perceptions, volitions and consciousness are not yours: give them up! Giving them up will be for your weal and happiness!'

We must recall here that it is the *attachment* to these five aggregates that has to be given up and that this is a gradual process. We must not expect our habitual likes and dislikes, our intellectual enjoyments and our desires, to vanish all at once; nor can or should they be broken by force. This seemingly compact and identifiable personality has been gradually built up by the intake of physical and mental nourishment. Again and again, thousands of times during a single day, we have approached and absorbed the physical and mental objects of our desire. One after the other we have made them 'our own' and believed them to be our own. This continuous process of accumulating attachments and self-identifications must now be reversed by a gradual process of detachment achieved by dissolving or stopping the false identifications. The Buddha's teaching chiefly consists of aids assisting us in that task of gradual detachment – aids to right living and right thinking. The simile of the snake's worn-out skin is one of these aids, and if seen as such it has much to teach. These are some ways in which its contemplation can be helpful:

1. We look at our skin encasing the body: it is now firm and taut, healthily alive, our warm blood pulsating beneath it. Imagine it now lying before you, empty and limp, like a snake's discarded slough. In such a manner you may visualize the feature *skin* among *the parts* of the body in the meditation on the body recommended by the Buddha.* When thus brought vividly to life, it will help you to alienate and detach yourself from the body.

*In this meditation the body is contemplated by way of its constituent parts, such as skin, muscles, sinews, bones, the internal organs, secretions and excretions.

2. Just as the serpent does not hesitate to fulfil the biological 'law of its kind' in shedding its old skin, so right renunciation will not waver or shrink from those acts of giving up which right understanding of reality demands. Just as the serpent does not mourn over the loss of its worn-out slough, so right renunciation has no regrets when it discards what has been seen as void of value and substance and replaces it by something new and more beautiful: the happiness of letting go, the exhilaration of the freedom won, the serenity of insight and the radiance of a mind purified and calmed. It is the growing strength of this new experience which will gradually clear the road to final emancipation.

3. According to the commentary quoted by us, the snake feels *disgust* towards its old skin when the sloughing is not yet complete and parts of the old skin still adhere to its body. Similarly, the disgust felt towards residual attachments and defilements will give to the disciple an additional urgency in his struggle for final liberation. Such disgust is a symptom of his growing detachment. It is strengthened by an increasing awareness of the perils inherent in the uneliminated defilements – perils to oneself and to others. On seeing these perils, the whole misery of man's situation – the saṁsāric predicament – will gain for him increasing poignancy; and the more he progresses in mental training and moral refinement, the stronger his distaste will become for what is still unamenable in him to that training and refinement. Therefore the Buddha advised his son Rāhula: 'Make disgust strong in you' (Sutta Nipāta, v. 340).

This disgust (*nibbidā*) is often mentioned in the Buddhist scriptures as an aid as well as a phase on the road to full detachment. In the early stages of insight, the experience of disgust may be tinged with feelings of revulsion. But as insight deepens and gathers strength, the revulsion gives way to dispassion: a fully conscious withdrawal and turning away from worldliness and from the residue of one's own defilements.

4. Just as the snake, in its effort to throw off its old skin, uses as support a stone or the root of a tree, similarly, the teachers of old say that the striving disciple should make full use of the support of noble friendship in his efforts towards full liberation. A friend's watchful concern, his wise counsel and his inspiring example may well be of decisive help in the arduous work of

freeing oneself from the burdensome encumbrance of passions, frailties and tenacious habits.

Often and emphatically, the Buddha praised the value of noble friendship. Once the venerable Ānanda, who was so deeply devoted to the Master, spoke of noble friendship as being 'half of the holy life', believing he had duly praised its worth. The Buddha replied: 'Do not say so, Ānanda, do not say so: it is the entire holy life to have noble friends, noble companions, noble associates' (Saṁyutta Nikāya, 45:2). If this holds true for the spiritual life of a monk, there are additional reasons for cherishing noble friendship within the common life of the world with all its harshness and perils, struggles and temptations, and its almost unavoidable contact with fools and rogues. Noble friendship, so rare and precious, is indeed one of the few solaces which this world can offer. But this world of ours would be truly 'disconsolate' if, besides the solace of friendship, it did not harbour the still greater solace of the Buddha's compassionate message of an open way to final deliverance from suffering.

THE MEANING OF MONK

The word *monk* (*bhikkhu*) has to be taken here in the same sense as explained in the old commentary on the Satipaṭṭhāna Sutta:

> *Monk* is a term to indicate a person who earnestly endeavours to accomplish the practice of the teaching. Though there are others, gods and men, who earnestly strive to accomplish the practice of the teaching, yet because of the excellence of the state of a monk by way of practice, the Master spoke here of a *monk*. . . . Verily, he who follows the teaching, be he a deity or a human being, is called a monk.

THE HERE AND THE BEYOND (*ora-pāraṁ*)

Now what is it that should be given up finally and without regret? Our text calls it 'the here and the beyond', using Pāli words that originally signified the two banks of a river. The 'here' is this world of our present life experience as human beings; the 'beyond' is any world beyond the present one to which our willed actions (*kamma*) may lead us in our future existences in saṁsāra, the round of rebirths. It may be a world

of heavenly bliss, or one of hell-like suffering, or a world which
our imagination creates and our heart desires; for life in any
world beyond the present one belongs as much to the totality of
existence as life on earth, Nibbāna alone being the 'beyond of
existence'.

The phrase 'the here and the beyond' also applies to all those
various discriminations, dichotomies and pairs of opposites in
which our minds habitually move: the lower and the higher, the
inner and the outer, the (life-affirming) good and the bad,
acceptance and rejection. In brief, it signifies the ever-recurring
play of opposites, and as this play maintains the game of life
with its unresolvable dissatisfactions, disappointment and
suffering, the Buddha calls on us to give it up.

The overcoming of the opposites, the detachment from 'both
sides', is one of the recurrent themes of the Sutta Nipāta.
Among the various pairs of opposites structuring our thoughts,
attitudes and feelings, the most prominent is that of 'the lower
and the higher'. All the numerous religious, ethical, social and
political doctrines devised by man employ this dichotomy, and
though their definitions of these two terms may differ
enormously, they are unanimous in demanding that we give up
the low and attach ourselves, firmly and exclusively, to
whatever they praise as 'high', 'higher' or 'highest'.

Espousing among views his own as highest,
Whatever he regards as 'best',
All else he will as 'low' condemn;
Thus one will never get beyond disputes.

Sutta Nipāta, v. 796

However, in any area of human concern, secular or religious,
clinging to discriminations of 'high and low' is bound to result
in suffering. When we are attached to anything as 'high', if the
object changes, we shall meet with sorrow; if our attitudes
change, we shall find ourselves feeling flustered and discontent.

But despite their repeated experience of transiency, and
despite all their prior disappointments, men still foster the vain
hope that what they cherish and cling to now will remain with
them forever. Only those few 'with little or no dust in their
eyes' understand that this play of opposites, on its own level, is
interminable; and only one, the Buddha, has shown us how to
step out of it. He, the Great Liberator, showed that the way to
genuine freedom lies in relinquishing both sides of the

dichotomy, even insisting that his own teaching is only a raft
built for crossing over and not for holding on to:

> You, O monks, who understand the Teaching's similitude to
> a raft, you should let go even good teachings, how much
> more the false ones.
>
> Majjhima Nikāya 22

> Do you see, my disciples, any fetter, coarse or fine, which I
> have *not* asked you to discard?
>
> Majjhima Nikāya 66

One should, however, know well and constantly bear in
mind that the relinquishing of both sides, the transcending of
the opposites, is the final goal – a goal which comes at the end of
a long journey. Because this journey unavoidably leads through
the ups and downs of saṁsāra, the traveller will repeatedly
encounter the play of opposites, within which he will have to
make his choices and select his values. He must never attempt to
soar above the realm of opposites while ill-equipped with feeble
wings or else his fate, like that of Icarus, will be a crash landing.
For a long time, to the best of his knowledge and strength, he
must firmly chose the side of the 'higher' against the 'lower',
following what is beneficial from the standpoint of the
Dhamma and avoiding what is harmful. But he should regard
his choices and values as a raft, not clinging to them for their
own sake, always ready to leave them behind to embark on the
next phase of the journey. While still on the mundane plane, he
must never forget or belittle the presence within himself of the
'lower', the dark side of his nature, and he must learn to deal
with this wisely, with caution as well as firmness.

To cross the ocean of life and reach 'the other shore' safely,
skill is needed in navigating its currents and cross-currents. In
adapting oneself to those inner and outer currents, however,
one must always be watchful. The currents can be powerful at
times and one must know when it is necessary to resist them.
Sometimes right effort has to be applied to avoid or overcome
what is evil and to produce and preserve what is good. At other
times it is wise to restrain excessive and impatient zeal and
revert to a receptive attitude, allowing the processes of inner
growth to mature at their own rate. By wisely directed
adaptation we can learn to give full weight to both sides of every
situation – to the duality in our own nature and in the objective

circumstances we face. Only by confronting and understanding the two sides within one's own experience can one master and finally transcend them.

An increasingly refined response to the play of opposites will teach one how to balance, harmonize and strengthen one's spiritual faculties (*indriya*) by reducing excess and making up deficiencies. When it concerns two equally positive qualities – such as the faculties of energy and calm – one will naturally prefer to strengthen the weaker side instead of reducing the stronger, thus re-establishing the balance of faculties on a higher level. Only by a harmonious balance of highly developed faculties can one move on to the next phase of progress: the 'transcending of both sides', the final comprehension and mastery of merely apparent opposites, such as firmness and gentleness, which appear opposed only when isolated or unbalanced.

This harmony, which is dynamic and not static, gains perfection in the equipoise and equanimity of the Arahat, the Liberated One, an equanimity far wider, deeper and stronger than any the ordinary man can even envision.

On the *emotional* level, the Arahat's equanimity is marked by perfect and unshakable equipoise in the midst of the vicissitudes of life and in the face of all the problems and conflicts which may come within the range of his experience. This equanimity is not indifferent aloofness but a balanced response to any situation – a response motivated and directed by wisdom and compassion.

On the *volitional and active* level, the Arahat's equanimity appears as freedom from partiality; as a thoughtful choice between action and non-action, again motivated by wisdom and compassion; and as perfect equipoise when the choice has been made.

On the *cognitive and intellectual* level, his equanimity shows up in a balanced judgement of any situation or idea, based on a mindful and realistic appraisal; it is the equipoise of insight that enables him to avoid the pitfalls of extreme conceptual viewpoints.

This is the triple aspect of the Arahat's equanimity as an embodiment of the middle path rising above the extremes and opposites.

THE STRUCTURE OF THE VERSES

In each verse of the poem, the giving up of 'the here and the beyond' mentioned in the refrain is connected with the abandonment of certain mental defilements (*kilesa*), basic distortions of attitude and understanding, mentioned in the first lines of the verses. The purport behind this connection is that only if the mental defilements mentioned in the first lines are eliminated *entirely* (*asesaṁ*, 'without remainder') – as stated expressly in verses 2, 3 and 4 – can one rise above the opposites involved in those defilements. Only by entire elimination are the defilements eradicated in their lower and higher, coarse and subtle forms, in their manifest and latent states. If even a minute residue of them is left, it will suffice to revive the full play of the opposites and a recurrence of the extremes. No member of a pair of opposites can exclude the influence of its counterpart and remain stationary within the same degree of strength or weakness. There is a constant fluctuation between 'high' and 'low' as to the degree of the defilements, as to evaluation of mental qualities and as to forms of existence to which the defilements may lead.

It is the *complete* uprooting of the defilements which will make an end of rebirth – of the here and the beyond, the high and the low, which remain in constant fluctuation as long as the defilements persist. When such an uprooting is made, the here and the beyond will be transcended, left behind as something empty, coreless and alien – 'just as a serpent sheds its worn-out skin.'

II *Reflections on the Verses*

1. He who can curb his wrath
    as soon as it arises,
    as a timely antidote will check
    snake's venom that so quickly spreads,
    – such a monk gives up the here and the beyond,
    just as a serpent sheds its worn-out skin.

This first verse compares *wrath*, which is vehement anger or rage, to a snake's poison that rapidly spreads in the body of the person bitten; for snakes, or at least some of the species, have always been regarded as irascible animals of venomous ire. Wrath is an outcome of hate, one of the three powerful roots of all evil and suffering.[2] The term 'hate' (*dosa*) comprises all degrees of antipathy, from the weakest dislike to the strongest fury. In fact, the Pāli word *kodha*, used in this verse and rendered here by 'wrath', actually extends to the whole scale of antagonistic emotions. We have, however, singled out its extreme form, 'wrath', because of the simile and in view of the fact that its less vehement forms will find their place under the heading of 'grudge', in verse 6.

Of the evil root hate in its entire range the Buddha says, 'it is a great evil but (relatively) easy to overcome.' (Anguttara Nikāya, 3. 68). It was perhaps for both these reasons that wrath is mentioned here first, preceding the other defilements which appear in the following verses. Hate is a great evil because of its consequences. Its presence poses a much greater danger of a straight fall into the lowest depths of inhuman conduct and into the lowest forms of existence than, for instance, greed (or lust), another of the three evil roots. On the other hand, hate is relatively easy to overcome, for it produces an unhappy state of mind which goes counter to the common human desire for happiness. But hate will be 'easy to overcome' only for those who also know of the need to purify their own hearts and are willing to make that effort. For those, however, who identify themselves fully with their aversions or even try to justify their outbursts of temper – for them hate, too, is very difficult to overcome and may well harden into a character trait of irritability.

Just as a snakebite needs prompt treatment to prevent the venom from spreading rapidly and widely through the body, so also any uprising of wrath should be curbed at once to prevent it from erupting into violent words and deeds of possibly grave consequence.

The true curative antidote for hate in all its forms is loving-kindness (*mettā*), assisted by patience, forbearance and compassion. But unless the mind is well-trained, when vehement wrath flares up it will rarely be possible to replace it immediately by thoughts of loving-kindness. Nevertheless, a mental brake should be applied at once and the thoughts of anger curbed[3] without delay; for if this is not done, the situation may be aggravated by continued outbursts of anger to the point where it gets completely out of control. This temporary curbing of wrath accords with the fifth method of removing undesirable thoughts as mentioned in the 20th Discourse of the Middle Length Sayings (Majjhima Nikāya),[4] namely, by vigorously restraining them. By such an act of firm restraint, time will be won to compose the mind for dealing with the situation thoughtfully and calmly. But if the anger thus suppressed is left smouldering under the ashes, it may well flare up on a future occasion with greater vehemence. Hence, in a quiet hour on the very same day, one should try to dissolve that anger fully, in a way appropriate to the situation. The Dhamma can offer many aids for doing so.

Hate can bind beings to each other as strongly as lust does, so that they drag each other along through repeated life situations of revenge and counter-revenge. This may first happen in the 'here', that is, within one life or in continued human rebirths. But persistent hate harbours the constant danger of dragging the hater down into a subhuman world of misery, 'beyond the human pale'; or the hater's fate might be a rebirth among the Asuras, the demonic titans of militant pride and aggressive power-urge, some of whom, in turn, seem to have taken human birth as great conquerors and rulers.

Whipped up by hate and wrath, towering waves of violence and fierce tempests of aggression have swept again and again through human history, leaving behind a wake of destruction. Though issuing from the same root of evil – hate – these upheavals have taken a multitude of forms: as racial, national, religious and class hatred as well as other varieties of factional and political fanaticism. Those who crave for leadership among men have always known that it is so much easier to unite people under the banner of a common hate than by a shared love. And all too often these leaders have made unscrupulous use of their knowledge to serve the ends of their burning ambition and power urge, even using millions of people as tools or victims of their own unquenchable hate for others or themselves. Untold misery has been wrought thus and is still being wrought today, as history books and the daily newspapers amply testify. Now mankind is faced by the mortal danger posed by tools of violence and aggression made utterly destructive through modern technology, and by a climate of hate made more infectious through modern mass media and subtle mind manipulation.

So there are, indeed, reasons enough for curbing wrath individually and for helping to reduce it socially. An appeal for the reduction of hate and violence in the world of today can no longer be dismissed as unrealistic moralizing. For the individual and for mankind, it has now become a question of survival, physically and spiritually.

He, however, who 'sees danger in the slightest fault', and knows that even slight but persistent resentments may grow into passionate hate and violence, will earnestly strive for the final eradication of the deepest roots of any aversion. This is achieved on the third stage of the path to liberation, called the stage of non-return (*anāgāmitā*). At that stage, return to the 'here' of existence in the sense sphere can no longer come about, while the end of the 'beyond', that is, of existence in the fine-material and immaterial spheres, will also be assured.[5]

> You must slay wrath if you would happily live;
> You must slay wrath if you would weep no more.
> The slaughter of anger with its poisoned source
> And fevered climax, murderously sweet –
> That is the slaughter noble persons praise;
> That you must slay in order to weep no more.
>
> Saṁyutta Nikāya, 11: 21

2. He who entirely cuts off his lust
    as entering a pond one uproots lotus plants,
    – such a monk gives up the here and the beyond,
    just as a serpent sheds its worn-out skin.

Lust (*rāga*) is here compared to the lotus flower as a symbol of beauty. Because of its loveliness one too easily forgets that the enchanting blossoms of sense enjoyment will soon wilt and lose their beauty and attraction. But the mere awareness of that impermanence is not enough, for it may even add to the enchantment and whet the desire to pluck the flowers of lust again and again as long as strength lasts. But desire often lasts longer than the strength to seek or obtain its fulfilment – and this is just one of the ways in which lust brings suffering and frustration.

In a single moment the roots of lust can sink deeply into man's heart; its fine hair-roots of subtle attachments are as difficult to remove as the great passions, or even more so. Thus the Buddha says that 'greed is hard to overcome'; but in the same text he also says that greed 'is a lesser evil' (or, literally rendered, 'less blameworthy').[6] This statement may appear strange in view of the fact that greed is one of the evil roots and also a form of craving, the fundamental cause of suffering. Yet greed is 'less blameworthy' than hate in all those cases where the gratification of lust does not violate basic morality and is not harmful to others; for instance, in the enjoyment of delicious food, sexual gratification within the bounds of the third precept and so forth.

Nevertheless, *all* forms of lust, be they inside or outside the moral norms, are still *unwholesome (akusala)*, as they chain man to kammic bondage and necessarily result in suffering. Therefore, for one who aspires to perfect purity and final liberation, all forms of lust, coarse or refined, are obstructions.

'All lust wants eternity' (Friedrich Nietzche) – but cannot obtain it. For, though lust itself may well go on eternally without ever being quenched, its objects are all inevitably evanescent. When the objects of lust perish, as they must, or are unattainable, as they often are, suffering results for the lusting person; and when his desire for a loved person fades and changes, suffering will result for the beloved.

Lust receives its full dimension of depth as an expression of craving, an inexhaustible neediness, the state of ever being in want. This craving is the subject of the next verse.

Lust is 'entirely cut off' at the stage of Arahatship, when desire even for the worlds of refined material form or the immaterial has vanished forever. With the elimination of lust, its unavoidable concomitants also disappear: the frustration, torment or despair of non-gratification and the listlessness, boredom or revulsion of surfeit. He who frees himself of lust is also free of its 'both sides', attraction and repulsion, like and dislike. He too has given up the here and the beyond.

3. He who entirely cuts off his craving
    by drying up its fierce and rapid flow,
    – such a monk gives up the here and the beyond,
    just as a serpent sheds its worn-out skin.

Craving (*taṇhā*) is the mighty stream of desire that flows through all existence, from the lowest microbes up to those sublime spheres free from coarse materiality. Craving is threefold: craving for sensuality, for continued existence and for annihilation or destruction.

Sensuous craving (kāma-taṇhā), within that mighty river of which our verse speaks, is a powerful whirlpool dragging everything into its depth. The infinity of all craving appears here as the bottomless abyss which vainly longs for fullness and fulfilment. But though it ceaselessly sucks into itself the objects of desire, it can never find satiety and peace. For like the hunger for food, this perpetual hunger of the senses daily craves afresh for gratification: 'The senses are greedy eaters.' The habit of daily sense gratification produces in us a *horror vacui*. We fear being left empty of sense experience, and this fear, an expression of the fear of death, stands dark and threatening behind each sensual craving as an additional driving force. We see the stark partnership of fear and desire in the pathological avarice, the hectic grasping and clinging of those old people so masterfully described by Molière and Balzac.

Driven by the burning sensation of a void within, by a feeling of constant lack and neediness, we try to suppress that painful sensation by swelling our ego. We strive to absorb into our ego what is non-ego or 'alien'; we chase hectically and insatiably after sense enjoyment, possessions or power; we yearn to be loved, envied or feared. In short, we try to build up our 'personality' – a *persona*, a hollow mask. But such attempts to satisfy sensual craving must fail. If the supposed ego expands its imagined boundaries, then, by the extension of its periphery, its points of contact with a hostile or tempting world also grow, inevitably bringing along a growth of both irritation and neediness. One believes that by the mere gratification of lust what has been 'appropriated' from the outside world of objects or people becomes a part of the ego or its property, becomes 'I' and 'mine'. But what the ego thus appropriates from outside, it can never fully assimilate. There remains an undissolved alien residue which accumulates and slowly but deeply alters the structure of body and mind. This process will finally end in the disruption of the organism – in death. To some extent this is normal, an ever-present process as it is also a formula for the intake and assimilation of food.[7] But if sensory craving grows excessive and becomes an uncontested or only weakly contested master, it may well happen that 'the food devours the eater': that the craving and search for sensual nourishment becomes so dominant that it weakens other functions of the human mind, and just those which are most refined and distinctively human. Unrestrained sensual craving makes a personality 'featureless' and 'impersonal'; it reduces human individuation and thus brings us into dangerous proximity to the animal level which is bare or poor of individuation. Specific sensual enjoyment may easily become habit-forming and even compulsive, again pulling us down to the animal level of instinctive behaviour at the cost of conscious control. A life dominated by sensual craving may turn into a monotonous automatism of sense-stimulus, craving and sense gratification. Uninhibited sensuality reduces our relative freedom of choice and may drag us, by way of rebirth, into subhuman realms of existence. We say this, not to moralize, but to emphasize the psychological effects of sensual craving and to show its implications for our progress towards true human freedom, that is, towards an increase of our mindfully responsible moral choices.

In the threatening effacement of individuation, in the rapturous submergence of individuality at moments of highest passion – in these features sensual craving approaches its apparent opposite, the craving for annihilation (*vibhava-taṇhā*). It is ancient knowledge: the affinity of Eros and Thanatos, of passionate love and death.

Craving for annihilation, for non-being, may be likened to the flooding of the river of individualized life. The waters revolt against the banks, the restricting boundaries of individuality. Suffering under their frustrating limitations, they seek to burst through all dams in quest of the great ocean, longing to be one with it, to submerge painful separateness in an imagined Oneness. It is the enticing melody of 'Unbewusst – hoechste Lust!' ('To be unconscious – oh highest lust!', Richard Wagner), the 'descent to the mother goddess', the cult of the night.

On a simpler level, the craving for annihilation is the outcome of sheer despair, the reverse of worldly enchantment. Worn out by the vicissitudes of life, one longs for a sleep without awakening, to obliterate oneself as a protest against a world that does not grant one's wishes. As an irrational revenge, one wants to destroy oneself or others. In some cases, fanatical creeds of violence and destruction stem from this very source.[8]

Finally, in its rationalized form, this craving appears as the view or theory of annihilationism (*uccheda-diṭṭhi*), expressed in various types of materialist philosophies throughout the history of human thought.

Craving for continued existence (*bhava-taṇhā*) is the unceasing, restless flow of the river of life towards goals hoped for, but never attained. It is fed by our persistent hope that happiness will come tomorrow, or in a heaven or golden age of our belief.

Even when all our toil gives little or no present satisfaction and happiness, we console ourselves with the thought that we work for our children or our nation or mankind; and each generation repeats that deferred hope.

As a longing for life eternal, desired and imagined in many forms, this craving for existence appears in many religions and philosophies. In Buddhist texts, it is called 'the eternalist view' (*sassata-diṭṭhi*).

Craving for existence is the driving force that keeps the Wheel of Life in rotation. If viewed by an unclouded eye, this wheel is seen as a treadmill kept in motion by those who have condemned themselves to that servitude. It is a contraption 'where you are perpetually climbing, but can never rise an inch' (Walter Scott). The beings who rotate in it are again and again victimized by their illusion that the stepping-board before their eyes is the cherished goal, the desired end of their toil. They do not know that within a turning wheel there is no final goal or destination, and that the end of the world with its suffering cannot be reached by walking on a treadmill. It can be attained only by stopping the driving forces within us – craving and ignorance. Yet those beings who have committed themselves to that wheel still believe that, within this truly vicious circle, they do 'get on in life', and hopefully speak of progress and evolution.

This is the sober and sobering view of existence and the craving for its continuation. But if there were not also a tempting aspect, beings would not cling to life and crave for it to go on. We need not dwell here on those tempting aspects high or low, as there have been, and still are, many eulogists of life and its beauties. Hence, we shall speak here only of some of the more subtle forms of allurement which the craving for existence takes.

Among its numerous forms, craving for existence may appear as a longing for variety. This longing frequently makes people seek for happiness somewhere other than in the here and now, and in some form other than the one they actually possess. The mirage of a 'happiness elsewhere' becomes a bait that moves further away the closer it is approached, ever eluding the hand that tries to grasp it. It is like the fate of Tantalus to which man has become so habituated that he even finds it pleasant, saying that 'it adds spice to life'.

There are others who thirst after ever-widening horizons of life, seeking new sensory or mental experiences for their own sake; some who are enamoured with their own prowess in confronting life; and some who enjoy their own creativity. The latter include many geniuses in diverse fields who may well be reborn as those deities of the Buddhist tradition who 'delight in their creations' (*nimmāna-rati-deva*). Characteristic of this mentality is Gotthold Ephraim Lessing's preference for the *search* for truth over the attainment of it; or Napoleon's words that he loved power just as the musician loves his instrument: for the sake of the music he produces on it. Those who enjoy life for its own sake proudly aver that they are willing to pay the price for it in life's coinage of suffering and pain, defeat and frustration. Often, however, this is just a heroic pose which hides feelings of frustration and pride. But even when that avowal is honest and stands firm against pain and failure, it will finally break down when body and mind lose their strength or when satiety and boredom set in.

It is one of the most subtle and effective ruses of the 'will to live' to lure man on and on, dangling before him hope, novelty or the gratification of pride. The allurement of 'far horizons', the search for the unknown, has tempted many imaginative and adventurous minds; and those of a heroic mould it has urged to meet the vicissitudes of life as a challenge, appealing to their pride to rise above them. Only in the Arahat, the Liberated One, will such detachment in the face of adversity be genuine and unshakable. Only he can truly say of himself that he has risen above the vicissitudes of existence; that his 'mind is unshaken by the eight worldly events' (Mahā Mangala Sutta): gain and loss, repute and disrepute, praise and blame, joy and woe. Being free from all three cravings, he is free of 'both sides': the longing for life and the longing for death, the fear of life and the fear of death. He who has conquered craving has conquered all the worlds, the 'here and the beyond'. For craving is the triune Lord of all the Worlds, their creator, sustainer and destroyer; and he who is craving's conqueror is also the true world conqueror.

4. He who entirely blots out conceit
    as the wind demolishes a fragile bamboo bridge,
    – such a monk gives up the here and the beyond,
    just as a serpent sheds its worn-out skin.

Human conceit is here compared with a fragile bamboo bridge. In countries of the East, such bridges often consist of just two or three bamboo poles, sometimes with a railing of the same material. On such bridges one has to be quite sure of one's balance in order to safely cross a roaring mountain brook or a deep gorge. Human pride is just as fragile and shaky. It may easily be upset by a whiff of public opinion, hurt by any fool's snide remark or hurled down deep by defeat, failure or misfortune.

Conceit has its roots in ego-belief, which may be either intellectually articulated or habitually and tacitly assumed. In return, conceit gives a very powerful support to ego-belief. It does not tolerate any doubt or challenge of what it prides itself on so much: the existence and the supreme value of that precious self. Any attempt to question its existence and its worth is regarded with as much violent resentment as a powerful ruler would exhibit if he were to be subjected to a body search at the border of his own country.

The noun *conceit* derives from the verb *conceiving*.[9] It is, indeed, a conceited conception to conceive oneself superior to others. But also to conceive oneself equal to another ('I am as good as you'), or as inferior (which often comes from frustrated pride) – these, too, are rooted in conceit, in an egocentric evaluation of oneself in relation to others. All three are modes of conceit: the superiority complex, the equality claim and the inferiority complex. This urge to compare oneself with others springs from an inner insecurity that deep within knows and fears the shakiness of the delusive ego image.

This triple conceit entirely vanishes only when even the most subtle ego reference disappears. This comes only with Arahatship, when the last vestige of the fetter of conceit (*māna-saṁyojana*) has been eliminated. The Arahat no longer needs the shaky bridge of ego conceit as he has given up 'both sides', the discrimination of self and others, and has transcended both the here and the beyond of worldly existence.

5. He who does not find core or substance
   in any of the realms of being,
   like flowers which are vainly sought
   in fig trees which have none,
   – such a monk gives up the here and the beyond,
   just as a serpent sheds its worn-out skin.

Like ignorant people who want to pick flowers where none can be expected, since time immemorial men have sought in vain for an abiding core and substance within themselves and in the world they inhabit. Or they have hoped to find it beyond their own world, in celestial realms and in their gods. Man is driven to that unceasing but futile quest for something immortal by his longing for a state of security, living as he does in an entirely insecure world which he constantly sees crumbling around him and below his own feet. Not that the vast majority of men would care for the boredom of living forever in the immobility which any stable and secure condition implies. But they long for it as a temporary refuge to which they can resort, as children resort to the soothing arms of their mothers after becoming sore and tired by their wild and reckless play.

Behind that longing for security, be it temporary or constant, there looms a still stronger driving force: the fear of death, the desire for self-preservation. This holds true for the coarsest as well as the subtlest form of that search for permanency, be it a wish for the perpetuation of sense enjoyment in a sensuous heaven, or the expression of a 'metaphysical need' or the deep yearning for a *unio mystica*. This quest for permanency and security may also manifest itself as an urge for absolute power or for absolute self-surrender, for absolute knowledge or for absolute faith.

Since man's early days, as soon as he first started to reflect upon his life situation, he turned his glance everywhere in search of something stable in a world of instability. He looked for it in the personified forces of nature, in stellar bodies, in the four great elements of matter, believing one or another to be the ultimate matrix of life. But chiefly he sought it in those changing forms and symbols of the divine which he had created in the image of his own longings, within the scope of his own understanding and for the furtherance of his own purposes, noble or low.

Firm belief in an Absolute, whether a god or the state, has appeared to man to be so absolutely necessary that he has used all subtleties of his intellect and all autosuggestive devices to persuade himself to accept this or that form of religious or political faith. He has also used every possible means, fair and foul, either to coax or to coerce others to recognize and worship his religious or political idols. Often not much coercion was needed, as there were always those who were only too glad to sacrifice their intellect and surrender their freedom at the altars of those idols, to win in return a feeling of security and doubt-free certainty.

Men have too easily believed, and made others believe, that when there is a word there must also be a 'real thing' corresponding to it: thence an abiding core, an eternal substance, within or behind this transient world. It was the Buddha who urged men to desist from their vain search for the non-existent and see reality as it is:

Entirely coreless is the world.

Sutta Nipāta, v. 927

He, the Awake, cleared the way to the open, leaving behind the towering edifices of ideologies and the debris in which they inevitably end. Showing up in their hollowness the claims of diverse Absolutes, he pointed out that only the hard way of critical examination, our precarious and limited freedom of choice and the road of morally responsible thought and action can lead us to freedom from suffering. And only a world that is entirely changeable can give us hope for final liberation. Anything permanent found in the world would necessarily bind us to it forever, making liberation impossible.

But one who is instructed by the Buddha, 'the Knower of the Worlds', will not find any core of permanency in any form of existence *high or low*, nor a core of lasting happiness or of an abiding personality. Such a one will not cling to the *here* nor yearn for a *beyond*; he will remain unattached to *either side*. Seeing world and self as void of an abiding core, he wins the unclouded vision of reality and, finally, the peace of Nibbāna.

6. He who bears no grudges in his heart,
   transcending all this 'thus' and 'otherwise',
   – such a monk gives up the here and the beyond,
   just as a serpent sheds its worn-out skin.

Grudge is felt towards people by whom one has been wronged or offended, or towards those who act against one's interests, even if in fair competition. Grudge may also have an impersonal character, as a resentful bitterness about one's life, if one feels that one has been treated unfairly in life by too long a chain of misfortunes. Such grudge and resentment may show up outwardly as angry words and deeds, or may rankle deep in the heart as a gnawing bitterness spreading a dark mood over all that one feels, thinks and speaks. With some temperaments it can foster vengeful and aggressive behaviour, with others an ever dissatisfied or melancholic and pessimistic mood. Habitual grudge and resentment can drain much joy from one's life. When growing into enmity, a deep personal grudge – just like strong attachment – may persist and grow from rebirth to rebirth, from the here to the beyond, repeatedly bringing dire misery to those linked in such an unhappy relationship. Also the impersonal grudge one bears against one's unhappy life experiences may well reappear in a young child as an innate mood of resentment and discontent. All these are certainly more than sufficiently harmful considerations for spurring us on to banish grudge from our hearts as soon as it arises.

Personal grudge arises from an unwise reaction to conflicts in human relationships. It is avoided and abandoned by forgiveness, forbearance and an understanding of the fact that people are heirs of their kamma.

Impersonal grudge is caused by an unwise reaction to the unavoidable vicissitudes of life – the 'thus' and 'otherwise' of our text. It is prevented and abandoned by understanding and accepting the impermanent nature of existence, and again by an understanding of kamma.

Fertile soil for the arising of a deep-seated grudge is political fanaticism, and national, racial, religious and class prejudices. Such grudges can have a personal or impersonal character, or both. For the elimination of this type of grudge the aid of both intellectual and ethical faculties is required: impartial examination of facts, together with tolerance and a feeling for the common human nature shared with others in spite of differences.

Grudge – like all other forms and degrees of aversion – is entirely discarded, like the snake's worn-out skin, at the stage of the non-returner. Then it loses forever its power to germinate in lives beyond – though even at the earlier stages of the stream-enterer and the once-returner it will have been greatly weakened. There is what may be called a 'higher' form of grudge, appearing as 'righteous indignation' and a resentful or even hostile attitude towards evil and evil-doers. But even this *'higher'* form of grudge, as well as its very common *lower* form, will be transcended in a mind that has grown mature in compassion and understanding.

7. He who has burned out his evil thoughts,
   entirely cut them off within his heart,
   – such a monk gives up the here and the beyond,
   just as a serpent sheds its worn-out skin.

Our verse speaks only of 'thoughts' (*vitakka*), without further qualification; but there is no doubt that only undesirable, unwholesome and evil thoughts are meant. Skilful and noble thoughts, particularly those aiming at liberation, should not be 'burned out' from the heart. The commentary to our verse speaks of the threefold wrong thoughts of sensuality, ill-will and cruelty, as opposed to the threefold right thought (*sammā-sankappa*) of the Noble Eightfold Path. The commentary mentions thoughts of gain, position and fame; concern for personal immortality; excessive attachment to home and country, to one's family or to other people. These latter types of thought apply chiefly to monks since, according to Buddhist lay ethics, concern for home and family, and even a moderate concern for gain and position, are not discouraged when they contribute toward the fulfilment of a layman's duties. Yet all these attachments are fetters binding us to the here and the beyond, and one day they have to be discarded if the heart's freedom is to be won.

But the root thoughts of everything harmful and evil are those of greed, hatred and delusion, which are expressly mentioned in the 'Discourse on the Quelling of Thoughts' (*Vitakkasaṇṭhāna Sutta*).[10] In that discourse, the Buddha sets forth five methods of removing such harmful thoughts from one's mind. They are given in a graded sequence from a subtle method of removal to increasingly coarser approaches.

The first method is that of immediately replacing undesirable, evil thoughts by their desirable and beneficial opposites: greedy thoughts should be superceded by thoughts of renunciation and selflessness; hate by thoughts of friendliness, love and compassion; delusion and confusion, by wise comprehension and clarity of thought. The discourse gives here the simile of driving out a coarse peg with a fine one, as carpenters do. This method will work best when there is a strong natural tendency to turn away quickly from any inner defilement or outer temptation, and to replace these thoughts immediately by their antidote. When this spontaneity of moral reaction is weak or absent, this method of *replacement* may still be workable if one has a fair degree of mind control, aided by alert mindfulness and firm determination. These latter qualities, however, can be gradually acquired or strengthened by mental training, until they ripen into a spontaneous advertence to the good.

The second method makes use of the mental impact of strong *repugnance* against evil, by impressing on the mind the ugliness, depravity, danger and unworthiness of evil thoughts. This may serve as a transition to, or preparation for, the first method. The simile in the discourse is that of a carcass thrown over the neck of a handsome young man or woman who will then feel 'horrified, humiliated and disgusted' by it and will do their utmost to get rid of it.

When these methods fail and undesirable thoughts still perturb the mind, one should deny them attention. One should not think about them or dwell on them in any way, but divert one's attention to any other thought or activity suitable to bind one's interest. This is the third method of *diverting* the mind by non-attention. Here the simile is that of closing one's eyes before a disagreeable sight or turning the glance in another direction. This approach, too, can prepare the mind for the application of the first method.

The fourth method is to go back to the thought-source from which those undesirable thoughts started and to remove them from one's mind. This might be easier than to cope directly with the resulting undesirable thought. Such a tracing back to the cause will also help to divert the mind and thus reduce the strength of the undesirable thoughts. The simile in the discourse speaks of reducing coarser movements of the body by calmer ones: a man who is running asks himself, 'Why should I run?', and he now goes slowly. He then continues the process of calming by successively standing still, sitting and lying down. The commentary explains this method as referring to a *tracing of the cause*, or of the starting point of the undesirable thoughts. [11] The simile, however, seems to admit an interpretation of this method as one of *sublimation* or gradual refinement.

The fifth and last method is vigorous *suppression*, the last resort when undesirable thoughts, e.g. extremely passionate ones, threaten to become unmanageable. This method, likened to a strong man pressing or forcing down a weaker person, shows the realistic and undogmatic approach of the Buddha, which does not exclude a method of suppression where the

situation demands it, lest a serious worsening of that situation
or a deterioration of one's character may occur.

By applying these methods, says the discourse, one may
become a 'master of the paths taken by one's thought processes.
The thought he then wants to think, that he will think; and the
thought he does not want to think, that he will not think. Thus,
having cut down craving, removed the fetter (binding to
existence), and fully mastered pride, he has made an end to
suffering.'

Hence the perfect mastery of defiled thoughts – their entire
'burning out' as our verse calls it – is identical with perfect
holiness (*arahatta*), in which all the here and beyond has been
transcended.

8.   He who neither goes too far nor lags behind,
     entirely transcending the diffuseness of the world,
     – such a monk gives up the here and the beyond,
     just as a serpent sheds its worn-out skin.

The first line of this stanza recurs five more times in the
following verses 9–13. This sixfold repetition indicates the
importance given to these few words by the creator of this
poem, the Buddha, who 'sees the deep meaning' (*nipuṇ-
atthadassī*) (Sutta Nipāta v. 377) and 'clads it in beautiful speech'
(*vaggu-vado*) (v. 955).

The first two lines of the stanza, if viewed closely, are
variations of the last two lines which speak of the transcending
of 'both sides' – taking the meaning of the Pāli words *ora-
pāraṁ* in their wider sense as explained above.

The range of meaning of these first few words is as wide as the
'world entire', the world of diffuseness or plurality (*papañca*). In
this context, it is significant that the Pāli word *papañca* has also
the connotation of 'lagging behind' or 'procrastination'.[12] Its
over-active partner within that pair, providing the extreme of
excessive movement, is craving, which tends to go far beyond
what the retarding force of objectified saṁsāra, or *papañca*, will
allow. Craving produces again and again the disillusioning
experience of its own futility; and yet again and again it seeks
'ever-new enjoyment, now here, now there'. The failure to
which craving is necessarily doomed is caused not only by its
own inherent illusions, but also, on the objective side, by the
unfathomable diffuseness of the world – that intricate saṁsāric
net of interactions in which the frantic flutterings of craving are

invariably caught, be it here or in a beyond, now or later.

The very same ideas as those of our verse are conveyed in the first text of the Saṁyutta Nikāya (Kindred Sayings). There we read:

'How, Lord, did you cross the flood (of saṁsāra)?'
'Without tarrying,[13] friend, and without struggling did I cross the flood.'
'But how could you do so, O Lord?'
'When tarrying, friend, I sank, and when struggling I was swept away. So, friend, it is by not tarrying and not struggling that I have crossed the flood.'[14]

What in our verse is called 'going too far' is here spoken of as 'struggling',[15] which has the attendant danger of being 'swept away' all over the wide expanse of the saṁsāric flood. The 'lagging behind' is here expressed by 'tarrying', which leads to 'sinking' or declining – possibly to the lowest depth. There is a similar metaphor in verses 938–939 of the Sutta Nipāta:

I saw what is so hard to see,
the dart embedded in the heart –
the dart by which afflicted we
in all directions hurry on.
If once this dart has been removed,
one will not hurry, will not sink.

These two extremes – going too far (struggling) and lagging behind (tarrying) – point also to basic tendencies of life and mind, manifesting themselves in various ways: as motory impulse and inertia; the phases of 'opening', developing, evolving, and of 'closing', shrinking, receding;[16] dispersal and contraction; dilution and hardening; distraction and concentration; hypertension and laxity; the flights of imagination and the confinement by habit and routine; the will to conquer and the desire for self-preservation; the wish for independence and for security ('freedom and bread'); an imperturbable will to believe and unappeasable scepticism, and so on.

The sets of paired terms given in the canonical texts considered here, that is:

going too far – lagging behind (Sutta Nipāta)
struggling – tarrying (Saṁyutta Nikāya)
being swept away – sinking (Saṁyutta Nikāya),

have been explained by the Buddhist commentators by corresponding dual concepts taken from the terminology of the
Dhamma. A selection of these explanations follows. Where it
serves greater clarity, the separate commentarial statements on
the two texts have been combined, paraphrased and amplified
by additional comments.

By *clinging* to the defiling passions, tarrying and seeking a
hold in them, beings will sink into a low and unhappy
existence in the course of future rebirths; and in this life, their
moral and mental standard will sink and deteriorate; or at
least they will 'lag behind', stagnate, in whatever higher aims
they have in their life.

Struggling for life's varied aims, for what is really a mere
accumulation of kammic bondage, beings are liable to 'go too
far' by aiming at unattainable goals, be it the gratification of
insatiable desires, the pursuit of insatiable ambitions, or the
fulfilment of unrealizable ideals. In that vain effort, beings are
swept away, carried along in all directions of the saṁsāric
ocean.

Driven by *craving for continued existence*, longing after the
bliss of a theistic heaven or for any other form of a happy
rebirth, one 'goes too far' by following one's wishful
thinking or one's desire for self-perpetuation; and when
turning to self-mortification of body or mind to achieve these
aims, one likewise goes to excess. When adopting a materialist creed, *the view of annihilationism*, one struggles for an
earthly paradise, fights fanatically against any religious
teaching and may even go so far as to deny dogmatically all
moral and spiritual values.

In performing *evil actions* one lags behind, falls short of the
basic human postulates; and deteriorating, one will finally
sink and be submerged by the saṁsāric floods. In struggling
for the performance of *worldly good actions*, with all their
inherent limitations and attachments, illusions and frus-
trations, one will be carried away endlessly into the ever-
receding horizon of the unattainable.

In *yearning after the past*, one strays too far from the present
and even struggles to bring back the past, as for instance
when one tries to 'appear young' or, in a more serious way,
to impose one's romantic notions of the past upon the
present. By doing so one is carried far away from a realistic

grasp of the present. *In hoping for the future*, for a heavenly beyond, a golden or messianic age to come, or even merely for 'better luck tomorrow', one neglects present effort, lags behind in meeting the demands of present situations, and sinks into a multitude of fears, hopes and vain worries.

Given to lassitude, one will lag behind, fall short in one's achievements, and be submerged in sloth and torpor. In the *excitement and restlessness* of struggling, one will be inclined to go too far and be carried away to extremes.[17]

But he who, avoiding all these extremes, walks the middle path and harmonizes the five spiritual faculties (the balancing of faith with wisdom, and energy with calm, while mindfulness watches over this process of harmonizing) – he is one 'who neither goes too far nor lags behind'.

After these specific illustrations, a few general observations may be made on what may be called the structural or functional nature of these pairs of opposites.

'Going too far' is the extreme development of one single aspect of many-sided actuality. But the desire for dominance and ever-continued expansion on the part of that one single aspect has also an activating effect on its counterpart: in the neglected or suppressed function, it will rouse the will to self-preservation and assertion. But apart from such opposition, any unrestrained one-sided expansion will finally weaken that 'extremist' factor itself. When 'going too far abroad', the distance from its original source of strength will grow, and there will be a loss of concentrated energy. The initial recklessly self-assertive factor that set out on a journey of conquest in order to impose itself on the world, will gradually be thinned out and diluted in the process. Through those thousand things which it absorbs in its conquering career, it will imperceptibly become alienated from its original nature; and those thousand influences, wrongly believed to have been mastered in the 'struggle', will carry their former master still further away into unrecognized and perilous self-alienation. This is a case of 'the eater being devoured by what he eats'. All these characteristics of 'going too far' hold good for external activities (political, social, etc.) as well as for the interplay of the inner forces of the mind.

In 'lagging behind', there is a preponderance of heaviness or inertia, a lack of self-impelling force, of powerful, springy tension, and even an aversion to it. As far as there is movement in that tarrying tendency, it is of a recoiling, centripetal nature. It is the cramped or contracted mind (*sankhitta-citta*) spoken of in the Satipaṭṭhāna Sutta. This centripetal and recoiling tendency is characteristic of an extremely introverted type of mind. Though an introvert type sometimes 'goes too far' in certain psychological and ideological attitudes, generally he is shy and timid, or resentful and contemptuous. Recoil from too close a social contact places him on the side of 'lagging behind'. An extreme introvert type tries to resist even those slight shiftings of his inner centre of gravity called for by the human or physical environment.

All manifestations of 'lagging behind' show a lack of reciprocity and of exchange with the outside world. We may even call it 'weak mental metabolism', since mental activity is also a process of nutrition.

While the opposite tendency towards excessive expansion may run the risk of being invaded by an excess of 'foreign bodies', there is here a deficiency of them; and this will make for poor adaptability and lack of stimulation for new developments. This may finally lead to such a degree of isolation and inbreeding that here, too, the neglected counterpart will rise in self-defence. If its counter-move succeeds, it may produce a harmonious balance of character, unless it starts on a one-sided development of its own. But if such a corrective is absent or remains unsuccessful, that particular life-process, by seriously 'lagging behind', will 'sink', that is, deteriorate, and may reach a point of complete stagnation.

Thus the strands of life's texture meet crosswise in their upward and downward path. In that way they weave the intricate net of the world's diffuseness (*papañca*), to which the interplay of these paired opposites adds uncountable meshes.

It is through balanced view and balanced effort that one can transcend all these extremes. If one has thus found the harmonizing centre in one's life and thought – the Noble Eightfold Path, the *middle way* – then the outer manifestations of the inner opposites and conflicts will also fall away, like the worn-out skin of the snake, never to be renewed again. Then there will be rebirth no more, neither in the lower nor in the higher realms, neither here nor beyond: both sides have been left behind. For the Liberated One, world migration, world creation, have utterly ceased.

He who neither goes too far nor lags behind,

9. and knows about the world: 'This is all unreal',
10. greedless he knows: 'This is all unreal',
11. lust-free he knows: 'This is all unreal',
12. hate-free he knows: 'This is all unreal',
13. delusion-free he knows: 'This is all unreal',
    – such a monk gives up the here and the beyond,
    just as a serpent sheds its worn-out skin.

The world is *unreal* in the sense of presenting a deceptive appearance, being quite different in actuality from the way it appears to a greedy, lustful, hating and ignorant mind. The Pāli word *vitatha*, here rendered by 'unreal', has both in Pāli and Sanskrit the meaning of 'untrue' or 'false'. These verses, however, are not meant to convey the idea that the world is mere illusion, a play of imagination. What underlies its deceptive appearance, the flux of mental and physical processes, is real enough in the sense that it is effect-producing. The unreality lies in what we attribute to the world, and not in the world itself.

What, now, is this 'world' (*loka*) and this 'all' (*sabba*), which should be seen as unreal, in the sense of being deceptive? When the Enlightened One was questioned about these two words, he gave the same answer for both:

1. 'One speaks of "the world", Lord. In how far is there a world or the designation "world"?'

'When there is the eye and visible forms, visual consciousness and things cognizable by visual consciousness; when there is the ear and sounds . . .; nose and smells . . .; tongue and flavours . . .; body and tangibles . . .; mind and ideas, mind-consciousness and things cognizable by mind-consciousness – then there is a world and the designation "world".'

Saṁyutta Nikāya, 35: 68

2. 'All' will I show you, O monks. And what is 'all'? The eye and visible forms, ear and sounds, nose and smells, tongue and flavours, body and tangibles, mind and ideas – this, O monks, is what is called 'all'.

Saṁyutta Nikāya, 35: 22

This twelvefold world process is kept going by craving for the six objects and by attachment to the six sense faculties deemed to belong to a 'self'. Craving itself is kindled by the discrimination between 'likes and dislikes', that is, choice and rejection motivated by greed, hatred and delusion.

What 'like and dislike' commonly is called,
induced by that, desire comes into being.

Sutta Nipāta, v. 867

It is this ego-centred discrimination of 'like and dislike' that gives to the world its deceptive colouring – its semblance of reality, meaning and value – which is derived from those subjective emotions. But he who is neither carried away by the unreal nor recoils from the real – and thus neither goes too far nor lags behind – he is able to remove that deceptive colouring (*rāgaratta*: coloured by passion) and to gain dispassion (*virāga*). When the colouring fades away, the bare processes of body and mind will appear in their true nature as being void of a core of permanence, happiness and selfhood. In the sense of that triple voidness, too, this world is unreal.

Look at the world as void, Mogharāja, ever mindful!
Uprooting the view of self you may thus be one who
overcomes death.

Sutta Nipāta, v. 119

Through freedom from lust and greed (vv. 10–11), there is the final fading away of the fictive reality bestowed by attraction.

Through freedom from hatred (v. 12), there is the final fading away of the fictive reality bestowed by aversion and aggression.

Through freedom from delusion (v. 13), greed and hatred come to an end, and there is the final fading away of all vain hopes and fears concerning the world and of all delusive ideologies about it.

A text in the Itivuttaka (No. 49) of the Pāli Canon speaks of the ideological extremes of eternity-belief and belief in annihilation, using figurative expressions similar to those of our Uraga Sutta:

There are two kinds of view, O monks, and when deities and human beings are obsessed by them, some stick fast and others run too far; only those with eyes see.

And how, O monks, do some stick fast? Deities and human beings for the most part love existence, delight in existence, rejoice in existence. When Dhamma is taught to them for the ceasing of existence, their minds do not take to it, do not accept it, and do not become firm and resolute (about that Dhamma). Thus it is that some stick fast (to their old attachments).

And how do some run too far? Some feel ashamed, humiliated and disgusted by that same existence, and they welcome non-existence in this way: 'Sirs, when with the breaking up of the body after death, this self is cut off, annihilated, does not become any more after death – that is peaceful, that is sublime, that is true.' Thus it is that some run too far.

And how do those with eyes see? Here a monk sees what has become as become, he has entered upon the way to dispassion for it, to the fading away of greed for it, to its cessation. This is how those with eyes see.

14. He who has no dormant tendencies whatever,
whose unwholesome roots have been expunged,
– such a monk gives up the here and the beyond,
just as a serpent sheds its worn-out skin.

'Dormant tendencies' (anusaya) are mental defilements which have become so strong that, from a state of latency, they easily become active in reaction to appropriate stimuli. These dormant tendencies are, as it were, the deepest strata of three levels on which defilements may exist.

At the first level, the most obvious and the coarsest, the defilements become manifest in unwholesome, evil deeds and words. This is called the level of moral transgression (vītikkama-bhūmi), which can be temporarily controlled by morality (sīla).

The second level is that of a purely mental involvement (pariyuṭṭhāna-bhūmi), namely in defiled thoughts. It can be temporarily suppressed by jhāna, meditative absorption.

The third level is that of the dormant tendencies (anusaya-bhūmi). These are gradually eliminated by wisdom (paññā), arising in the four stages of final emancipation.

At the first stage of emancipation, stream-entry, the tendencies to false views and sceptical doubt are eliminated.

At the second stage, once-return, the gross forms of the tendencies of sensual desire and ill-will are eliminated.

At the third stage, non-return, the residual tendencies of sensual desire and ill-will are eliminated.

At the fourth stage, Arahatship, all remaining unwholesome tendencies have disappeared – those of conceit, desire for any new becoming and ignorance.

Our clinging to habitual desires and their objects on the one hand, and our emotional rejections and aversions on the other – these are the main feeders of the hidden but powerful tendencies in our minds. The tendencies in turn strengthen our habitual reactions of grasping and repelling, making them almost automatic. Thence they become potent unwholesome roots of evil (*akusala-mūla*) by way of greed or hate, while the unthinking state of mind in which we so react is the third evil root, delusion.

It is mindfulness that can check the unrestricted growth of those unwholesome tendencies. At the beginning mindfulness may not be strong enough to prevent the arising of every instance and degree of mental defilement. But when these defilements in their manifestation are confronted by awareness and resistance, they will no longer bring an increase in the strength of the dormant tendencies.

They are finally silenced, however, only by the Arahat, in whom all 'unwholesome roots have been expunged'. The Arahat has abandoned 'both sides' of the tendencies, those of attraction and repulsion. Being freed of all fetters that bind to existence, he has given up the here and the beyond, the high and the low, of samsāra.

15. States born of anxiety he harbours none,
   which may condition his return to earth,

16. States born of attachment he harbours none,
   which cause his bondage to existence,
   – such a monk gives up the here and the beyond,
   just as a serpent sheds its worn-out skin.

'Anxiety' (*daratha*) and 'attachment' (*vanatha*), from which similar states of mind are born (*jā*), can be interpreted here as forms of dormant tendencies, as basic moods causing appropriate manifestations.

Anxiety appears as anguish, fear and worry, and as feelings of tension, oppression and depression caused by those emotions. Also inner conflict may be included here, especially as the Pāli word *daratha* has the primary meaning of 'split'. Hence the range of what we have called 'anxiety' may extend to the dark moods resulting from:

cares and worries, which make the heart heavy;
depression and melancholy which paralyse it;
anxieties proper: fears for oneself and for others, fear of death and fear of life;
the tension and agitation caused by inner conflict;
the feelings of insecurity, helplessness and loneliness;
the primordial or metaphysical anguish, rooted in those former three and in the fear of the unknown.

All these moods and feelings create a negative emotional background in the character, which may colour one's human relationships and influence decisions of consequence. It may also throw a deep shadow over one's attitude to life in general, and may lead to a shirking of reality, to a recoil from it. When anguish and worry continue to grow in the mind without finding relief, they may become a cause of the anxiety neurosis which is so widespread in times of emotional and social insecurity.

But anguish and anxiety are inherent in human life itself, and their presence in the human mind is not limited to times of particular stress and turbulence. How poignantly the weight of anguish was felt even in ancient India, has found a moving expression in words that were once addressed to the Buddha:

The heart is always in a state of fear,
And is always full of anguish drear,
Concerning things that now have taken place
And things that shortly I shall have to face.
If there's a place that's free from ev'ry fear,
That fear-free place will thou to me make clear?

Saṁyutta Nikāya, 2: 17. Tr. Soma Thera

Attachment, via 'states born of attachment' (*vanathajā*), leads to entanglements in the thicket (*vanatha*) of life. These entanglements through attachment are of many kinds and they throw over man the widespread 'catch-net' of craving (v. 527). Apart from those that are openly seductive, others appear in an innocuous or respectable guise, or are rationalized in more or less convincing ways. Attachments can be pursued actively or enjoyed passively. Of the innumerable forms they may take, only a very few will be mentioned here.

There is the whole scale of five-sense enjoyment, with sex as its strongest; sex in all its varieties, coarse and refined, with all its trappings and subservient arts and enticements.

There is the enchantment of beauty, in nature and art with man's creative or receptive response.

There is the insatiable craze to get and to grasp, the fierce determination to hold and hoard; thirst for power and domination, in the smallest circle and on a world-wide scale.

On the passive side, there is the felt need and the inner satisfaction to obey and submit; the gregarious instinct, and the wish to creep under the protective shelter of this or that personal or group relationship; the comfortable feeling of following habits and custom; hero worship and leader cult.

And there is also the mystic's loving surrender to his god, which, of course, can have an ennobling effect on the mind, and yet is an 'intoxication of the soul', just like the attachment to the bliss of meditation (jhāna-nikanti) for its own sake.

'States born of attachment' are at the very root of the entire life process, on all its levels. Hence their variety is inexhaustible. Some may show man at his lowest and others at his most refined level. There are attachments that can inspire man to noble virtues, such as loyalty or self-sacrificing love, and to sublime creativity in many fields. But even the most lofty heights reached by refined attachment are no safeguard against a plunge into the lowest depths if one unwarily entrusts oneself to the dangerous gradient of attachment. Therefore, the wise will strive to detach themselves from the high as well as the low, from the here of earthly attachments and from the beyond of their 'divine' and subtle forms. The Master said: 'Do you see, my disciples, any fetter, coarse or fine, which I have *not* asked you to discard?'

Anxiety (fear) and attachment (craving) produce each other, but they also set limits to each other. 'Craving breeds anxiety; craving breeds fear', says the Dhammapada. And fear and anxiety on their part give rise to an intensified attachment to what is threatened and to a craving for the means to attain security. On the other hand, greed may sometimes be restrained by fear, both in individuals and in nations. But greed may also put shackles on fear: thus, disregarding fear's warnings, a person may set out on a perilous course to satisfy his desires.

Anxiety and attachment – these two well up from an unfathomable past, and again and again become, as our text says, conditions for renewed existence, here and beyond. For 'anxiety', our text specifies a rebirth *here* (*oraṁ*), in this human existence. Anxiety, in all the aspects we have mentioned, is so deeply embedded in the human situation that it may sometimes 'drag to rebirth' as strongly as craving does. To illustrate that typical human mood of anguish, we have quoted earlier a voice from the Buddha's own days. Closer to our own days, it was that great and radical Christian, Søren Kierkegaard, who held that the human predicament demanded from those who seriously desired salvation, an 'anxious concern' and even 'despair'. The Buddha, however, as a teacher of the middle way, advocated neither a mood of despair nor of facile appeasement. In his earnest disciples he instilled a 'sense of urgency' (*saṁvega*), like that of one 'whose turban is on fire'. And on the side of 'attachment', he urged his disciples to show 'keen desire' (*tibba-chanda*) for the task of liberation.

The Arahat, however, has transcended 'both sides' even in their beneficial aspects. He is free from 'anxious concern' (*asoko*) and free from any clinging (*anupādāno*).

17. He who has the five hindrances discarded,
     is doubt-free and serene, and free of inner barbs,
     – such a monk gives up the here and the beyond,
     just as a serpent sheds its worn-out skin.

When, in the Arahat, all defiling tendencies have been silenced and become nonexistent, they can no longer provide a soil for the growth of the 'five hindrances' (*nīvaraṇa*), which in jhāna and in the worldling's insight are only temporarily suppressed. The pair of opposites in the moral sphere, *sense-desire* and *ill-will*, can no longer impede, and these painful 'inner barbs' can no longer irritate. The extremes in temperament, *sloth* and *agitation*, cannot arise and disturb the serenity of one who has reached the perfect equipoise of the faculties of energy and calm; nor can there by any *doubtful wavering* in one of perfect wisdom.

It is for these reasons that, in this last verse of our text, the Arahat is portrayed as being 'doubt-free and serene, and free of inner barbs'.

The five hindrances illustrate once more some of the strands that keep the skin – be it fresh or partly worn-out – attached to the body. Unhindered by them and free from all that has been 'worn out', the Liberated One serenely goes his way into the Trackless – Nibbāna.

Notes

1.   These are the 'five aggregates' (*pañcakkhandhā*) into which the Buddha analyzes the individual personality.
2.   See Irene Quittner, 'Hate as Unwholesome Root', (BODHI LEAVES No. A 16).
3.   The words *he can curb* in verse 1 are a rendering of the Pāli word *vineti*, which, among other connotations, may have the two nuances of 'restraining' and 'removing'.
4.   See *The Removal of Distracting Thoughts*, tr. by Soma Thera, (WHEEL No. 21).
5.   Buddhist cosmology orders the planes of sentient existence into three spheres – the sense sphere, the fine-material sphere and the immaterial sphere. Human existence belongs to the sense sphere. Human beings who pass away after attaining the stage of non-return are reborn in the higher spheres, where they attain final liberation.
6.   Anguttara Nikāya, 3: 68.
7.   See below, 'The Four Nutriments of Life'.
8.   On these necrophilic, 'death-loving' tendencies, see Erich Fromm, *The Heart of Man* (New York: Harper and Row, 1964), pp. 37 ff.
9.   Quite similarly, in the Pāli language, *māna* (conceit) and *maññati* (conceiving).
10.   Majjhima Nikāya 20. Translated as *The Removal of Distracting Thoughts*, by Soma Thera, (WHEEL No. 21).
11.   In the discourse, the relevant Pāli term is *citta-sankhāra-saṇṭhāna*, and the commentary explains here *sankhāra* by condition (*paccaya*), cause (*kāraṇa*), and root or source (*mūla*). This phrase, however, could also be rendered by 'stilling the thought formations (or processes)'.
12.   Another important connotation of the term *papañca*, i.e. 'conceptual proliferation', has been emphasized and ably explained by Bhikkhu Ñāṇananda in his book *Concept and Reality* (Buddhist Publication Society, Kandy, 1971), which mainly deals with that term. But we feel that this meaning chiefly applies to a psychological context and not, as the author thinks (*ibid*. p. 26), also to our present text where the range of reference is wider than the topic of delusive concepts. The first line of the verse, for instance, refers to extremes of conduct and not only to those of conceptual thought. The concluding two lines, too, point to a wider significance.
13.   *appatiṭṭhaṁ*, 'without standing still' or 'without seeking a hold'.
14.   See the translation of this text with notes by Bhikkhu Ñāṇananda in *Saṁyutta Nikāya Anthology, Part II*, (WHEEL No. 183/185).
15.   The Pāli word *āyūhana* also means 'accumulation' of rebirth – producing actions (*kamma*), and thereby, of new lives.
16.   Here one may think too of the cosmic periods of evolving and shrinking

(*vivaṭṭa-saṃvaṭṭa*) within one world-cycle (*kappa*).

17.   This relates our paired terms to two of the five hindrances (*nīvaraṇa*), shown explicitly in verse 17 and its commentary.

The Power of
Mindfulness

Introduction

Is mindfulness actually a power in its own right as claimed by the title of this essay? Seen from the viewpoint of the ordinary pursuits of life, it does not seem so. From that angle mindfulness, or attention, has a rather modest place among many other seemingly more important mental faculties serving the purpose of variegated wish-fulfilment. Here, mindfulness means just 'to watch one's steps' so that one may not stumble or miss a chance in the pursuit of one's aims. Only in the case of specific tasks and skills is mindfulness sometimes cultivated more deliberately, but here too it is still regarded as a subservient function, and its wider scope and possibilities are not recognized.

Even if one turns to the Buddha's doctrine, taking only a surface view of the various classifications and lists of mental factors in which mindfulness appears, one may be inclined to regard this faculty just as 'one among many'. Again one may get the impression that it has a rather subordinate place and is easily surpassed in significance by other faculties.

Mindfulness in fact has, if we may personify it, a rather unassuming character. Compared with it, mental factors such as devotion, energy, imagination and intelligence are certainly more colourful personalities, making an immediate and strong impact on people and situations. Their conquests are sometimes rapid and vast, though often insecure. Mindfulness, on the other hand, is of an unobtrusive nature. Its virtues shine inwardly, and in ordinary life most of its merits are passed on to other mental faculties which generally receive all the credit. One must know mindfulness well and cultivate its acquaintance before one can appreciate its value and its silent penetrative influence. Mindfulness walks slowly and deliberately, and its daily task is of a rather humdrum nature. Yet where it places its feet it cannot easily be dislodged, and it acquires and bestows true mastery of the ground it covers.

Mental faculties of such a nature, like actual personalities of a similar type, are often overlooked or underrated. In the case of mindfulness, it required a genius like the Buddha to discover the 'hidden talent' in the modest garb, and to develop the vast inherent power of that potent seed. It is, indeed, the mark of a genius to perceive and to harness the power of the seemingly small. Here, truly, it happens that 'what is little becomes much'. A revaluation of values takes place. The standards of greatness and smallness change. Through the master mind of the Buddha, mindfulness is finally revealed as the Archimedean point where the vast revolving mass of world suffering is levered out of its twofold anchorage in ignorance and craving.

The Buddha spoke of the power of mindfulness in a very emphatic way:

> 'Mindfulness, I declare, is all-helpful.' (Saṁyutta Nikāya, 46: 59)
> 'All things can be mastered by mindfulness.' (Anguttara Nikāya, 8: 83)

Further, there is that solemn and weighty utterance opening and concluding the Satipaṭṭhāna Sutta, the Discourse on the Foundations of Mindfulness:

> This is the only way, monks, for the purification of beings, for the overcoming of sorrow and lamentation, for the destruction of pain and grief, for reaching the right path, for the attainment of Nibbāna, namely, the four foundations of mindfulness.

In ordinary life, if mindfulness, or attention, is directed to any object, it is rarely sustained long enough for the purpose of careful and factual observation. Generally it is followed immediately by emotional reaction, discriminative thought, reflection or purposeful action. In a life and thought governed by the Buddha's teaching too, mindfulness (sati) is mostly linked with clear comprehension (sampajañña) of the right purpose or suitability of an action, and other considerations. Thus again it is not viewed in itself. But to tap the actual and potential *power* of mindfulness it is necessary to understand and deliberately cultivate it in its basic, unalloyed form, which we shall call *bare attention*.

By bare attention we understand the clear and single-minded awareness of what actually happens *to* us and *in* us, at the successive moments of perception. It is called 'bare' because it attends to the bare facts of a perception without reacting to them by deed, speech or mental comment. Ordinarily, that purely receptive state of mind is, as we said, just a very brief phase of the thought process of which one is often scarcely aware. But in the methodical development of mindfulness aimed at the unfolding of its latent powers, bare attention is sustained for as long a time as one's strength of concentration permits. Bare attention then becomes the key to the meditative practice of Satipaṭṭhāna, opening the door to mind's mastery and final liberation.

Bare attention is developed in two ways: (1) as a methodical meditative practice with selected objects; (2) as applied, as far as practicable, to the normal events of the day, together with a general attitude of mindfulness and clear comprehension. The details of the practice have been described elsewhere, and need not be repeated here.[1]

The primary purpose of this essay is to demonstrate and explain the efficacy of this method, that is, to show the actual power of mindfulness. Particularly in an age like ours, with its superstitious worship of ceaseless external activity, there will be those who ask: 'How can such a passive attitude of mind as that of bare attention possibly lead to the great results claimed for it?' In reply, one may be inclined to suggest to the questioner that he should not rely on the words of others, but should put these assertions of the Buddha to the test of personal experience. But those who do not yet know the Buddha's teaching well enough to accept it as a reliable guide, may hesitate to take up – without good reasons – a practice that, on account of its radical simplicity, may appear strange to them. In the following a number of such 'good reasons' are therefore proffered for the reader's scrutiny. They are also meant as an introduction to the general spirit of Satipaṭṭhāna and as pointers to its wide and significant perspectives. Furthermore, it is hoped that he who has taken up the methodical training will recognize in the following observations certain features of his own practice, and be encouraged to cultivate them deliberately.

Four Sources of Power in Bare Attention

We shall now deal with four aspects of bare attention, which are the mainsprings of the power of mindfulness. They are not the only sources of its strength, but they are the principal ones to which its efficacy as a method of mental development is due. These four are:

1. the functions of 'tidying up' and 'naming' exercised by bare attention;
2. its non-violent, non-coercive procedure;
3. the capacity of stopping and slowing down;
4. the directness of vision bestowed by bare attention.

1. THE FUNCTIONS OF 'TIDYING' AND 'NAMING'

Tidying Up the Mental Household

If anyone whose mind is not harmonized and controlled through methodical meditative training should take a close look at his own everyday thoughts and activities, he will meet with a rather disconcerting sight. Apart from the few main channels of his purposeful thoughts and activities, he will everywhere be faced with a tangled mass of perceptions, thoughts, feelings and casual bodily movements, showing a disorderliness and confusion which he would certainly not tolerate in his living-room. Yet this is the state of affairs that we take for granted within a considerable portion of our waking life and our normal mental activity. Let us now look at the details of that rather untidy picture.

First we meet a vast number of casual sense-impressions such as sights and sounds, passing constantly through our minds. Most of them remain vague and fragmentary; some are even based on faulty perceptions and misjudgements. Carrying these inherent weaknesses, they often form the untested basis for judgements and decisions on a higher level of consciousness. True, all these casual sense-impressions need not and cannot be objects of focused attention. A stone on the road that happens to meet our glance will have a claim on our attention only if it obstructs our progress or is of interest to us for some reason. Yet if we neglect these casual impressions too often, we may stumble over many stones lying on our road and also overlook many gems.

Besides the casual sense impressions, there are those more significant and definite perceptions, thoughts, feelings and volitions, which have a closer connection with our purposeful life. Here too, we find that a very high proportion of them are in a state of utter confusion. Hundreds of cross-currents flash through the mind, and everywhere there are 'bits and ends' of unfinished thoughts, stifled emotions and passing moods. Many meet a premature death. Owing to their innately feeble nature, our lack of concentration or their suppression by new and stronger impressions, they do not persist and develop. If we observe our own minds, we shall notice how easily diverted our thoughts are, how often they behave like undisciplined disputants constantly interrupting each other and refusing to listen to the other side's arguments. Again, many lines of thought remain rudimentary or are left untranslated into will and action, because courage is lacking to accept their practical, moral or intellectual consequences. If we continue to examine more closely our average perceptions, thoughts or judgements, we shall have to admit that many of them are unreliable. They are just the products of habit, led by prejudices of intellect or emotion, by our pet preferences or aversions, by faulty or superficial observations, by laziness or by selfishness.

Such a look into long-neglected quarters of the mind will come as a wholesome shock to the observer. It will convince him of the urgent need for methodical mental culture extending below the thin surface layer of the mind to those vast twilight regions of consciousness we have just visited. The observer will then become aware that the relatively small sector of the mind that stands in the intense light of purposeful will and thought is not a reliable standard of the inner strength and lucidity of consciousness in its totality. He will also see that the quality of individual consciousness cannot be judged by a few optimal results of mental activity achieved in brief, intermittent periods. The decisive factor in determining the quality of consciousness is self-understanding and self-control: whether that dim awareness characteristic of our everyday mind and the uncontrolled portion of everyday activity tends to increase or decrease.

It is the daily little negligence in thoughts, words and deeds going on for many years of our lives (and as the Buddha teaches, for many existences), that is chiefly responsible for the untidiness and confusion we find in our minds. This negligence creates the trouble and allows it to continue. Thus the old Buddhist teachers have said: 'Negligence produces a lot of dirt. As in a house, so in the mind, only a very little dirt collects in a day or two, but if it goes on for many years, it will grow into a vast heap of refuse.'[2]

The dark, untidy corners of the mind are the hideouts of our most dangerous enemies. From there they attack us unawares, and much too often succeed in defeating us. That twilight world peopled by frustrated desires and suppressed resentments, by vacillations, whims and many other shadowy figures, forms a background from which upsurging passions – greed and lust, hatred and anger – may derive powerful support. Besides, the obscure and obscuring nature of that twilight region is the very element and mother-soil of the third and strongest of the three roots of evil (*akusala mūla*), ignorance or delusion.

Attempts at eliminating the mind's main defilements – greed, hate and delusion – must fail as long as these defilements find refuge and support in the uncontrolled dim regions of the mind; as long as the close and complex tissue of those half-articulate thoughts and emotions forms the basic texture of mind into which just a few golden strands of noble and lucid thought are woven. But how are we to deal with that unwieldy, tangled mass? Usually we try to ignore it and to rely on the counter-acting energies of our surface mind. But the only safe remedy is to face it – with mindfulness. Nothing more difficult is needed than to acquire the habit of directing bare attention to these rudimentary thoughts as often as possible. The working principle here is the simple fact that two thoughts cannot exist together at the same time: if the clear light of mindfulness is present, there is no room for mental twilight. When sustained mindfulness has secured a firm foothold, it will be a matter of comparatively secondary importance how the mind will then deal with those rudimentarty thoughts, moods and emotions. One may just dismiss them and replace them by purposeful thoughts; or one may allow and even compel them to complete what they have to say. In the latter case they will often reveal how poor and weak they actually are, and it will then not be difficult to dispose of them once they are forced into the open. This procedure of bare attention is very simple and effective; the difficulty is only the persistence in applying it.

Observing a complex thing means identifying its component

parts, singling out the separate strands forming that intricate tissue. If this is applied to the complex currents of mental and practical life, automatically a strong regulating influence will be noticeable. As if ashamed in the presence of the calmly observing eye, the course of thoughts will proceed in a less disorderly and wayward manner; it will not be so easily diverted, and will resemble more and more a well-regulated river.

During decades of the present life and throughout millennia of previous lives traversing the round of existence, there has steadily grown within each individual a closely knit system of intellectual and emotional prejudices, of bodily and mental habits that are no longer questioned as to their rightful position and useful function in human life. Here again, the application of bare attention loosens the hard soil of these often very ancient layers of the human mind, preparing thus the ground for sowing the seed of methodical mental training. Bare attention identifies and pursues the single threads of that closely inter-woven tissue of our habits. It sorts out carefully the subsequent justifications of passionate impulses and the pretended motives of our prejudices. Fearlessly it questions old habits often grown meaningless. It uncovers their roots, and thus helps abolish all that is seen to be harmful. In brief, bare attention lays open the minute crevices in the seemingly impenetrable structure of unquestioned mental processes. Then the sword of wisdom wielded by the strong arm of constant meditative practice will be able to penetrate these crevices, and finally to break up that structure where required. If the inner connections between the single parts of a seemingly compact whole become intelligible, they then cease to be inaccessible.

When the facts and details of the mind's conditioned nature are uncovered by meditative practice, there is an increased chance to effect fundamental changes in the mind. In that way, not only those hitherto unquestioned habits of the mind, its twilight regions and its normal processes as well, but even those seemingly solid, indisputable facts of the world of matter – all will become 'questionable' and lose much of their self-assurance. Many people are so impressed and intimidated by that bland self-assurance of assumed 'solid facts', that they hesitate to take up any spiritual training, doubting that it can effect anything worthwhile. The application of bare attention to the task of tidying and regulating the mind will bring perceptible results – results which will dispel their doubts and encourage in them the confidence to enter a spiritual path.

The tidying or regulating function of bare attention, we should note, is of fundamental importance for that 'purification of beings' mentioned by the Buddha as the first aim of Satipaṭṭhāna. This phrase refers, of course, to the purification of their minds, and here the very first step is to bring initial order into the functioning of the mental processes. We have seen how this is done by bare attention. In that sense, the commentary to the Discourse on the Foundations of Mindfulness explains the words 'for the purification of beings' as follows:

> It is said: 'Mental taints defile beings; mental clarity purifies them.' That mental clarity comes to be by this way of mindfulness.

Naming

We said before that bare attention 'tidies up' or regulates the mind by sorting out and identifying the various confused strands of the mental process. That identifying function, like any other mental activity, is connected with a verbal formulation. In other words, 'identifying' proceeds by way of expressly 'naming' the respective mental processes.

Primitive man believed that words could exercise a magical power: 'Things that could be named had lost their secret power over man, the horror of the unknown. To know the name of a force, a being or an object was (to primitive man) identical with the mastery over it.'[3] That ancient belief in the magical potency of names appears also in many fairy tales and myths, where the power of a demon is broken just by facing him courageously and pronouncing his name.

There is an element of truth in the 'word-magic' of primitive man, and in the practice of bare attention we shall find the power of naming confirmed. The 'twilight demons' of the mind – our passionate impulses and obscure thoughts – cannot bear the simple but clarifying question about their 'names', much less the knowledge of these names. Hence this is often alone sufficient to diminish their strength. The calmly observant glance of mindfulness discovers the demons in their hiding-places. The practice of calling them by their names drives them out into the open, into the daylight of consciousness. There they will feel embarrassed and obliged to justify themselves, although at this stage of bare attention they have not yet even been subjected to any closer questioning except about their names, their identity. If forced into the open while still in an incipient stage, they will be incapable of withstanding scrutiny and will just dwindle away. Thus a first victory over them may be won, even at an early stage of the practice.

The appearance in the mind of undesirable and ignoble thoughts, even if they are very fleeting and only half-articulate, has an unpleasant effect upon one's self-esteem. Therefore such thoughts are often shoved aside, unattended to and unopposed. Often they are also camouflaged by more pleasing and respectable labels which hide their true nature. Thoughts disposed of in either of these two ways will strengthen the accumulated power of ignoble tendencies in the subconscious. Furthermore, these procedures will weaken one's will to resist the arising and the dominance of mental defilements, and strengthen the tendency to evade the issues. But by applying the simple method of clearly and honestly naming or registering any undesirable thoughts, these two harmful devices, ignoring and camouflage, are excluded. Thence their detrimental consequences on the structure of the subconscious and their diversion of mental effort will be avoided.

When ignoble thoughts or personal shortcomings are called by their right names, the mind will develop an inner resistance and even repugnance against them. In time it may well succeed in keeping them in check and finally eliminating them. Even if these means do not bring undesirable tendencies fully under control at once, they will stamp upon them the impact of repeated resistance which will weaken them whenever they reappear. To continue our personification, we may say that unwholesome thoughts will no longer be the unopposed masters of the scene, and this diffidence of theirs will make them considerably easier to deal with. It is the power of moral shame (*hiri-bala*) that has been mustered here as an ally, methodically strengthened by these simple yet subtle psychological techniques.

The method of naming and registering also extends, of course, to noble thoughts and impulses which will be encouraged and strengthened. Without being given deliberate attention, such wholesome tendencies often pass unnoticed and remain barren. But when clear awareness is applied to them, it will stimulate their growth.

It is one of the most beneficial features of right mindfulness, and particularly of bare attention, that it enables us to utilize all external events and inner mental events for our progress. Even the unsalutary can be made a starting point for the salutary if, through the device of naming or registering, it becomes an object of detached knowledge.

In several passages of the Satipaṭṭhāna Sutta the function of naming or 'bare registering' seems to be indicated by formulating the respective statements by way of direct speech. There are no less than four such instances in the discourse:

(1) 'When experiencing a pleasant feeling, he knows "I experience a pleasant feeling",' etc.;
(2) 'He knows of a lustful (state of) mind, "Mind is lustful",' etc.;
(3) 'If (the hindrance of) sense desire is present in him, he knows, "Sense desire is present in me",' etc.;
(4) 'If the enlightenment factor mindfulness is present in him, he knows, "The enlightenment factor mindfulness is present in me",' etc.

In concluding this section, we briefly point out that the *tidying up* and the *naming* of mental processes is the indispensable preparation for fully understanding them in their true nature, the task of insight (*vipassanā*). These functions, exercised by bare attention, will help dispel the illusion that the mental processes are compact. They will also help us to discern their specific nature or characteristics, and to notice their momentary rise and fall.

2. THE NON-COERCIVE PROCEDURE

Obstacles to Meditation

Both the world surrounding us and the world of our own minds are full of hostile and conflicting forces causing us pain and frustration. We know from our own bitter experience that we are not strong enough to meet and conquer all these antagonistic forces in open combat. In the external world we cannot have everything exactly as we want it, while in the inner world of the mind, our passions, impulses and whims often override the demands of duty, reason and our higher aspirations.

We further learn that often an undesirable situation will only worsen if excessive pressure is used against it. Passionate desires may grow in intensity if one tries to silence them by sheer force of will. Disputes and quarrels will go on endlessly and grow fiercer if they are fanned again and again by angry retorts or by vain attempts to crush the other man's position. A disturbance during work, rest or meditation will be felt more strongly and will have a longer-lasting impact if one reacts to it by resentment and anger and attempts to suppress it.

Thus, again and again, we meet with situations in life where we cannot *force* issues. But there are ways of mastering the vicissitudes of life and conflicts of mind without application of force. Non-violent means may often succeed where attempts at coercion, internal or external, fail. Such a non-violent way of mastering life and mind is Satipaṭṭhāna. By the methodical application of bare attention, the basic practice in the development of right mindfulness, all the latent powers of a non-coercive approach will gradually unfold, with their beneficial results and their wide and unexpected implications. In this context we are mainly concerned with the benefits of Satipaṭṭhāna for the mastery of mind, and for the progress in meditation that may result from a non-coercive procedure. But we shall also cast occasional side glances at its repercussions on everyday life. It will not be difficult for a thoughtful reader to make more detailed application to his own problems.

The antagonistic forces that appear in meditation and that are liable to upset its smooth course are of three kinds:

1. external disturbances, such as noise;
2. mental defilements (*kilesa*), such as lust, anger, restlessness, dissatisfaction or sloth, which may arise at any time during meditation; and
3. various incidental stray thoughts, or surrender to daydreaming.

These distractions are the great stumbling blocks for a beginner in meditation who has not yet acquired sufficient dexterity to deal with them effectively. To give thought to those disturbing factors only when they actually arise at the time of meditation is insufficient. If caught unprepared in one's defence, one will struggle with them in a more or less haphazard and ineffective way, and with a feeling of irritation which will itself be an additional impediment. If disturbances of any kind and unskilful reactions to them occur several times during one session, one may come to feel utterly frustrated and irritated and give up further attempts to meditate, at least for the present occasion.

In 'fact, even meditators who are quite well informed by books or a teacher about all the details concerning their subject of meditation often lack instruction on how to deal skilfully with the disturbances they may meet. The feeling of helplessness in facing them is the most formidable difficulty for a beginning meditator. At that point many accept defeat, abandoning prematurely any further effort at methodical practice. As in worldly affairs, so in meditation, one's way of dealing with the 'initial difficulties' will often be decisive for success or failure.

When faced by inner and outer disturbances, the inexperienced or uninstructed beginner will generally react in two ways. He will first try to shove them away lightly, and if he fails in that, he will try to suppress them by sheer force of will. But these disturbances are like insolent flies: by whisking – first lightly and then with increasing vigour and anger – one may perhaps succeed in driving them away for a while, but usually they will return with an exasperating constancy, and the effort and vexation of whisking will have produced only an additional disturbance of one's composure.

Satipaṭṭhāna, through its method of bare attention, offers a non-violent alternative to those futile and even harmful attempts at suppression by force. A successful non-violent procedure in mind-control has to start with the right attitude. There must be first the full cognizance and sober acceptance of the fact that those three disturbing factors are co-inhabitants of the world we live in, whether we like it or not. Our disapproval of them will not alter the fact. With some we shall have to come to terms, and concerning the others – the mental defilements – we shall have to learn how to deal with them effectively until they are finally conquered.

1. Since we are not the sole inhabitants of this densely populated world, there are bound to be *external disturbances* of various kinds, such as noise and interruptions by visitors. We cannot always live in 'splendid isolation', 'from noise of men and dogs untroubled', or in 'ivory towers' high above the crowd. Right meditation is not escapism; it is not meant to provide hiding-places for temporary oblivion. Realistic meditation has the purpose of training the mind to face, to understand and to conquer this very world in which we live. And this world inevitably includes numerous obstacles to the life of meditation.

2. The Burmese meditation master, the Venerable Mahāsi Sayadaw, said: 'In an unliberated worldling *mental defilements* are sure to arise again and again. He has to face that fact and know these defilements well in order to apply again and again the appropriate remedy of Satipaṭṭhāna. Then they will grow weaker, more short-lived and will finally disappear.' To know the occurrence and nature of defilements is therefore as important for a meditator as to know the occurrence of his noble thoughts.

By facing one's own defilements one will be stirred to increase the effort to eliminate them. On the other hand, if out of a false shame or pride one tries to avert one's glance when they arise, one will never truly join issue with them, and will always evade the final and decisive encounter. By hitting blindly at them, one will only exhaust or even hurt oneself. But by observing carefully their nature and behaviour when they arise in one's own mind, one will be able to meet them well prepared, often to forestall them and finally to banish them fully. Therefore meet your defilements with a free and open glance! Be not ashamed, afraid or discouraged!

3. The third group of intruders disturbing the meditator's mind are *stray thoughts* and *daydreams*. These may consist of various memories and images of the past, recent or remote, including those emerging from subconscious depths; thoughts of the future – planning, imagining, fearing, hoping; and the casual sense-perceptions that may occur at the very time of meditation, often dragging after them a long trail of associated ideas. Whenever concentration and mindfulness slacken, stray thoughts or daydreams appear and fill the vacuum. Though they seem insignificant in themselves, through their frequent occurrence they form a most formidable obstacle, not only for the beginner, but in all cases when the mind is restless or distracted. However, when these invaders can be kept at bay, even long continuous periods of meditation can be achieved. As in the case of the mental defilements, stray thoughts will be entirely excluded only at the stage of Arahatship, when the perfect mindfulness thereby obtained keeps unfailing watch at the door of the mind.

If they are to shape our attitude, all these facts about the three kinds of disturbing factors must be given full weight and be fully absorbed by our minds. Then, in these three disturbing factors, the noble truth of suffering will manifest itself to the meditator very incisively through his own personal experience: 'Not to obtain what one wants is suffering.' The three other noble truths should also be exemplified by reference to the same situation. In such a way, even when dealing with impediments, the meditator will be within the domain of Satipaṭṭhāna. He will be engaged in the mindful awareness of the Four Noble Truths – part of the contemplation of mental objects (*dhammānupas-sanā*).[4] It is characteristic of right mindfulness, and one of its tasks, to relate the actual experiences of life to the truths of the Dhamma, and to use them as opportunities for its practical realization. Already at this preliminary stage devoted to the shaping of a correct and helpful attitude, we have the first successful test of our peaceful weapons: by understanding our adversaries better, we have consolidated our position which was formerly weakened by an emotional approach; and by transforming these adversaries into teachers of the truths, we have won the first advantage over them.

Three Countermeasures

If we are mentally prepared by a realistic view of these three factors antagonistic to meditation, we shall be less inclined to react at once with irritation when they actually arise. We shall be emotionally in a better position to meet them with the non-violent weapons of which we shall now speak.

There are three devices for countering disturbances that arise in meditation. The three should be applied in succession whenever the preceding device has failed to dispose of the disturbance. All three are applications of bare attention; they differ in the degree and duration of attention given to the disturbance. The guiding rule here is: to give no more mental emphasis to the respective disturbance than is actually required by circumstances.

1. First, one should notice the disturbance clearly, but lightly: that is, without emphasis and without attention to details. After that brief act of noticing, one should try to return to the original subject of meditation. If the disturbance was weak or one's preceding concentration fairly strong, one may well succeed in resuming contemplation. At that stage, by being careful not to get involved in any 'conversation' or argument with the intruder, we shall on our part not give it a reason to stay long; and in a good number of cases the disturbance will soon depart like a visitor who does not receive a

very warm welcome. That curt dismissal may often enable us to return to our original meditation without any serious disturbance to the composure of mind.

The non-violent device here is: to apply bare attention to the disturbance, but with a minimum of response to it, and with a mind bent on withdrawal. This is the very way in which the Buddha himself dealt with inopportune visitors, as described in the Mahāsuññata Sutta: '. . . with a mind bent on seclusion . . . and withdrawn, his conversation aiming at dismissing (those visitors).' Similar is Śā[or:Shā]ntideva's advice on how to deal with fools: if one cannot avoid them, one should treat them 'with the indifferent politeness of a gentleman'.

2. If, however, the disturbance persists, one should repeat the application of bare attention again and again, patiently and calmly; and it may be that the disturbance will vanish when it has spent its force. Here the attitude is to meet the repeated occurrence of a disturbance by a reiterated 'No', a determined refusal to be deflected from one's course. This is the attitude of patience and firmness. The capacity for watchful observation has to be aided here by the capacity to wait and to hold one's ground.

These two devices will generally be successful with incidental stray thoughts and daydreams, which are feeble by nature, but the other two types of disturbances, the external ones and defilements, may also yield quite often.

3. But if, for some reason, they do *not* yield, one should deliberately turn one's full attention to the disturbance and make it an object of knowledge. Thus one transforms it from a *disturbance* to meditation into a legitimate *object* of meditation. One may continue with that new object until the external or internal cause for attending to it has ceased; or, if it proves satisfactory, one may even retain it for the rest of that session.

For instance, when disturbed by a persistent noise, we should give the noise our undivided attention, but we should take care to distinguish the object itself from our reaction to it. For example, if resentment arises, it should be clearly recognized in its own nature whenever it arises. In doing so we shall be practising the contemplation of mind-objects (*dhammānupassanā*) according to the following passage of the Satipaṭṭhāna Sutta: 'He knows the ear and sounds, and the fetter (e.g. resentment) arising through both.' If the noise is intermittent or of varying intensity, one will easily be able to discern the rise

63

and fall (*udayabbaya*) in its occurrence. In that way one will add to one's direct insight into impermanency (*aniccatā*).

The attitude towards recurrent mental defilements, such as thoughts of lust and restlessness, should be similar. One should face them squarely, but distinguish them from one's reaction to them, e.g. connivance, fear, resentment, irritation. In doing so, one is making use of the device of 'naming', and one will reap the benefits mentioned above. In the recurrent waves of passion or restlessness, gradually one will likewise learn to distinguish phases of 'high' and 'low', their 'ups and downs', and may also gain other helpful knowledge about their behaviour. By that procedure, one again remains entirely within the range of Satipaṭṭhāna by practising the contemplation of the state of mind (*cittānupassanā*) and of mind-objects (*dhammānupassanā*: attention to the hindrances).

This method of transforming disturbances to meditation into objects of meditation, as simple as it is ingenious, may be regarded as the culmination of non-violent procedure. It is a device very characteristic of the spirit of Satipaṭṭhāna, to make use of all experiences as aids on the path. In that way enemies are turned into friends; for all these disturbances and antagonistic forces become our teachers, and teachers, whoever they may be, should be regarded as friends.

We cannot forego quoting here a passage from a noteworthy little book, *The Little Locksmith* by Katherine Butler Hathaway, a moving human document of fortitude and practical wisdom acquired by suffering:

> I am shocked by the ignorance and wastefulness with which persons who should know better throw away the things they do not like. They throw away experiences, people, marriages, situations, all sorts of things because they do not like them. If you throw away a thing, it is gone. Where you had something you have nothing. Your hands are empty, they have nothing to work on. Whereas, almost all those things which get thrown away are capable of being worked over by a little magic into just the opposite of what they were . . . But most human beings never remember at all that in almost every bad situation there is the possibility of a transformation by which the undesirable may be changed into the desirable.

We said before that the occurrence of the three disturbing

elements cannot always be prevented. They are parts of our world, and their coming and going follows its own laws irrespective of our approval or disapproval. But by applying bare attention we can avoid being swept away or dislodged by them. By taking a firm and calm stand on the secure ground of mindfulness, we shall repeat in a modest degree, but in an essentially identical way, the historic situation under the Bodhi Tree. When Māra the Evil One, at the head of his army, claimed the soil on which the future Buddha sat, the latter refused to budge. Trusting in the power of mindfulness, we may confidently repeat the Bodhisatta's aspiration on that occasion: *Mā maṁ ṭhānā acavi!* 'May he (*Māra*) not dislodge me from this place' (Padhāna Sutta).

Let the intruders come and go. Like all the other members of that vast unceasing procession of mental and physical events that passes before our observant eyes in the practice of bare attention, they arise, and having arisen, they pass away.

Our advantage here is the obvious fact that two thought moments cannot be present at the same time. Attention refers, strictly speaking, not to the present but to the moment that has just passed away. Thus, as long as mindfulness holds sway, there will be no 'disturbance' or 'defiled thought'. This gives us the chance to hold on to that secure ground of an 'observer's post', our own potential 'throne of enlightenment'.

By the quietening and neutralizing influence of detached observation as applied in our three devices, the interruptions of meditation will increasingly lose the sting of irritation, and thereby their disturbing effect. This will prove to be an act of true *virāga* (dispassion), which literally means 'decolouring'. When these experiences are stripped of the emotional tinge that excites towards lust, aversion, irritation and other defilements of the mind, they will appear in their true nature as bare phenomena (*suddha-dhammā*).

The non-violent procedure of bare attention endows the meditator with the light but sure touch so essential for handling the sensitive, evasive and refractory nature of the mind. It also enables him to deal smoothly with the various difficult situations and obstacles met with in daily life. To illustrate the even quality of energy required for attaining to the meditative absorptions, *The Path of Purification* (*Visuddhimagga*) describes a test which students of surgery in ancient days had to undergo as a proof of their skill. A lotus leaf was placed in a bowl of water, and the pupil had to make an incision through the length of the leaf, without cutting it entirely or submerging it. He who applied an excess of force either cut the leaf into two or pressed it into the water, while the timid one did not even dare to scratch it. In fact, something like the gentle but firm hand of the surgeon is required in mental training, and this skilful, well-balanced touch will be the natural outcome of the non-violent procedure in the practice of bare attention.

3. STOPPING AND SLOWING-DOWN

Keeping Still

For a full and unobstructed unfoldment of the mind's capacities, the influence of two complimentary forces is needed: *activating* and *restraining*. That twofold need was recognized by the Buddha, the great knower of mind. He advised that the faculties of energy (*viriy'indriya*) and of concentration (*samādh'indriya*) should be kept equally strong and well balanced.[5] Furthermore, he recommended three of the seven factors of enlightenment (*bojjhanga*) as suitable for rousing the mind, and another three for calming it.[6] In both cases, among the spiritual faculties and the enlightenment factors, it is mindfulness that not only watches over their equilibrium, but also activates those that are sluggish and restrains those that are too intense.

Mindfulness, though seemingly of a passive nature, is in fact an activating force. It makes the mind alert, and alertness is indispensable for all purposeful activity. In the present inquiry, however, we shall be mainly concerned with the *restraining* power of mindfulness. We shall examine how it makes for disentanglement and detachment and how it positively helps in the development of the mental qualities required for the work of deliverance.

In practising bare attention, we *keep still* at the mental and spatial place of observation, amidst the loud demands of the inner and outer world. Mindfulness possesses the strength of tranquillity, the capacity for deferring action and applying the brake, for *stopping* rash interference and for suspending judgement while pausing to observe facts and to reflect upon them wisely. It also brings a wholesome *slowing-down* in the impetuosity of thought, speech and action. Keeping still and stopping, pausing and slowing-down – these will be our key words when speaking now of the restraining effect of bare attention.

An ancient Chinese book states:

In making things end, and in making things start,
there is nothing more glorious than *keeping still*.

In the light of the Buddha's teaching, the true 'end of things' is Nibbāna which is called the '*stilling* of formations' (*sankhārānaṁ vūpasamo*), that is, their final end or cessation. It is also called 'the stopping' (*nirodha*). The 'things' or 'formations' meant here are the conditioned and impersonal phenomena rooted in craving and ignorance. The end of formations comes to be by the end of 'forming', that is, by the end of world-creating kammic activities. It is the 'end of the world' and of suffering, which the Buddha proclaimed cannot be reached by walking, migrating or transmigrating, but can be found within ourselves. That end of the world is heralded by each deliberate act of *keeping still*, *stopping* or *pausing*. 'Keeping still', in that highest sense, means stopping the accumulation of kamma, abstaining from our unceasing concern with evanescent things, abstaining from perpetually adding to our entanglements in saṁsāra – the round of repeated birth and death. By following the way of mindfulness, by training ourselves to keep still and pause in the attitude of bare attention, we refuse to take up the world's persistent challenge to our dispositions for greed or hatred. We protect ourselves against rash and delusive judgements; we refrain from blindly plunging into the whirlpool of interfering action with all its inherent dangers.

He who abstains from interfering is everywhere secure.

Sutta Nipāta v. 953

He who keeps still and knows where to stop will not meet danger.

Tao-Te-Ching, Chapter 44

The Chinese saying quoted earlier states in its second part that there is nothing more glorious in *making things start* than in keeping still. Explained in the Buddhist sense, these things effectively started by keeping still are 'the things (or qualities) making for decrease of kammic accumulation'. In dealing with them, we may follow the traditional division of mental training into morality (or conduct), concentration (or tranquillity) and wisdom (or insight). All three are decisively helped by the attitude of *keeping still* cultivated by bare attention.

1. *Conduct.* How can we improve our conduct, its moral quality and its skill in taking right decisions? If we earnestly desire such an improvement, it will generally be wisest to choose the line of least resistance. If we turn too quickly against those shortcomings deeply rooted in old habits or in powerful impulses, we might suffer discouraging defeat. We should pay attention first to our blemishes of action and speech and our errors of judgement caused by thoughtlessness and rashness. Of these there are many. In our lives there are numerous instances where one short moment of reflection might have prevented a false step, and thereby warded off a long chain of misery or moral guilt that started with a single moment of thoughtlessness. But how can we curb our rash reactions, and replace them by moments of mindfulness and reflection? To do so will depend on our capacity to *stop and pause*, to apply the brakes at the right time, and this we can learn by practising bare attention. In that practice we shall train ourselves 'to look and wait', to suspend reactions or slow them down. We shall learn it first the easy way, in situations of our own choice, within the limited field of experiences met with during the periods of meditative practice. When facing again and again the incidental sense-impressions, feelings or stray thoughts which interrupt our concentration; when curbing again and again our desire to respond to them in some way; when succeeding again and again in keeping still in face of them – we shall be preparing ourselves to preserve that inner stillness in the wider and unprotected field of everyday life. We shall have acquired a presence of mind that will enable us to pause and stop, even if we are taken by surprise or are suddenly provoked or tempted.

Our present remarks refer to those blemishes of conduct liable to arise through thoughtlessness and rashness, but which may be more or less easily checked through mindfulness. Dexterity in dealing with these will also affect those more obstinate deviations from moral conduct rooted in strong passionate impulses or in deeply ingrained bad habits. The increased tranquillity of mind achieved in keeping still for bare attention will restrain the impetuosity of passions. The acquired habit of pausing and stopping will act as a brake to the ingrained habits of indulging in unwholesome deeds.

By being able to keep still for bare attention, or to pause for wise reflection, very often the first temptation to lust, the first wave of anger, the first mist of delusion, will disappear without causing serious entanglement. At which point the current of unwholesome thought processes is stopped will depend on the quality of mindfulness. If mindfulness is keen, it will succeed at a very early point in calling a stop to a series of defiled thoughts or actions before we are carried along by them too far. Then the respective defilements will not grow beyond their initial strength, less effort will be required to check them and fewer kammic entanglements, or none, will follow.

Let us take the example of a pleasant visual object which has aroused our liking. At first that liking might not be very active and insistent. If at this point the mind is already able to keep still for detached observation or reflection, the visual perception can easily be divested of its still very slight admixture of lust. The object becomes registered as 'just something seen that has caused a pleasant feeling', or the attraction felt is sublimated into a quiet aesthetic pleasure. But if that earliest chance has been missed, the liking will grow into attachment and into the desire to possess. If now a stop is called, the thought of desire may gradually lose its strength; it will not easily turn into an insistent craving, and no actual attempts to get possession of the desired object will follow. But if the current of lust is still unchecked, then the thought of desire may express itself by speech in asking for the object or even demanding it with impetuous words. That is, unwholesome mental kamma is followed by unwholesome verbal kamma. A refusal will cause the original current of lust to branch out into additional streams of mental defilements, either sadness or anger. But if even at that late stage one can stop for quiet reflection or bare attention, accept the refusal, and renounce wish-fulfilment, further complications will be avoided. However, if clamouring words are followed by unwholesome bodily kamma, and if, driven by craving, one tries to get possession of the desired object by stealth or force, then the kammic entanglement is complete and its consequences must be experienced in their full impact. But still, if even after the completion of the evil act, one stops for reflection, it will not be in vain. For the mindfulness that arises in the form of remorseful retrospection will preclude a hardening of character and may prevent a repetition of the same action. The

Exalted One once said to his son, Rāhula (Majjhima Nikāya, 61):

> Whatever action you *intend* to perform, by body, speech or mind, you should consider that action. . . . If, in considering it, you realize: 'This action which I intend to perform will be harmful to myself, or harmful to others, or harmful to both; it will be an unwholesome action, producing suffering, resulting in suffering' – then you should certainly not perform that action.

> Also *while* you are performing an action, by body, speech or mind, you should consider that action. . . . If, in considering it, you realize: 'This action which I am performing is harmful to myself, or harmful to others, or harmful to both; it is an unwholesome action, producing suffering, resulting in suffering' – then you should desist from such an action.

> Also *after* you have performed an action, by body, speech or mind, you should consider that action. . . . If, in considering it, you realize: 'This action which I have performed has been harmful to myself, or harmful to others, or harmful to both; it was an unwholesome action producing suffering, resulting in suffering' – then you should in future refrain from it.

2. *Tranquillity.* We shall now consider how stopping for bare attention also helps one to attain and strengthen tranquillity (*samatha*) in its double sense: general peace of mind and meditative concentration.

By developing the habit of pausing for bare attention, it becomes increasingly easier to withdraw into one's own inner stillness when unable to escape bodily from the loud, insistent noises of the outer world. It will be easier to forego useless reactions to the foolish speech or deeds of others. When the blows of fate are particularly hard and incessant, a mind trained in bare attention will find a refuge in the haven of apparent passivity or watchful non-action, from which position it will be able to wait patiently until the storms have passed. There are situations in life when it is best to allow things to come to their natural end. He who is able to keep still and wait will often succeed where aggressiveness or busy activity would fail. Not only in critical situations, but also in the normal course of life, the experience won by observant keeping still will convince us that we need not actively respond to every impression we receive, or regard every encounter with people or things as a challenge to our interfering activity.

By refraining from busying ourselves unnecessarily, external frictions will be reduced and the internal tensions they bring will loosen up. Greater harmony and peace will pervade the life of every day, bridging the gap between normal life and the tranquillity of meditation. Then there will be fewer of those disturbing inner reverberations of everyday restlessness which, in a coarse or subtle form, invade the hours of meditation, producing bodily and mental unrest. Consequently, the hindrance of agitation, a chief obstacle to concentration, will appear less often and will be easier to overcome when it arises.

By cultivating the attitude of bare attention as often as opportunity offers, the centrifugal forces of mind, making for mental distraction, will peter out; the centripetal tendency, turning the mind inward and making for concentration, will gather strength. Craving will no longer run in pursuit of a variety of changing objects.

Regular practice of sustained attention to a continuous series of events prepares the mind for sustained concentration on a *single* object, or a limited number of objects, in the strict practice of meditation. Firmness or steadiness of mind, another important factor in concentration, will likewise be cultivated.

Thus, the practice of keeping still, pausing and stopping for bare attention, fosters several salient components of meditative tranquillity: calmness, concentration, firmness and reduction of the multiplicity of objects. It raises the average level of normal consciousness and brings it closer to the level of the meditative mind. This is an important point because often too wide a gap between these two mental levels repeatedly frustrates attempts at mental concentration and hinders the achievement of smooth continuity in meditative practice.

In the sequence of the seven factors of enlightenment, we find that the enlightenment factor of tranquillity (*passaddhi-sambojjhaṅga*) precedes that of concentration (*samādhi-sambojjhaṅga*). Expressing the same fact, the Buddha says: 'If tranquillized within, the mind will become concentrated.' Now in the light of our previous remarks, we shall better understand these statements.

3. *Insight.* It has been said by the Exalted One: 'He whose mind is concentrated sees things as they really are.' Therefore, all those ways by which bare attention strengthens concentration also provide a supporting condition for the development

of insight. But there is also a more direct and specific help which insight receives from keeping still in bare attention.

Generally, we are more concerned with handling and using things than with knowing them in their true nature. Thus we usually grasp in haste the very first few signals conveyed to us by a perception. Then, through deeply ingrained habit, those signals evoke a standard response by way of judgements such as good-bad, pleasant-unpleasant, useful-harmful, right-wrong. These judgements, by which we define the objects in relation to ourselves, lead to corresponding reactions by word or deed. Only rarely does attention dwell upon a common or familiar object for any longer time than is needed to receive the first few signals. So, for the most part, we perceive things in a fragmentary manner and thence misconceive them. Further, only the very first phase of the object's life-span, or a little more, comes into the focus of our attention. One may not even be consciously aware that the object is a process with an extension in time – a beginning and an end; that it has many aspects and relations beyond those casually perceived in a limited situation; that, in brief, it has a kind of evanescent individuality of its own. A world perceived in this superficial way will consist of shapeless little lumps of experiences marked by a few sub-jectively selected signs or symbols. The symbols chosen are determined mainly by the individual's self-interest; sometimes they are even misapplied. The shadow-like world that results includes not only the outer environment and other persons, but also a good part of one's own bodily and mental processes. These, too, become subjected to the same superficial manner of conceptualization. The Buddha points out four basic mis-conceptions that result from distorted perceptions and un-methodical attention: taking the impure for pure, the imperma-nent for lasting, the painful and pain-bringing for pleasant and the impersonal for a self or something belonging to the self. When the seal of self-reference is thus stamped again and again upon the world of everyday experience, the basic miscon-ception, 'This belongs to me' (attaniya) will steadily put forth roots into all the bodily and mental factors of our being. Like the hair-roots of a plant, these will be fine, but firm and widespread – to such an extent, in fact, that the notions of 'I' and 'mine' will hardly be shaken by merely intellectual convictions about the non-existence of a self (anattā).

These grave consequences issue from the fundamental

perceptual situation: our rush into hasty or habitual reactions after receiving the first few signals from our perceptions. But if we muster the restraining forces of mindfulness and pause for bare attention, the material and mental processes that form the objects of mind at the given moment will reveal themselves to us more fully and more truly. No longer dragged at once into the whirlpool of self-reference, allowed to unfold themselves before the watchful eye of mindfulness, they will disclose the diversity of their aspects and the wide net of their correlations and interconnections. The connection with self-interest, so narrow and often falsifying, will recede into the background, dwarfed by the wider view now gained. The processes observed display in their serial occurrence and in their component parts a constant birth and death, a rise and a fall. Thereby the facts of change and impermanence impress themselves on the mind with growing intensity. The same discernment of rise and fall dissolves the false conceptions of unity created under the influence of the egocentric attitude. Self-reference uncritically overrides diversity; it lumps things together under the preconceptions of *being* a self or *belonging* to a self. But bare attention reveals these sham unities as impersonal and conditioned phenomena. Facing thus again and again the evanescent, dependent and impersonal nature of life-processes within and without, we shall discover their monotony and unsatisfactory nature: in other words, the truth of suffering. Thus, by the simple device of slowing down, pausing and keeping still for bare attention, all three of the characteristics of existence – impermanence, suffering and non-self – will open themselves to penetrative insight (*vipassanā*).

Spontaneity

An acquired or strengthened habit of pausing mindfully before acting does not exclude a wholesome spontaneity of response. On the contrary, through training, the practice of pausing, stopping and keeping still for bare attention will itself become quite spontaneous. It will grow into a selective mechanism of the mind that, with an increasing reliability and swiftness of response, can prevent the upsurge of evil or unwise impulses. Without such a skill we may intellectually realize those impulses to be unwholesome, but still succumb to them owing to their own powerful spontaneity. The practice of pausing mindfully serves, therefore, to replace unwholesome spontaneity or habits by wholesome ones grounded in our better knowledge and nobler intentions.

Just as certain reflex movements automatically protect the body, similarly the mind needs spontaneous spiritual and moral self-protection. The practice of bare attention will provide this vital function. A person of average moral standards instinctively shrinks from thoughts of theft or murder. With the help of the method of bare attention, the range of such spontaneous moral brakes can be vastly extended and ethical sensitivity greatly heightened.

In an untrained mind, noble tendencies and right thoughts are often assailed by the sudden outbreak of passions and prejudices. They either succumb or assert themselves only with difficulty after an inner struggle. But if the spontaneity of the unwholesome is checked or greatly reduced, as described above, our good impulses and wise reflections will have greater scope to emerge and express themselves freely and spontaneously. Their natural flow will give us greater confidence in the power of the good within us; it will also carry more conviction for others. That spontaneity of the good will not be erratic, for it will have deep and firm roots in previous methodical training. Here appears a way by which a premeditated good thought (*sasaṅkhārika-kusala-citta*) may be transformed into a spontaneous good thought (*asaṅkhārika-kusala-citta*). According to the psychology of the Abhidhamma Piṭaka, such a thought, if combined with knowledge, takes the first place in the scale of ethical values. In this way we shall achieve a practical understanding of a saying in *The Secret of the Golden Flower*:[7] 'If one attains intentionally to an unintentional state one has comprehension.' This saying invites a paraphrase in Pāli terms: *Sasaṅkhārena asaṅkhārikaṁ pattabbaṁ*, 'By premeditated intentional effort spontaneity can be won.'

If the numerous aids to mental growth and liberation found in the Buddha's teachings are wisely utilized, there is actually nothing that can finally withstand the Satipaṭṭhāna method; and this method starts with the simple practice of learning to pause and stop for bare attention.

Slowing-down

Against the impetuosity, rashness and heedlessness of the untrained mind, the practice of pausing and stopping sets up a deliberate slowing-down. The demands of modern life, however, make it impracticable to introduce such a slowing-down of functions into the routine of the average working day. But as an antidote against the harmful consequences of the hectic speed of modern life, it is all the more important to cultivate that practice in one's leisure hours, especially in periods of strict Satipaṭṭhāna practice. Such practice will also bestow the worldly benefits of greater calm, efficiency and skill in one's daily round of work.

For the purposes of meditative development, slowing-down serves as an effective training in heedfulness, sense-control and concentration. But apart from that, it has a more specific significance for meditative practice. In the commentary to the Satipaṭṭhāna Sutta, it is said that the slowing-down of movements may help in *regaining lost concentration* on a chosen object. A monk, so we read, had bent his arm quickly without remembering his subject of meditation as his rule of practice demanded. On becoming aware of that omission he took his arm back to its previous position and repeated the movement mindfully. The subject of meditation referred to was probably 'clearly comprehending action', as mentioned in the Sati-paṭṭhāna Sutta: 'In bending and stretching he acts with clear comprehension.'

The slowing-down of certain bodily movements during strict meditative training is particularly helpful in gaining *insight-knowledge (vipassanā-ñāṇa)*, especially the direct aware-ness of change and non-self. To a great extent, it is the rapidity of movement that strengthens the illusion of unity, identity and substantiality in what is actually a complex evanescent process. Therefore, in the strict practice of Satipaṭṭhāna, the slowing down of such actions as walking, bending and stretching, so as to discern the several phases of each movement, provides a powerful aid for direct insight into the three characteristics of all phenomena. The meditator's contemplation will gain increas-ing force and significance if he notices clearly how each partial phase of the process observed arises and ceases by itself, and nothing of it goes over or 'transmigrates' to the next phase.

Under the influence of pausing for bare attention, the average rhythm of our everyday actions, speech and thoughts will also become more quiet and peaceful. Slowing-down the hurried rhythm of life means that thoughts, feelings and perceptions will be able to complete the entire length of their natural lifetime. Full awareness will extend up to their end phase: to their last vibrations and reverberations. Too often that end phase is cut off by an impatient grasping at new impressions, or by hurrying on to the next stage of a line of thought before the earlier one has been clearly comprehended. This is one of the main reasons for the disorderly state of the average mind, which is burdened by a vast amount of indistinct or fragmentary perceptions, stunted emotions and undigested ideas. Slowing-down will prove an effective device for recovering the fullness and clarity of consciousness. A fitting simile, and at the same time an actual example, is the procedure called for in the practice of mindfulness of breathing (*ānāpānasati*): mindfulness has to cover the whole extent of the breath, its beginning, middle and end. This is what is meant by the passage in the sutta, 'Experiencing the *whole* (breath-) body, I shall breathe in and out.' Similarly, the entire 'breath' or rhythm of our lives will become deeper and fuller if, through slowing-down, we get used to sustained attention.

The habit of prematurely cutting off processes of thought, or slurring over them, has assumed serious proportions in the man of modern urban civilization. Restlessly he clamours for ever new stimuli in increasingly quicker succession just as he demands increasing speed in his means of locomotion. This rapid bombardment of impressions has gradually blunted his sensitivity, and thus he always needs new stimuli, louder, coarser and more variegated. Such a process, if not checked, can end only in disaster. Already we see at large a decline of finer aesthetic susceptibility and a growing incapacity for genuine natural joy. The place of both is taken by a hectic, short-breathed excitement incapable of giving any true aesthetic or emotional satisfaction. 'Shallow mental breath' is to a great extent responsible for the growing superficiality of 'civilized man' and for the frightening spread of nervous disorders in the West. It may well become the start of a general deterioration of human consciousness in its qualitative level, range and strength. This danger threatens all those, in the East as well as in the West, who lack adequate spiritual protection from the impact of technical civilization. Satipaṭṭhāna can make an important contribution to remedying this situation, in the way we have briefly indicated here. Thus the method will prove beneficial from the worldly point of view as well.

Here, however, we are chiefly concerned with the psycho-logical aspects of mindfulness and their significance for meditative development. Sustained attention, helped by slowing-down, will affect the quality of consciousness mainly in three ways: (a) in intensifying consciousness; (b) in clarifying the object's characteristic features; and (c) in revealing the object's relatedness.

(a) An object of sustained attention will exert a particularly *strong* and *long-lasting* impact on the mind. Its influence will be felt not only throughout the thought-series immediately following the particular perception, but may also extend far into the future. It is that causal efficacy which is the measure of the *intensity of consciousness.*

(b) Sustained attention leads to a *fuller picture* of the object in all its aspects. Generally, the first impression we gain of any new sense-object or idea will be its most striking feature; it is this aspect of the object which captures our attention up to the culminating point of the impact. But the object also displays other aspects or characteristics, and is capable of exercising functions, other than those we initially notice. These may be less obvious to us or subjectively less interesting; but they may be even more important. There will also be cases where our first impression is entirely deceptive. Only if we sustain our attention beyond that first impact will the object reveal itself more fully. In the downward course of the first perceptual wave the prejudicing force of the first impact lessens; and it is only then, in that end phase, that the object will yield a wider range of detail, a more complete picture of itself. It is therefore only by sustained attention that we can obtain a *clearer understanding of an object's characteristic features.*

(c) Among the characteristic features of any object, physical or mental, there is one class we often overlook due to hasty or superficial attention, and which therefore needs to be treated separately. This is the *relatedness* of the object. The object's relatedness extends back to its past – to its origin, causes, reasons and logical precedents; it also extends outward to embrace the total context – its background, environment and presently active influences. We can never fully understand things if we view them in artificial isolation. We have to see them as part of a wider pattern, in their conditioned and conditioning nature; and this can be done only with the help of sustained attention.

Subliminal Influences
The three ways of heightening consciousness just discussed

77

are clearly of prime importance for the development of insight. When consciousness is intensified, and its objective field clarified and discerned in its relational structure, the ground is prepared for 'seeing things according to reality'. But besides its obvious direct influence, this threefold process also has an indirect influence which is no less powerful and important: it strengthens and sharpens the mind's subliminal faculties of subconscious organization, memory and intuition. These again, on their part, nourish and consolidate the progress of liberating insight. The insight aided by them is like the mountain lake of the canonical simile: it is fed not only by the outside rains, but also by springs welling up from within its own depths. The insight nourished by these 'underground' subliminal resources of the mind will have deep roots. The meditative results that it brings cannot be lost easily, even with unliberated worldlings who are still subject to relapse.

1. Perceptions or thoughts which have been objects of sustained attention make a stronger impact on the mind and reveal their characteristic features more distinctly than when attention is slack. Thus, when they sink into the subconscious, they occupy a special position there. This holds true for all three ways of enhancing the consciousness of an object. (a) In a process of consciousness, if attention is as strong in the end phase as in the earlier phases, then when the process is finished and the mind lapses back into subconsciousness, the latter will be more amenable to conscious control. (b) If an impression or idea has been marked by numerous distinct characteristics, then when it fades from immediate awareness, it will not be so easily lost in the vague contents of the subconscious or dragged by passionate biases into false subconscious associations. (c) Similarly the correct comprehension of the object's related-ness will protect the experience from being merged with indistinct subconscious material. Perceptions or thoughts of enhanced intensity and clarity, absorbed into the subconscious, remain more articulate and more accessible than contents originating from hazy or 'stunned' impressions. It will be easier to convert them into full consciousness and they will be less unaccountable in their hidden effects upon the mind. If, through an improvement in the quality and range of mindful-ness, the number of such matured impressions increases, the results might be a subtle change in the very structure of subconsciousness itself.

2. It will be evident from our earlier remarks that those impressions that we have called 'matured' or 'more accessible and convertible', lend themselves more easily and more correctly to recollection – more easily because of their greater intensity, more correctly because their clearly marked features protect them from being distorted by false associative images or ideas. Remembering them in their context and relatedness works both ways – it promotes both easier and more correct recollection. Thus *sati* in its meaning and function of mindfulness helps to strengthen *sati* in its meaning and function of *memory*.

3. The influence of sustained attention on the subconscious and on memory brings a deepening and strengthening of the faculty of intuition, particularly the intuitive insight which chiefly concerns us here. Intuition is not a gift from the unknown. Like any other mental faculty, it arises out of specific conditions. In this case the primary conditions are latent memories of perceptions and thoughts stored in the sub-conscious. Obviously, the memories providing the most fertile soil for the growth of intuition will be those marked by greater intensity, clarity and wealth of distinctive marks; for it is these that are most accessible. Here, too, the preserved relatedness of the impressions will contribute much. Recollections of that type will have a more organic character than memories of bare or vague isolated facts, and they will fall more easily into new patterns of meaning and significance. These more articulate memory images will be a strong stimulation and aid for the intuitive faculty. Silently, in the hidden depths of the subliminal mind, the work of collecting and organizing the subconscious material of experience and knowledge goes on until it is ripe to emerge as an *intuition*. The break-through of that intuition is sometimes occasioned by quite ordinary happenings. How-ever, though seemingly ordinary, these events may have a strong evocative power if previously they had been made objects of sustained attention. Slowing-down and pausing for bare attention will uncover the depth dimension of the simple things of everyday life, and thus provide potential stimuli for the intuitive faculty. This applies also to the intuitive pene-tration of the Four Noble Truths that culminates in liberation (*arahatta*). The scriptures record many instances of monks who could not arrive at intuitive penetration when engaged in the actual practice of insight meditation. The flash of intuition struck them on quite different occasions: when stumbling

against a rock or catching sight of a forest fire, a mirage or a lump of froth in a river. We meet here another confirmation of that seemingly paradoxical saying that 'intentionally an unintentional state may be won'. By deliberately turning the full light of mindfulness on the smallest events and actions of everyday life, eventually the liberating wisdom may arise.

Sustained attention not only provides the nourishing soil for the *growth* of intuition, it also makes possible the fuller utilization and even repetition of the intuitive moment. Men of inspiration in various fields of creative activity have often deplored their common experience; the flash of intuition strikes so suddenly and vanishes so quickly that frequently the slow response of the mind hardly catches the last glimpse of it. But if the mind has been trained in observant pausing, in slowing-down and sustained attention, and if – as indicated above – the subconscious has been influenced, then the intuitive moment too might gain that fuller, slower and stronger rhythm. This being the case, its impact will be strong and clear enough to allow for full use of that flash of intuitive insight. It might even be possible to lead its fading vibrations upward again to a new culmination, similar to the rhythmic repetition of a melody rising again in harmonious development out of the last notes of its first appearance.

The full utilization of a single moment of intuitive insight could be of decisive importance for one's progress toward full realization. If one's mental grip is too weak and one lets those elusive moments of intuitive insight slip away without having utilized them fully for the work of liberation, then they might not recur until many years have passed, or perhaps not at all during the present life. Skill in sustained attention, however, will allow one to make full use of such opportunities, and slowing-down and pausing during meditative practice is an important aid in acquiring that skill.

Through our treatment of pausing, stopping and slowing-down, one of the traditional definitions of mindfulness found in the Pāli scriptures will have become more intelligible in its far-reaching implications: that is, its function of *anapilāpanatā*, meaning literally, 'not floating (or slipping) away'. 'Like pumpkin-pots on the surface of water', add the commentators, and they continue: 'Mindfulness enters deeply into its object, instead of hurrying only over its surface.' Therefore, 'non-superficiality' will be an appropriate rendering of the above Pāli term, and a fitting characterization of mindfulness.

4. DIRECTNESS OF VISION

I wish I could disaccustom myself from everything, so that I might see anew, hear anew, feel anew. Habit spoils our philosophy.

G. C. Lichtenberg (1742–1799)

In an earlier section we spoke about the impulsive spontaneity of the unwholesome. We have seen how stopping for bare and sustained attention is able to counter, or reduce, our rash impulsive reactions, thus allowing us to face any situation with a fresh mind, with a *directness of vision* unprejudiced by those first spontaneous responses.

By *directness of vision* we understand a direct view of reality, without any colouring or distorting lenses, without the intrusion of emotional or habitual prejudices and intellectual biases. It means: coming face to face with the bare facts of actuality, seeing them as vividly and freshly as if we were seeing them for the first time.

The Force of Habit

Those spontaneous reactions which so often stand in the way of direct vision do not derive only from our passionate impulses. Very frequently they are the product of *habit*. In that form, they generally have an even stronger and more tenacious hold on us – a hold which may work out either for our good or for our harm. The influence habit exercises for the *good* is seen in the 'power of repeated practice'. This power protects our achievements and skills – whether manual or mental, worldly or spiritual – against loss or forgetfulness, and converts them from casual, short-lived imperfect acquisitions into the more secure possession of a quality thoroughly mastered. The *detrimental* effect of habitual spontaneous reactions is manifest in what is called in a derogative sense the 'force of habit': its deadening, stultifying and narrowing influence productive of compulsive behaviour of various kinds. In our present context we shall be concerned only with that negative aspect of habit as impeding and obscuring the directness of vision.

As remarked earlier, habitual reactions generally have a

stronger influence upon our behaviour than impulsive ones. Our passionate impulses may disappear as suddenly as they have arisen. Though their consequences may be very grave and extend far into the future, their influence is in no way as long-lasting and deep-reaching as that of habit. Habit spreads its vast and closely meshed net over wide areas of our life and thought, trying to drag in more and more. Our passionate impulses, too, might be caught in that net and thus be transformed from passing outbursts into lasting traits of character. A momentary impulse, an occasional indulgence, a passing whim may by repetition become a habit we find difficult to uproot, a desire hard to control and finally an automatic function we no longer question. Repeated gratification turns a desire into a habit, and a habit left unchecked grows into a compulson.

It sometimes happens that, at first, we regard a particular activity or mental attitude as without any special personal importance. The activity or attitude may be morally indifferent and inconsequential. At the start we might find it easy to abandon it or even to exchange it for its opposite, since neither our emotions nor reason bias us towards either alternative. But by repetition, we come to regard the chosen course of action or thought as 'pleasant, desirable and correct', even as 'righteous'; and thus we finally identify it with our character or personality. Consequently, we feel any break in this routine to be unpleasant or wrong. Any outside interference with it we greatly resent, even regarding such interference as a threat to our 'vital interests and principles'. In fact at all times primitive minds, whether 'civilized' or not, have looked at a stranger with his 'strange customs' as an enemy, and have felt his mere unaggressive presence as a challenge or threat.

At the beginning, when no great importance was ascribed to the specific habit, the attachment that gradually formed was directed not so much to the action proper as to the pleasure we derived from undisturbed routine. The strength of that attachment to routine derives partly from the force of physical and mental inertia, so powerful a motive in man; we shall presently refer to another cause for attachment to routine. By force of habit, the particular concern – whether a material object, an activity or a way of thinking – comes to be invested with such an increase of emotional emphasis, that the attachment to quite unimportant or banal things may become as tenacious as that to our more fundamental needs. Thus the lack of conscious control can turn even the smallest habits into the uncontested masters of our lives. It bestows upon them the dangerous power to limit and rigidify our character and to narrow our freedom of movement – environmental, intellectual and spiritual. Through our subservience to habit, we forge new fetters for ourselves and make ourselves vulnerable to new attachments, aversions, prejudices and predilections; that is, to new suffering. The danger for spiritual development posed by the dominating influence of habit is perhaps more serious today than ever before; for the expansion of habit is particularly noticeable in our present age when specialization and standardization reach into so many varied spheres of life and thought.

Therefore, when considering the Satipaṭṭhāna Sutta's words on the formation of fetters, we should also think of the important part played by habit:

> . . . and what fetter arises dependent on both (i.e. the sense organs and sense objects), that he knows well. In what manner the arising of the unarisen fetter comes to be, that he knows well.

In Buddhist terms, it is pre-eminently the hindrance of sloth and torpor (thīna-middha nīvaraṇa) which is strengthened by the force of habit, and it is the mental faculties such as agility and pliancy of mind (kāya and citta-lahutā, etc.)[8] that are weakened.

This tendency of habits to extend their range is anchored in the very nature of consciousness. It stems not only from the aforementioned passive force of inertia, but in many cases from an active will to dominate and conquer. Certain active types of consciousness, possessing a fair degree of intensity, tend to repeat themselves. Each one struggles to gain ascendancy, to become a centre around which other weaker mental and physical states revolve, adapting themselves to and serving that central disposition. This tendency is never quite undisputed, but still it prevails, and even peripheral or subordinate types of consciousness exhibit the same urge for ascendancy. This is a striking parallel to the self-assertion and domineering tendency of an egocentric individual in his contact with society. Among biological analogies, we may mention the tendency toward expansion shown by cancer and other pathological growths; the tendency toward repetition we meet in the freak mutations which loom as a grave danger at the horizon of our atomic age.

Because of that will to dominate inherent in many types of

consciousness, a passing whim may grow into a relatively constant trait of character. If still not satisfied with its position, it may break away entirely from the present combination of life forces until finally, in the process of rebirths, it becomes the very centre of a new personality. There are within us countless seeds for new lives, for innumerable potential 'beings', all of whom we should vow to liberate from the wheel of saṁsāra, as the Sixth Zen Patriarch expressed it.[9]

Detrimental physical or mental habits may grow strong, not only if fostered deliberately, but also if left unnoticed or unopposed. Much of what has now strong roots in our nature has grown from minute seeds planted in a long-forgotten past (see the Simile of the Creeper, Majjhima Nikāya 45). This growth of morally bad or otherwise detrimental habits can be effectively checked by gradually developing another habit: that of attending to them mindfully. If we now do deliberately what had become a mechanical performance, and if prior to doing it we pause a while for bare attention and reflection – this will give us a chance to scrutinize the habit and clearly comprehend its purpose and suitability (sātthaka and sappāya-sampajañña). It will allow us to make a fresh assessment of the situation, to see it directly, unobscured by the mental haze that surrounds a habitual activity with the false assurance: 'It is right because it was done before.' Even if a detrimental habit cannot be broken quickly, the reflective pause will counter its unquestioned spontaneity of occurrence. It will stamp it with the seal of repeated scrutiny and resistance, so that on its recurrence it will be weaker and will prove more amenable to our attempts to change or abolish it.

It need hardly be mentioned that habit, which has been rightly called 'the wet-nurse of man', cannot and should not disappear from our lives. Let us only remember what a relief it is, particularly in the crowded day and complex life of a city-dweller, to be able to do a great number of things fairly mechanically with, as it were, only 'half-powered attention'. Habit brings considerable simplification to our lives. It would be an unbearable strain if all our little humdrum activities had to be done with deliberate effort and close attention. In fact, many operations of manual labour, much of the technique in art, and even standard procedures in complex intellectual work, generally bring better and more even results through skilled routine performance. Yet that evenness of habitual performance will also reach its end point. Unless enlivened by the creation of new interest, it will show symptoms of fatigue and start to decline.

Of course it would be absurd to advocate that all our little habits be abolished, for many are innocuous and even useful. But we should regularly ask ourselves whether we still have control over them; whether we can give them up or alter them at will. We can answer this question for ourselves in two ways: first, by attending to our habitual actions mindfully for a certain period of time, and second, by actually giving them up temporarily in cases where this will not have any harmful or disturbing effects upon ourselves or others. If we turn on them the light of *direct vision*, looking at them or performing them as if for the first time, these little routine activities, and the habitual sights around us, will assume a new glow of interest and stimulation. This also holds good for our professional occupations and their environment, and for our close human relationships if they should have become stale by habit. The relationship to one's marriage partner, to friends and to colleagues may thus receive a great rejuvenation. A fresh and direct vision will also reveal that one can relate to people or do things in a different and more beneficial way than one did before by force of habit.

An acquired capacity to give up minor habits will prove its worth in the fight against more dangerous proclivities. It will also come to our aid at times when we are faced with serious changes in our lives which forcefully deprive us of fundamental habits. Loosening the hardened soil of our routine behaviour and thoughts will have an enlivening effect on our vital energy, our mental vigour and our power of imagination. But what is most important, into that loosened soil we shall be able to plant the seeds of vigorous spiritual progress.

Associative Thought

Mental habituation to standard reactions, to sequences of activity and to judgements of people or things, proceeds by way of associative thinking. From the objects, ideas, situations and people that we encounter, we select certain distinctive marks, and associate these marks with our own response to them. If these encounters recur, they are associated first with those marks selected earlier, and then with our original, or strongest response. Thus these marks become a signal for releasing a standard reaction, which may consist of a long sequence of connected acts or thoughts familiar through repeated practice or experience. This way of functioning makes it unnecessary for us to apply new effort and painstaking scrutiny to each single step in such a sequence. The result is a great simplification of life, permitting us to release energy for other tasks. In fact, in the evolution of the human mind, associative thinking was a progressive step of decisive importance. It enabled us to learn from experience, and thus led up to the discovery and application of causal laws.

Yet along with these benefits, associative thinking can also bring many grave dangers if it is applied faultily or thoughtlessly and not carefully controlled. Let us draw up a partial list of these danger points:

1. Associative thinking, recurring again and again in similar situations, may easily perpetuate and strengthen faulty or incomplete initial observations, errors of judgement and emotional prejudices such as love, hate and pride.

2. Incomplete observations and restricted viewpoints in judgement, sufficient to deal with one particular situation, may prove quite inadequate and entail grave consequences if mechanically applied to changed circumstances.

3. Due to misdirected associative thinking, a strong instinctive dislike may be felt for things, places or people which in some way are merely reminiscent of unpleasant experiences, but actually have no connection with them.

These briefly-stated instances show how vital it is for us to scrutinize from time to time the mental grooves of our associative thoughts, and to review the various habits and stereotype reactions deriving from them. In other words, we must step out of our ruts, regain a direct vision of things and make a fresh appraisal of our habits in the light of that vision.

If we look once again over the list of potential dangers deriving from uncontrolled associative thinking, we shall better understand the Buddha's insistence upon getting to the bedrock of experience. In the profound and terse stanzas called 'The Cave', included in the Sutta Nipāta, the Buddha says that the 'full penetration of *sense impression* (*phassa*) will make one free from greed' and that 'by understanding *perception* (*saññā*), one will be able to cross the flood of saṁsāra' (Stanza 778 ff.[10].) By placing mindfulness as a guard at the very first gate through which thoughts enter the mind, we shall be able to control the incomers much more easily, and shut out unwanted intruders. Thus the purity of 'luminous consciousness' can be maintained against 'adventitious defilements' (Anguttara Nikāya, 1: 51).

The Satipaṭṭhāna Sutta provides a systematic training for inducing direct, fresh and undistorted vision. The training covers the entire personality in its physical and mental aspects, and includes the whole world of experience. The methodical application of the several exercises to oneself (*ajjhatta*), to others (*bahiddhā*) and alternatingly to both, will help uncover erroneous conceptions due to misdirected associative thinking and misapplied analogies.

The principal types of false associative thinking are covered, in the terminology of the Dhamma, by the four kinds of *misapprehension* or *perverted views* (*vipallāsa*): i.e. wrongly taking (1) what is impermanent for permanent, (2) what is painful, or conducive to pain, for happiness, (3) what has no self and is unsubstantial for a self or an abiding substance, and (4) what is impure for beautiful. These perverted views arise through a false apprehension of the characteristic marks of things. Under the influence of our passions and false theories, we perceive things selectively in a one-sided or erroneous way, and then associate them wrongly with other ideas. By applying bare attention to our perceptions and impressions, gradually we can free them from these misapprehensions, progressing steadily towards the *direct vision* of things as they really are.

The Sense of Urgency

One who has clear and direct vision, stirred to a sense of urgency (*saṁvega*) by things which are deeply moving, will experience a release of energy and courage enabling him to break through his timid hesitations and his rigid routine of life and thought. If that sense of urgency is kept alive, it will bestow the earnestness and persistence required for the work of liberation. Thus said the teachers of old:

This very world here is our field of action.
It harbours the unfoldment of the holy path,
And many things to break complacency.
Be stirred by things which may well move the heart,
And being stirred, strive wisely and fight on!

Our closest surroundings are full of stirring things. If we generally do not perceive them as such, that is because habit has made our vision dull and our heart insensitive. The same thing happens to us even with the Buddha's teaching. When we first encounter the teaching, we receive a powerful intellectual and emotional stimulation; but gradually the impetus tends to lose its original freshness and impelling force. The remedy is to constantly renew it by turning to the fullness of life around us, which illustrates the Four Noble Truths in ever new variations. A direct vision will impart new lifeblood even to the most common experiences of every day, so that their true nature appears through the dim haze of habit and speaks to us with a fresh voice. It may well be just the long accustomed sight of the beggar at the street corner, or a weeping child, or the illness of a friend, which startles us afresh, makes us think, and stirs our sense of urgency in treading resolutely the path that leads to the cessation of suffering.

We know the beautiful account of how Prince Siddhattha first came face to face with old age, illness and death while driving his chariot through the royal city after a long period of isolation in a make-believe world. This ancient story may well be historical fact, for we know that in the lives of many great men common events often gain a symbolic significance and lead to major consequences far beyond their ordinary appearance. Great minds find significance in the seemingly commonplace and invest the fleeting moment with far-reaching efficacy. But, without contesting the inner truth of that old story, we may reasonably believe that the young prince had actually seen before, with his fleshy eyes, old people, sick people and those who had succumbed to death. However, on all these earlier occasions, he would not have been touched very deeply by these sights – as is the case with most of us most of the time. That earlier lack of sensitivity may have been due to the carefully protected, artificial seclusion of his petty, though princely, happiness – the hereditary routine of his life into which his father had placed him. Only when he broke through that golden cage of easy-going habits could the facts of suffering strike him as forcibly as if he had seen them for the first time. Then only was he stirred by them to a sense of urgency that led him out of the home life and set his feet firmly on the road to enlightenment.

The more *clearly* and *deeply* our minds and hearts respond to the truth of suffering manifest in the very common facts of our existence, the less often shall we need a repetition of the lesson and the shorter will be our migration through saṁsāra. The *clarity* of perception evoking our response will come from an undeflected directness of vision, bestowed by bare attention (*sati*); and the *depth* of experience will come from wise reflection or clear comprehension (*sampajañña*).

The Road to Insight

Directness of vision is also a chief characteristic of the methodical practice of insight meditation. There it is identified with the direct or experiential knowledge bestowed by meditation, as distinguished from the inferential knowledge obtained by study and reflection. In the meditative development of insight, one's own physical and mental processes are directly viewed, without the interference of abstract concepts or the filtering screens of emotional evaluation. For in this context these only obscure or camouflage the naked facts, detracting from the strong immediate impact of reality. Conceptual generalizations from experience are very useful in their place; but if they interrupt the meditative practice of bare attention, they tend to 'shove aside' or dispose of the particular fact, by saying, as it were: 'It is nothing else but this.' Generalizing thought inclines to become impatient with a recurrent type, and after having it classified, soon finds it boring.

Bare attention, however, being the key instrument of methodical insight, keeps to the particular. It follows keenly the rise and fall of successive physical and mental processes. Though all phenomena of a given series may be true to type (e.g., inhalations and exhalations), bare attention regards each of them as distinct, and conscientiously registers its separate birth and death. If mindfulness remains alert, these repetitions of type will, by their multiplication, exert not a reduced but an intensified impact on the mind. The three characteristics – impermanence, suffering and voidness of self – inherent in the process observed, will stand out more and more clearly. They will appear in the light shed by the phenomena themselves, not in a *borrowed* light; not even a light borrowed from the Buddha, the peerless and indispensable guide to these experiences. These physical and mental phenomena, in their 'self-luminosity' will then convey a growing sense of urgency to the meditator: revulsion, dissatisfaction and awareness of danger, followed by detachment – though certainly, joy, happiness and calm, too, will not be absent throughout the practice. Then, if all other

89

conditions of inner maturity are fulfilled, the first direct vision of final liberation will dawn with the stream-winner's (*sotāpanna*) indubitable knowledge: 'Whatever has the nature of arising, has the nature of vanishing.'

Thus, in the unfoldment of the power of mindfulness, Satipaṭṭhāna will prove itself as the true embodiment of the Dhamma, of which it was said:

Well-proclaimed is the Dhamma by the Blessed One, visible here and now, not delayed, inviting inspection, onward-leading, to be directly experienced by the wise.

Notes

1. See Nyanaponika Thera, *The Heart of Buddhist Meditation*, (Rider & Co., 1962).
2. Comy. to Sutta Nipāta v. 334.
3. Anagarika Govinda, *The Psychological Attitude of Early Buddhist Philosophy*, (Rider & Co., 1961).
4. *The Way of Mindfulness*, Bhikkhu Soma, (Kandy: Buddhist Publication Society, 1975), p. 83.
5. See *Path of Purification*, pp. 135 ff.
6. *Ibid.* pp. 136 ff. The three rousing factors are investigation, energy and rapture; the three calming ones, tranquillity, concentration and equanimity.
7. A treatise of Chinese Taoism, strongly influenced by Mahāyāna Buddhism.
8. About these important qualitative constituents of good, wholesome (*kusala*) consciousness, see the author's *Abhidhamma Studies*, (Kandy: Buddhist Publication Society, 1965), pp. 51 ff.
9. This may be a somewhat ironical reference by that great sage to the fact that the well-known Mahāyānic Bodhisattva vow of liberating all beings of the universe is often taken much too light-heartedly by many of his fellow Mahāyānists.
10. Compare also the passage on the significance of sense impression (or contact) in the concluding sections of the Brahmajāla Sutta (Digha Nikāya 1).

The Roots of Good
and Evil

Introduction

The Buddha has taught that there are three roots of evil: greed, hatred and delusion. These three states comprise the entire range of evil, whether of lesser or greater intensity, from a faint mental tendency to the coarsest manifestations in action and speech. In whatever way they appear, these are the basic causes of suffering.

These roots have their opposites: non-greed, non-hatred and non-delusion. These are the three roots of good: of all acts of unselfishness, liberality and renunciation; of all expressions of loving-kindness and compassion; of all achievements in knowledge and understanding.

These six mental states are the roots from which everything harmful and beneficial sprouts. They are the roots of the Tree of Life with its sweet and bitter fruits.

Greed and hatred, maintained and fed by delusion, are the universal impelling forces of all animate life, individually and socially. Fortunately, the roots of good also reach into our world and keep the forces of evil in check, but the balance is a precarious one needing to be preserved by constant watchfulness and effort. On the level of inanimate nature, too, we find counterparts to greed and hatred in the forces of attraction and repulsion, kept in their purposeless reactive movement by inherent nescience which cannot provide a motive for cessation of the process. Thus, through an unfathomable past, the macrocosm of nature and the microcosm of mind have continued their contest between attraction and repulsion, greed and hatred; and unless stopped by voluntary effort and insight, they will so continue for aeons to come. This cosmic conflict of opposing energies, unsolvable on its own level, is one aspect of *dukkha* (unsatisfactoriness): the ill of restless, senseless movement as felt by a sensitive being.

On the human level, too, we see that man, who proudly

believes himself to be a 'free agent' – the master of his life and even of nature – is in his spiritually undeveloped state actually a passive patient driven about by inner forces he does not recognize. Pulled by his greed and pushed by his hatred, in his blindness he does not see that the brakes for stopping these frantic movements are in his reach, within his own heart. The brakes are the roots of good themselves, which can be cultivated to such a degree that greed, hatred and delusion are utterly destroyed.

Though we have spoken of the six roots as being 'roots of good and evil', our use of the terms 'good' and 'evil' is provisional, a simplification chosen to introduce this teaching by familiar terms. In the Buddhist texts they are called the roots of the wholesome (*kusala-mūla*) and the roots of the unwholesome (*akusala-mūla*). And thus we, too, shall generally call them.

This differentiation of terms marks an important distinction, for the 'spread' of the mental states called roots is much wider and deeper than the moral realm to which the words 'good' and 'evil' refer. The distinction may be defined as follows. An intentional action performed by body or speech is immoral – an evil or a 'sin' – when it is motivated by the unwholesome roots and is *intentionally and directly harmful to others*. This constitutes *socially* significant immorality, for which it is the criterion. Such actions are termed *unwholesome bodily or verbal kamma*. Thoughts associated with these unwholesome roots, wishing the harm of others, constitute *individually* significant immorality, for which they are the criterion. They include thoughts such as those of injury, murder, theft, fraud and rape, and also false ideologies leading to the harm of others or condoning such harm. Whether or not these thoughts are followed by deeds or words, they constitute *unwholesome mental kamma*.

When greed, hatred and delusion, in any degree, do *not* cause intentional harm to others, they are not evil or immoral in the strict sense of our definition. However, they are still kammically unwholesome in that they maintain bondage and lead to unpleasant results. Similarly, the term 'wholesome' extends beyond socially significant morality to comprise also what is individually beneficial, such as acts of renunciation and attempts to understand the nature of reality.

The recent crisis of theistic faith which has taken hold in the West has brought in its trail a moral crisis as well. For many, belief in God has been shattered, and often those who lose their belief in God fail to see any convincing reason for morality without a divine sanction coming down from above. Left without a sound foundation for ethics, they either accept materialistic political ideologies or allow their conduct to be guided by self-interest. Yet we also find today a growing number of people seeking better alternatives. To them the Buddha's teaching on the wholesome and unwholesome roots provides a criterion of good and evil that is neither theological nor authoritarian but experiential, one with a sound psychological basis offering an autonomous pragmatic motivation for avoiding evil and choosing the good.

The social and political motivations for moral conduct proposed to modern man may not openly contradict the basic sentiments of morality, but as their structures are bound to specific historical conditions and reflect the varying self-interests and prejudices of the dominant social group, the values they propose are highly relative, lacking universal validity. In contrast, Buddhist ethics, being based on psychological fact and not on external contingencies, provides a core of moral principles inherently free from relativistic limitations, valid for all time and under all circumstances. By introspection and observation, we can understand that the unwholesome roots are undesirable mental states, productive of suffering for ourselves and others; and since it is our common nature to avoid suffering and to desire happiness, we can understand that it serves our own long-range interest as well as the good of others to restrain actions born of these roots and to act in ways motivated by their wholesome opposites. A brief survey of the evil roots will make this clear.

Greed is a state of lack, need and want. It is always seeking fulfilment and lasting satisfaction, but its drive is inherently insatiable, and thus as long as it endures it maintains the sense of lack.

Hatred, in all its degrees, is also a state of dissatisfaction. Though objectively it arises in response to undesired people or circumstances, its true origins are subjective and internal, chiefly frustrated desire and wounded pride. Buddhist psychology extends the range of hatred beyond simple anger and enmity to include a variety of negative emotions – such as disappointment, dejection, anxiety and despair – representing misguided reactions to the impermanence, insecurity and imperfection inherent in all conditioned existence.

Delusion, taking the form of ignorance, is a state of confusion, bewilderment and helplessness. In its aspect of false views, delusion issues in dogmatism; it takes on a fanatical, even obsessive, character, and makes the mind rigid and encapsulated.

All three unwholesome roots lead to inner disharmony and social conflict. In Tibetan paintings they are depicted at the very hub of the Wheel of Life,[1] symbolically represented by a cock, a pig and a snake, turning round and round, catching each other's tails. The three unwholesome roots, indeed, produce and support each other.

The root of greed gives rise to resentment, anger and hatred against those who obstruct the gratification of desire or compete in the chase to gain the desired objects – whether sensual enjoyment, power, dominance or fame. In this way greed leads to conflict and quarrels. When frustrated, instead of producing enmity and aversion, greed may bring about grief, sadness, despair, envy and jealousy – states which also come under the heading of hatred. The pain of deprivation and frustration again sharpens the keenness of desire, which then seeks an escape from pain by indulging in other kinds of enjoyment.

Both greed and hatred are always linked with delusion. They are grounded upon delusion and, on their part, produce still more delusion as we pursue the objects we desire or flee from those we dislike. Both love and hate blind us to the dangers besetting our pursuits; they lead us away from our true advantage. It is the delusion beneath our love and hate that really blinds us, delusion that leads us astray.

The basic delusion, from which all its other forms spring, is the idea of an abiding self: the belief in an ego. For the sake of this illusory ego men lust and hate; upon this they build their imagination and pride. This ego-belief must first be clearly comprehended as a delusive viewpoint. One must pierce through the illusion of self by cultivating right understanding through penetrative thought and meditative insight.

Though the wholesome and unwholesome roots are individual mental states, their manifestations and repercussions have the greatest social significance. Each individual in society rises up at once to protect himself, his loved ones, his property, security and freedom, from the greed, hatred and delusions of others. His own greed, hatred and ignorance may in turn arouse others to anxious concern and resentment, though he may not be aware of this or care about it. From all this there results an intricate interlocking of suffering – suffering caused to others and suffering experienced oneself. Hence the Buddha repeatedly said that the unwholesome roots cause harm both to oneself and to others, while the wholesome roots are sources of benefit for both the individual and society (See Texts 16–20).

The wholesome and unwholesome roots are of paramount human concern on all levels. As the originating causes of kamma, our life-affirming and rebirth-producing intentional actions, they are the motive powers and driving forces of our deeds, words and thoughts. They mould our character and our destiny and hence determine the nature of our rebirth. Being dominant features in the structure of the mind, the unwholesome roots are used in the Abhidhamma Piṭaka for the classification of unwholesome consciousness and also for a typology of temperaments. All stages of the path to deliverance are closely concerned with the wholesome and unwholesome roots. At the very beginning, the coarsest forms of greed, hatred and irresponsible ignorance have to be abandoned through virtue (sīla), while in the advanced stages the aids of meditation (samādhi) and wisdom (paññā) have to be applied to a deeper-reaching removal of the unwholesome roots and to the cultivation of the wholesome ones. Even Arahatship and Nibbāna – the consummation of the great quest – are both explained in terms of the roots: as the extinction of greed, hatred and delusion.

This wide-ranging significance of the Buddha's teaching on the roots places it at the very core of the Dhamma. Showing the distinct marks of a fully enlightened mind, it is a teaching simple as well as profound, and hence accessible on many levels. The fact that greed, hatred and delusion, in their extreme forms, are the root causes of much misery and evil should be painfully obvious to every morally sensitive person. Such an initial understanding, open to commonsense, may well grow into full comprehension. It may then become the insight that moves one to enter the path to deliverance – the eradication of greed, hatred and delusion.

Within the framework of the Buddha's teaching, the Roots of Good and Evil have found their place in a great variety of contexts. To illustrate this by an ample selection of Buddhist texts – almost entirely taken from the discourses of the Buddha – is the intention of the following pages.

I   Basic Explanations

1.   DEFINITIONS

There are three roots of the unwholesome: greed, hatred and delusion; and there are three roots of the wholesome: non-greed, non-hatred and non-delusion.

Dīgha Nikāya 33 (Sangīti Sutta)

Comment

These two sets of three are, respectively, the roots of unwholesome and wholesome volitional action (*kamma*), by way of deeds, words or thoughts.

The term 'root' (*mūla*), the commentaries explain, has the sense of firm support, cause, condition and producer. The figurative character of the term suggests that the roots can also be taken as conveyors of the 'nourishing sap' of the wholesome or unwholesome. They convey this sap to the mental factors and functions existing simultaneously with themselves, as well as to the wholesome or unwholesome actions in which they issue. They are *producers* by being productive of rebirth.

The words 'unwholesome' and 'wholesome', as used here, are renderings of the Pāli terms *akusala* and *kusala*, respectively. Alternative renderings used by other translators are, for the wholesome: profitable, skilful; for the unwholesome: unprofitable, unskilful. The terms 'wholesome' and 'unwholesome' comprise all volitional actions that bind living beings to saṃsāra, the round of rebirth and suffering. The actions having these roots may, therefore, be called *kammically* wholesome or unwholesome. Hence the range of the unwholesome is wider than that of the immoral, as it includes forms of the root-defilements which are not immoral in the strict sense explained above. The wholesome, as dealt with here and in most, though not all, of the following texts, is that of the mundane type. The wholesome of the supramundane type is not productive of kamma and therefore does not result in rebirth (See Text 14).[2]

The commentators to the Pāli scriptures explain *kusala*, the wholesome, as a healthy state of mind (*ārogya*), as morally faultless (*anavajja*), and as having favourable or pleasant kamma-results (*sukha-vipāka*). Another connotation of *kusala*, 'dexterous' or 'skilful', according to the commentators, does not apply in this context. Yet kammically wholesome actions may also be described as skilful insofar as they lead to happiness in the present and future, and to progress on the path to liberation.

Akusala, the unwholesome, has the opposite characteristics: it is an unhealthy or sickly state of mind (*gelañña*), morally faulty and blameworthy (*sāvajja*), and has unpleasant kamma-results (*dukkha-vipāka*). For all these reasons, unwholesome actions in thoughts, words and deeds can also be said to be unskilful responses to life.

The Range of the Six Roots

(a) The Unwholesome – The three unwholesome roots are not restricted to the strong manifestations suggested by the English terms greed, hatred and delusion. To understand their range it is important to know that in the Pāli these three terms stand for all degrees of intensity, even the weakest, of the three defilements, and for all varieties in which these appear. In their weak degrees their unwholesome influence on character and kammic consequences is, of course, not as grave as that of their stronger forms. But even weak forms may carry the risk of either growing stronger or of making a person's character more susceptible to their graver manifestations. A fuller view of the various forms the unwholesome roots assume may be gained from a list of their synonyms, partly taken from the *Dhamma-saṅgaṇī*, the first book of the Abhidhamma Piṭaka.

Greed: liking, wishing, longing, fondness, affection, attachment, lust, cupidity, craving, passion, self-indulgence, possessiveness, avarice; desire for the five sense objects; desire for wealth, offspring, fame, etc.

Hatred: dislike, disgust, revulsion, resentment, grudge, ill-humour, vexation, irritability, antagonism, aversion, anger, wrath, vengefulness.

Delusion: stupidity, dullness, confusion, ignorance of essentials (e.g. the Four Noble Truths), prejudice, ideological dogmatism, fanaticism, wrong views, conceit.

(b) The Wholesome – Though formulated negatively, the three wholesome roots signify positive traits:

Non-greed: unselfishness, liberality, generosity; thoughts and actions of sacrifice and sharing; renunciation, dispassion.

Non-hatred: loving-kindness, compassion, sympathy, friendliness, forgiveness, forbearance.

Non-delusion: wisdom, insight, knowledge, understanding, intelligence, sagacity, discrimination, impartiality, equanimity.

2. THE COMMENTARIAL DEFINITIONS OF THE UNWHOLESOME ROOTS

Greed has the characteristic of grasping an object, like bird-lime (lit. 'monkey-lime'). Its function is sticking, like meat put in a hot pan. It is manifested as not giving up, like the dye of lamp-black. Its proximate cause is seeing enjoyment in things that lead to bondage. Swelling with the current of craving, it should be regarded as carrying beings along with it to states of misery as a swift-flowing river does to the great ocean.

Hatred has the characteristic of savageness, like a provoked snake. Its function is to spread, like a drop of poison, or its function is to burn up its own support, like a forest fire. It is manifested as persecuting like an enemy that has got his chance. Its proximate cause is the grounds for annoyance (*āghāta-vatthu*). It should be regarded as being like stale urine mixed with poison.

Delusion has the characteristic of blindness, or it has the characteristic of unknowing. Its function is non-penetration, or its function is to conceal the true nature of an object. It is manifested as the absence of right view,[3] or it is manifested as darkness. Its proximate cause is unwise (unjustified) attention. It should be regarded as the root of all that is unwholesome.

Visuddhimagga: The Path of Purification, pp. 529 ff., 532.

3. THE COMMENTARIAL DEFINITIONS OF THE WHOLESOME ROOTS

Non-greed has the characteristic of the mind's lack of desire for an object, or it has the characteristic of non-adherence, like a water drop on a lotus leaf. Its function is not to lay hold (or not to grasp), like a liberated bhikkhu. It is manifested as not treating (the desire-evoking object) as a shelter (or non-cleaving), as a man who has fallen into filth (will not cling to it).

Non-hatred has the characteristic of lack of savagery, or the characteristic of non-opposing, like a congenial friend. Its function is to remove annoyance, or its function is to remove fever, as sandalwood does. It is manifested as agreeableness, like the full moon.

Non-delusion has the characteristic of penetrating (things) according to their true nature, or it has the characteristic of sure penetration, like the penetration of an arrow shot by a skilful archer. Its function is to illuminate the objective field, like a lamp. It is manifested as non-bewilderment, like a forest guide.

The three should be regarded as the roots of all that is wholesome.

Visuddhimagga: The Path of Purification, p. 525.

4. THE NATURE OF THE WHOLESOME ROOTS

Non-greed is opposed to the taint of avarice; *non-hatred* to the taint of immorality; *non-delusion* to an undeveloped state of wholesome qualities.

Non-greed is a condition of giving (*dāna*); *non-hatred* is a condition of virtue (*sīla*); *non-delusion* is a condition of mental development (or meditation; *bhāvanā*).

Through *non-greed* one does not overrate (an attractive object), as the lustful person does. Through *non-hatred* one does not underrate or deprecate (an unattractive or disagreeable object), as the hater does. Through *non-delusion* one has an undistorted view of things, while one who is deluded conceives things in a distorted way.

With *non-greed* one will admit an existing fault (in an attractive object) and will behave accordingly, while a greedy or lustful person will hide that fault. With *non-hatred* one will admit an existing virtue (in a disagreeable or hostile object) and will behave accordingly, while the hater will disparage that virtue. With *non-delusion* one will admit facts as they are and behave accordingly, while a deluded man holds the true for false (the factual for non-factual) and the false for true (the non-factual for factual).

With *non-greed* one does not have the suffering through

separation from the beloved; but the greedy and lustful person identifies himself with the beloved and hence cannot bear separation from him. With *non-hatred* one does not have the suffering through association with the unbeloved; but the hater identifies himself with (his aversion against) the unbeloved and cannot bear association with him. With *non-delusion* one does not have the suffering through not obtaining what one wishes, because the undeluded person will be able to reflect in this way: 'How can it be possible that what is subject to decay should not enter into decay!'

With *non-greed* one does not encounter the suffering of birth, because non-greed is the opposite of craving, and craving is at the root of the suffering of birth. With *non-hatred* the suffering of ageing is not felt (strongly, or prematurely); because it is one harbouring strong hate who ages quickly. With *non-delusion* there is no suffering in dying; because it is dying with a confused or deluded mind that is suffering, but this does not happen to one who is undeluded.

Non-greed makes for a happy life among lay people (who often quarrel about property). *Non-delusion* makes for a happy life among ascetics and monks (who often quarrel about opinions). *Non-hatred* makes for happy living with all.

Through *non-greed* there is no rebirth in the realm of the famished ghosts (*preta*); because generally beings are reborn there through their craving, and non-greed (unselfishness, renunciation) is opposed to craving. Through *non-hatred* there is no rebirth in the hells; for it is through hate and a fierce temperament that beings are reborn in hell, which is congenial to hate; but non-hate (loving-kindness) is opposed to hate. Through *non-delusion* there is no rebirth in the animal world, for it is generally through delusion that beings are reborn as animals who are always deluded; but non-delusion (wisdom) is opposed to delusion.

Among these three, *non-greed* prevents approach in lust, *non-hatred* prevents alienation through hate, *non-delusion* prevents the loss of equipoise (or impartiality) due to delusion.

Furthermore, to these three roots, in the order given, correspond the following sets of three perceptions: the perception of renunciation, of good-will, and of non-violence; and also the perception of bodily foulness, of boundless love and compassion, and of the elements.

Through *non-greed* the extreme of sense-indulgence is avoided; through *non-hatred* the extreme of self-mortification; through *non-delusion* a middle course is practised.

Non-greed breaks the bodily bondage of covetousness, *non-hatred* breaks the bodily bondage of ill-will, and *non-delusion* breaks the other two bondages (i.e. that of clinging to rites and rituals, and of dogmatic fanaticism).

By virtue of the first two wholesome roots, the practice of the first two foundations of mindfulness (i.e. body and feelings) will succeed; by virtue of the third wholesome root (non-delusion), the practice of the last two foundations of mindfulness (state of mind and contents of mind) will succeed.

Non-greed is a condition of health, because one who is not greedy will not partake of something unsuitable, even if it is tempting, and hence he will remain healthy. *Non-hatred* is a condition of youthfulness, because one who is free from hate is not consumed by the fires of hate that cause wrinkles and grey hair, and thus he remains youthful for a long time. *Non-delusion* is a condition of longevity, because one who is undeluded will know what is beneficial and what is harmful, and by avoiding the harmful and resorting to the beneficial he will have a long life.

Non-greed is a condition of the boon of wealth, because one who is not greedy will obtain wealth through his liberality (as its kammic result). *Non-hatred* is a condition of the boon of friendship, because through loving-kindness one will win friends and not lose them. *Non-delusion* is a condition of the boon of self-development, because he who is undeluded and does only what is beneficial will perfect himself.

Through *non-greed* one has detachment to persons and things belonging to one's own group; because even in the case of their destruction, one will not feel the suffering that is caused by strong attachment. With *non-hatred*, the same will hold true in the case of persons and things belonging to a hostile group; because he who is free of hatred will have no thoughts of enmity even towards those who are hostile. With *non-delusion*, the same holds true concerning persons and things belonging to a neutral group; because in him who is undeluded there is no strong attachment to anybody or anything.

Through *non-greed* one will understand impermanence; for

a greedy man, in his longing for enjoyment, will not see the impermanence of transitory phenomena. Through *non-hatred* one will understand suffering; for one inclined to non-hate, in comprehending the grounds of annoyance discarded by him, sees phenomena as suffering. Through *non-delusion* one will understand not-self; for one who is undeluded is skilled in grasping the nature of reality, and he knows that the five aggregates are without an internal controller. Just as the understanding of impermanence, etc. is effected by non-greed, etc., so are also non-greed, etc. produced by the understanding of impermanence, etc. Through the understanding of impermanence arises non-greed; through the understanding of suffering arises non-hatred; through the understanding of not-self arises non-delusion. For who will allow attachment to arise for something which he fully well knows is impermanent? And, when knowing phenomena to be suffering, who would produce the additional and exceedingly pungent suffering of anger? And, when knowing phenomena as void of self, who would again plunge into confusion of mind?

From the *Aṭṭhasālinī* (commentary to the *Dhammasangaṇī* of the Abhidhamma Piṭaka), Pāli Text Society edition, pp. 127 ff.

5. THE DIVERSITY OF THE UNWHOLESOME ROOTS

There may be outsiders, O monks, who will ask you: 'There are, friends, three states of mind: greed, hatred and delusion. What is their distinction, their diversity, their difference?'

Questioned thus, O monks, you may explain it to those outsiders in this way:

'Greed is a lesser fault and fades away slowly; hatred is a great fault and fades away quickly; delusion is a great fault and fades away slowly.'

Anguttara Nikāya, 3: 68 (extract)

Comment

The statements in this text about greed being a lesser fault, and so on, have to be taken in a relative sense. The commentary explains: 'Greed (or lust) is a lesser fault in a twofold way: (1) in public opinion (*loka*; i.e. in the 'eyes of the world'), and (2) with regard to kamma-result (*vipāka*), i.e., the rebirth resulting from the kamma (impelled by greed). (1) If, for instance, parents give their children in marriage, according to the standards of worldly life no fault is involved (though greed enters into the parents' affection and sexuality in marriage). (2) If in marriage one is satisfied with one's own marriage-partner (and thus observes the third percept), there is thereby no rebirth in the lower worlds. Thus greed or lust can be a lesser fault in regard to kamma-result. Greed, however, is "slow in fading away", being as hard to remove as oily soot. Greed for particular objects or sensual lust for a certain person may persist throughout life. It may even continue for two or three existences without disappearing.'

Thus, relative to hatred and delusion, greed is a lesser evil. For if it remains within the bounds of basic morality, and does not entail a violation of the five precepts, it will not exclude a favourable rebirth caused by good kamma. Greed, however, is very hard to overcome entirely. Its fine hair-roots reach deep into our nature, and it may clad itself in many alluring garments, assuming subtle disguises and sublime forms of beauty. As 'lust for life' or 'the will to live' it is the very core of existence. As life-affirming craving it is the origin of suffering.

'Hatred', according to the commentary, 'may lead to wrong-doings towards parents, brothers, sisters, ascetics (i.e. people of religious calling), etc. Wherever such an offender goes, blame and bad reputation will follow him. If, through hatred, he even commits one of the heinous offences (*ānantariya-kamma*), such as parricide, etc., he will suffer in hell for aeons.[4] In that way, hatred is a great fault both in public opinion and by its kamma-result. Yet hatred may quickly fade away; for soon after committing an offence out of hatred or anger one may repent, ask those whom one has wronged for forgiveness, and if that is granted, the act is atoned for (as far as the offender's state of mind is concerned.)'

Hatred is a disruptive and anti-social factor, a source of untold misery for individuals and all human groups. One would thus expect society to regard it as a 'great fault', as the great enemy of societal welfare, and make every effort to weaken and eliminate it. But on the contrary we find that human institutions, large and small, have often promoted hate for their own selfish ends, or have fostered deeds, words and thoughts of hate motivated by delusive ideologies. Throughout history, leaders seeking the support of the masses have always found it easier to unite people by means of a common hate than by a common love.

On the individual level, hatred in all its degrees is often roused by conflicting self-interests and by other kinds of ego-centric antagonism. Hatred can grow as obsessive as lustful passion, but it is generally more destructive for both the hater and his victim. It can take deep roots in the mind, be it in the form of smouldering resentment or the enjoyment of outbursts of violence. Through hatred, man's mind may sink to a sub-human level, and thus for the hater there is always the risk of being reborn in a sub-human realm of existence.

Yet for one who does not identify himself with all his states of mind, but sees the need and has the will to transform himself – for such a one it will not be difficult to control his hatred or anger before it grows stronger. Hatred causes irritation, tension and distress; and since men are basically beings 'desirous of happiness and averse to unhappiness', those who do understand the consequences of hatred will normally wish to get rid of it.

'Delusion', according to the commentary, 'is a great fault for both reasons, that is, in the eyes of public opinion and with regard to its unhappy kamma-result (in the same ways as mentioned above for hatred). If an action is done under the impact of delusion, such action will set man free only very slowly; it can be likened to bear skin, which will not become bright even if washed seven times.'

If unrestrained acts of unlawful greed or lust are performed without a feeling of guilt, but are, on the contrary, justified by such prejudiced views as the claim that might makes right, such deluded greed will obviously not be easy to eliminate. It will not be given up even under the impact of repeated failures to satisfy it, which may only strengthen the greed through frustration and resentment. There are also forms of deluded greed supported by a religious (or pseudo-religious) sanction (See Comment to Text 14). All these forms of deluded greed can be eliminated only when the delusive false views and principles are discarded. But even in cases where greed is not backed by wrong theory, when self-indulgence has the ininhibited innocence of ignorance or when the delusive view involved is just the naive belief that 'this is the right and natural thing to do' – in these cases, too, our bondage by such deluded greed will be hard to break.

It is similar when delusion instigates hatred and keeps it alive with wrong views or attitudes. If, for instance, due to delusive views, people regard others belonging to certain races, classes or religions as legitimate objects of hate, this will be a much stronger bondage than any impassioned but temporary outburst of anger having only the normal admixture of delusion.

Without the presence of delusion, no greed or hatred can arise. The unwholesome roots of greed and hatred always occur associated with delusion. Delusion, however, may occur by itself and can be a very powerful source of evil and suffering. In view of that omnipresence of delusion in the unwholesome, the Dhammapada says that there is no entanglement equal to the widespread net of delusion (v. 251), and that ignorance (a synonym of delusion) is the greatest taint of the mind (v. 243). Hence the Buddha declares: 'All unwholesome states have their root in ignorance, they converge upon ignorance, and by the abolishing of ignorance, all the other unwholesome states are abolished' (Saṁyutta Nikāya 20: 1).

Ignorance, of course, does not mean a mere lack of information about this or that subject of worldly knowledge. It is, rather, the lack of right understanding concerning the Four Noble Truths: namely, the ignorance (or wilful ignoring) of the full range and depth of suffering, of its true cause, of the fact that there can be an end of suffering and of the path that leads to the end of suffering.

The truth of suffering is hidden by the four distortions of reality (vipallāsa), the four great illusions of seeing permanence in the impermanent, happiness in what is truly suffering, selfhood in what is void of a self and beauty in the unbeautiful. These distortions, powerful universal manifestations of ignorance and delusion, shut out an understanding of the truth of suffering, and thereby obscure the other truths, too. The four may appear on any of three levels: at the level of quite ordinary misperceptions (saññā-vipallāsa), or as wrong ways of thinking (citta-vipallāsa) or as expressed in definite wrong ideas and theories (diṭṭhi-vipallāsa). Tenaciously held wrong views can forge the strongest chain fettering beings to pain-fraught saṁsāra. If these views go so far as to deny the moral relevance of any action, they will lead in the next existence to a 'fixed destiny' of rebirth in a world of misery.[5]

Sheer stupidity is, of course, also a form of delusion, and it can stultify a man's inner growth throughout life and for many lives to come. But there can be an escape from it, if that dull person's good roots of non-greed (selflessness) and non-hate (kindness, compassion) are strong enough to become active.

The most deep-rooted and powerful aspect of delusion, and the most consequential of wrong views, is personality-belief. Personality-belief is the belief in an abiding self or soul, with its attendant conceits and conceptions. The belief may be naive and unreflective, or supported by definite theories and convictions. But however it is held, this personality-belief makes delusion a barrier hard to overcome and slow to fade away, while the moral implications of egocentricity make it a 'great fault'.

Considering the wide range and universal influence of delusion, it is understandable that, under the name of ignorance, it appears as the first factor in the chain of dependent origination (*paṭicca-samuppāda*). As the chief impelling force that keeps the wheel of existence in rotation, delusion is, indeed, 'a great fault and slow to fade away'.

II *General Texts*

6. OVERCOMING BIRTH AND DEATH

If three things were not found in the world, the Perfect One, the Holy One who is fully enlightened, would not appear in the world, nor would his teaching and discipline shed their light over the world.

What are these three things? They are birth, old age and death. Because these three are found in the world, the Perfect One, the Holy One who is fully enlightened, has appeared in the world, and his teaching and discipline shed their light over the world.

It is, however, impossible to overcome birth, old age and death without overcoming another three things, namely: greed, hatred and delusion.

Anguttara Nikāya, 10: 76.

7. MĀRA'S PRISONER[6]

He who has not abandoned greed, hatred and delusion, is called Māra's prisoner, captured in Māra's snares, subject to the Evil One's will and pleasure.

But he who has abandoned greed, hatred and delusion, is

no longer Māra's prisoner; he is freed from Māra's snares, no longer subject to the Evil One's will and pleasure.

Itivuttaka 68

8. CROSSING THE OCEAN

A monk or a nun who has not abandoned greed, hatred and delusion, such a one has not crossed the ocean (of saṁsāra), with its waves and whirlpools, monsters and demons.

But a monk or a nun who has abandoned greed, hatred and delusion, such a one has crossed the ocean (of saṁsāra), with its waves and whirlpools, monsters and demons, has traversed it and gone to the other shore (Nibbāna), standing on firm ground as a true saint.

Itivuttaka 69

9. THE THREE FIRES

There are three fires: the fire of lust, the fire of hatred and the fire of delusion.

The fire of lust burns lustful mortals
  Who are entangled in the sense-objects.
The fire of hate burns wrathful men
  Who urged by hate slay living beings.
Delusion's fire burns foolish folk
  Who cannot see the holy Dhamma.

Those who delight in the embodied group[7]
  Do not know this triple fire.
They cause the worlds of woe to grow:
  The hells, and life as animal,
The ghostly and demoniac realms;
  Unfreed are they from Māra's chains.
But those who live by day and night
  Devoted to the Buddha's law,
They quench within the fire of lust
  By seeing the impurity of body.
They quench within the fire of hate
  By loving-kindness, loftiest of men.
Delusion's fire they also quench
  By wisdom ripening in penetration.[8]

When they extinguish these three fires,
  Wise, unremitting day and night,
Completely they are liberated,
  Completely they transcend all ill.

Seers of the holy realm,[9]
  Through perfect knowledge[10] wise,
By direct vision ending all rebirth,
  They do not go to any new existence.

Itivuttaka 93

From the commentary by Bhadantācariya Dhammapāla

Because greed, when it arises, burns and consumes living beings, therefore it is called a fire; and so it is with hatred and delusion. Just as a fire consumes the fuel through which it has arisen, and grows into a vast conflagration, similarly it is with greed, hatred and delusion: they consume the life-continuity in which they have arisen and grow into a vast conflagration that is hard to extinguish.

Innumerable are the beings who, with hearts ablaze with the fire of lust, have come to death through the suffering of unfulfilled desire. This is greed's burning power. For the burning power of hatred, a special example is the 'deities ruined by their angry minds' (manopadosika-devā), and for delusion, the 'deities ruined by their playful pleasures' (khiḍḍapadosika-devā).[11] In their delusion, the latter become so forgetful that they miss their meal-time and die. This is the burning power of greed, hatred and delusion, as far as the present life is concerned. In future lives these three are still more terrible and hard to endure, in so far as greed, etc., may cause rebirth in the hells and the other worlds of woe.

10.   THREE INNER FOES

There are three inner taints, three inner foes, three inner enemies, three inner murderers, three inner antagonists. What are these three? Greed is an inner taint. . . . Hatred is an inner taint. . . . Delusion is an inner taint, an inner foe, an inner enemy, an inner murderer, an inner antagonist.

Greed is a cause of harm,
  Unrest of mind it brings

This danger that has grown within,
   Blind folk are unaware of it.

A greedy person cannot see the facts,
   Nor can he understand the Dhamma.
When greed has overpowered him,
   In complete darkness he is plunged.

But he who does not crave and can forsake
   This greed and what incites to greed,
From him quickly greed glides off
   Like water from a lotus leaf.

Hate is a cause of harm,
   Unrest of mind it brings.
This danger that has grown within,
   Blind folk are unaware of it.

A hater cannot see the facts,
   Nor can he understand the Dhamma.
When hate has overpowered him,
   In complete darkness he is plunged.

But he who does not hate and can forsake
   This hatred and what incites to hate,
From him quickly hatred falls off
   As from a palm tree falls the ripened fruit.

Delusion is a cause of harm,
   Unrest of mind it brings.
This danger that has grown within,
   Blind folk are unaware of it.

He who is deluded cannot see the facts,
   Nor can he understand the Dhamma.
If a man is in delusion's grip,
   In complete darkness he is plunged.

But he who has shed delusion's veil
   Is undeluded where confusion reigns;
He fully scatters all delusion,
   Just as the sun dispels the night.

                     Itivuttaka 88

Comment

Greed, hatred and delusion strong enough to lead to sub-human rebirths are abandoned by the first path, that of stream-entry. Sensual desire and hatred, in their coarse forms, are abandoned by the second path (of once-return), and in their subtle forms, by the third path (of non-return). All remaining greed and delusion, along with their associated defilements, are abandoned by the fourth path – that of Arahatship.

III *The Roots and Kamma*

11. THE CAUSE OF ACTION

There are, O monks, three causes for the origin of action (*kamma*): greed, hatred and delusion.

From greed, O monks, no greedlessness will arise; it is greed that arises from greed. From hatred no hatelessness will arise; it is hatred that arises from hatred. From delusion no non-delusion will arise; it is delusion that arises from delusion.

Due to actions born of greed, born of hatred, born of delusion, neither divine beings will appear, nor humans, nor any other kind of happy existence.[12] Rather the hells, the animal kingdom, the realm of ghosts or some other kind of woeful existence will appear due to actions born of greed, hatred and delusion.

These are, O monks, three causes for the origin of action.

There are, O monks, three other causes for the origin of action: non-greed, non-hatred and non-delusion.

From non-greed, O monks, no greed will arise; it is non-greed that arises from non-greed. From non-hatred no hatred will arise; it is non-hatred that arises from non-hatred. From non-delusion no delusion will arise; it is non-delusion that arises from non-delusion.

Due to actions born of non-greed, non-hatred and non-delusion, neither the hells will appear, nor the animal kingdom, the realm of ghosts, nor any other kind of woeful existence. Rather divine beings, humans or some other kind of happy existence will appear due to actions born of non-greed, non-hatred and non-delusion.

These are, O monks, three other causes for the origin of actions.

Anguttara Nikāya, 6: 39

Comment

In this text the Buddha implicitly rejects the maxim that 'the end justifies the means' – a doctrine widely followed in politics and sometimes even by religious institutions. Our text further declares as groundless the hope of those who apply this maxim in the belief that they will be rewarded in a future life for serving their cause by uprighteous means in this life, or in the case of non-religious application, that a future generation will reap the reward of present violence and repression in an ideal society or 'paradise on earth'.

Our text further negates the notion that lustful passion, or actions usually regarded as immoral or sinful, need not be obstacles to liberation or salvation, and can even aid their attainment. Such ideas, in varying formulations, have been mooted in the antinomian sects belonging to several of the world's great religions.[13] The notion that the end justifies the means occurs also in the basic principle of the intentional theory of ethics: 'Whatever is done with the intention of doing good to the world is right or virtuous.' All such notions, the Buddha's statement implies, are untenable, undermined by the deep psychological connections of the roots.

12. THE TEN WAYS OF ACTION

If a noble disciple knows what is unwholesome and knows the root of the unwholesome; if he knows what is wholesome and knows the root of the wholesome – he is then, to that extent, one of right understanding; he is one whose understanding is correct, who has firm confidence in the teaching, and has arrived at (the core of) the good law.

And what is unwholesome? Killing is unwholesome, taking what is not given is unwholesome, sexual misconduct is unwholesome; lying is unwholesome, tale-bearing is unwholesome, harsh language is unwholesome, vain talk is unwholesome; covetousness is unwholesome, ill-will is unwholesome, wrong views are unwholesome.

And what is the root of the unwholesome? Greed is a root

of the unwholesome, hatred is a root of the unwholesome, delusion is a root of the unwholesome.

And what is wholesome? Abstaining from killing is wholesome, abstaining from taking what is not given is wholesome, abstaining from sexual misconduct is wholesome; abstaining from lying . . . from tale-bearing . . . from harsh language . . . from vain talk is wholesome; non-covetousness is wholesome, non-ill-will is wholesome, right understanding is wholesome.

And what is the root of the wholesome? Non-greed is a root of the wholesome, non-hatred is a root of the wholesome, non-delusion is a root of the wholesome.

Majjhima Nikāya 9 (Sammādiṭṭhi Sutta)

Comment

In this discourse, spoken by the venerable Sāriputta, the unwholesome and the wholesome are explained by the 'ten ways of unwholesome and wholesome action' (*akusala-kusala-kamma-patha*), which extend to deeds, words and thoughts. They are also called the ten bad and ten good ways of conduct.

This explanation of the unwholesome enumerates ten cases of definite immoral behaviour. Even the last three items, referring to unwholesome *mental* kamma, have in this context an immoral character. As ways of unwholesome mental action, they signify the covetous desire to appropriate others' property; the hateful thoughts of harming, hurting or killing others; and those wrong views which deny moral causality and thus give room and justification for immoral acts.

These ten, however, do not exhaust the range of the term *unwholesome*. As mentioned earlier, the range of the unwholesome is wider than that of the immoral. It is not restricted to violations of the ten bad courses, but comprises all deeds, words and thoughts motivated by any degree of greed, hate and delusion.

To give a few examples: fondness for good food, music or physical comfort is not immoral, but as an attachment which binds us to the world of sense experience, it is kammically unwholesome. The same holds true for sexual acts, words and thoughts directed to one's marriage partner. These, too, according to the moral code of lay society, are not immoral. Yet as strong manifestations of craving, they fall under the unwholesome root 'greed'. One's personal stupidity, narrowness of view, ignorance of what is truly beneficial and similar limitations of mind are not immoral and need not have immediate immoral consequences. Yet they are great impediments to the acquisition of liberating wisdom and bind one firmly to saṁsāra. Therefore, they too are unwholesome, being forms of the unwholesome root 'delusion'.

3. THE ROOTS OF THE TEN UNWHOLESOME WAYS

Killing, I declare, O monks, is of three kinds: motivated by greed, motivated by hatred, motivated by delusion.

Also the taking of what is not given, sexual misconduct, lying, tale-bearing, harsh language, vain talk, covetousness, ill-will and wrong views – all these, I declare, are of three kinds: motivated by greed, motivated by hatred, motivated by delusion.

Thus, O monks, greed is an originator of the kamma-concatenation, hatred is an originator of the kamma-concatenation, delusion is an originator of the kamma-concatenation. But by the destruction of greed, hatred and delusion, the kamma-concatenation comes to an end.

Anguttara Nikāya, 10: 174

14. REBIRTH AND ITS CESSATION

I

There are, O monks, three causes for the origin of action (*kamma*): greed, hatred and delusion.

An action performed out of greed, born of greed, caused by greed, originating in greed;

an action performed out of hatred, born of hatred, caused by hatred, originating in hatred;

an action performed out of delusion, born of delusion, caused by delusion, originating in delusion –

such an action will ripen wherever the individual is reborn; and wherever the action ripens, there the individual will reap the fruit thereof, be it in this life, in the next or in future lives.

It is as with seeds that are undamaged and unspoiled, unimpaired by wind and heat, capable of sprouting, sown well in a good field, planted in well-prepared soil. If there is plentiful rain, these seeds will come to growth, increase and reach full development. Similarly, an action performed out of greed, hatred or delusion will ripen wherever the individual is reborn; and wherever the action ripens, the individual will reap the fruit thereof, be it in this life, in the next life or in future lives.

II

There are three other causes for the origin of action: non-greed, non-hatred and non-delusion.

If an action is performed out of non-greed, born of non-greed, caused by non-greed, originating in non-greed, and if greed has entirely gone;

if performed out of non-hatred, born of non-hatred, caused by non-hatred, originating in non-hatred, and if hatred has entirely gone;

if performed out of non-delusion, born of non-delusion, caused by non-delusion, originating in non-delusion, and if delusion has entirely gone –

such an action is thereby given up, cut off at its root, made (barren) like a palm-stump, brought to non-existence and is no longer liable to arise in the future again.

It is as with seeds that are undamaged and unspoiled, unimpaired by wind and heat, capable of sprouting, sown well in a good field. If now a man were to burn them, reduce them to ashes and then scatter the ashes in a strong wind or throw them into a stream's rapid current which carried them away – then these seeds would have been utterly destroyed, made unable to sprout again.

Similarly, if an action is performed out of non-greed, non-hatred and non-delusion, and if greed, hatred and delusion have entirely gone – such an action is thereby given up, cut off at its root, made (barren) like a palm-stump, brought to non-existence and is no longer liable to arise in the future again.

Anguttara Nikāya, 3: 33

Comment on Section II

Greed and delusion in their weakest forms are entirely eliminated on attaining Arahatship, while hatred down to its weakest form is fully abandoned at the stage of the non-returner. Section

II of our text applies, therefore, only to actions performed at these stages of final emancipation. Only then are these actions finally 'given up' so that they can no longer lead to a future rebirth. It is thus only at Arahatship that all three unwholesome roots are 'entirely gone', though they are decisively weakened at the earlier three stages of emancipation.

The Arahat's action, as no longer productive of rebirth, occurs also as the fourth item in a fourfold division of kamma:

Dark action that brings dark results;
bright action that brings bright results;
partly bright and partly dark action which brings partly
  bright and partly dark results;
action neither bright nor dark which brings neither bright nor
  dark results and leads to the exhaustion of action.

Anguttara Nikāya, 4: 232;
Majjhima Nikāya 57

The text explains that this last type of action is the volition of giving up all acts of kammic formation, that is, the volition present in the states of consciousness pertaining to the four paths of emancipation. But this fourth type can also be understood as the actions an Arahat performs in ordinary life, for these do not lead him into kammic involvement or bind him to a future rebirth. His good actions may appear quite similar to the moral deeds of noble (though unliberated) worldlings, but the Arahat's actions are not motivated by the slightest trace of craving and ignorance. In the Arahat's mind there is no greed (craving) by way of wishing that his virtue be recognized and appreciated, no delusion (ignorance) by way of a proud satisfaction in 'being good', no illusionary expectations as to the result of these good actions; nor is there any other self-reference in any form whatever. An Arahat's good actions are a spontaneous outflow of a fully purified mind and heart, responding without hesitation to situations where help is needed and possible. But though his actions may be inspired by sympathy and compassion, beneath them there is detachment and deep serenity instead of emotional involvement. As long as the momentum of his life-force lasts, the Arahat lives on as an embodiment of wisdom and compassion. But as the Arahat's mind no longer clings to anything, not even to the results of his actions, there is no potentiality left for any future rebirth. The life-nourishing sap conveyed by the roots has ceased to flow, and the roots of continued existence themselves are cut off.

15. THE EXPOSITION OF PREVALENCE (*ussada-kittana*)

In some beings greed is prevalent, in others hatred or delusion; and again in others, non-greed, non-hatred or non-delusion are prevalent. What is it that governs this prevalence? It is the root-cause in the previous life that governs the prevalence of roots in the present life.

There is differentiation at the very moment of the accumulating of kamma. In one person, at the moment of (rebirth-producing) kamma-accumulation, greed is strong and non-greed is weak, non-hatred and non-delusion are strong and hatred and delusion are weak; then his weak non-greed is unable to prevail over his greed, but non-hatred and non-delusion being strong, can prevail over his hatred and delusion. Hence when a being is born through rebirth-linking caused by that kamma, he will be greedy, good-natured, not irascible, intelligent and having knowledge that can be likened to a lightning flash.

In another case, at the moment of kamma-accumulation, greed and hatred are strong, and non-greed and non-hatred are weak, but non-delusion is strong and delusion weak; then, in the way stated, that person will have both greed and hatred, but he will be intelligent and have flash-like knowledge like the Elder Datta-Abhaya.

When, at the moment of kamma-accumulation, greed, non-hatred and delusion are strong and the other roots are weak, then, in the way stated, that person will be greedy and dull-witted, but he will be good-natured and not irascible.

When, at the moment of kamma-accumulation, the three roots, greed, hatred and delusion are strong and non-greed, etc. are weak, then, in the way stated, that person will be greedy, given to hatred and given to delusion.

When, at the moment of kamma-accumulation, non-greed, hatred and delusion are strong and the others are weak, then, in the way stated, that person will have few (lustful) defilements, being unmoved even when seeing a heavenly sense-object; but he will be given to hatred and his understanding will be slow.

When, at the moment of kamma-accumulation, non-greed, non-hatred and delusion are strong, and the others weak, then, in the way stated, that person will not be greedy and will be good-natured, but he will be slow of understanding.

When, at the moment of kamma-accumulation, non-greed, hatred and non-delusion are strong, and the others weak, then, in the way stated, that person will not be greedy; he will be intelligent, but given to hatred and irascibility.

But when, at the moment of kamma-accumulation, the three (wholesome roots), non-greed, non-hatred and non-delusion are strong, and greed etc., are weak, then, in the way stated, he has no greed and no hate and he is wise, like the Elder Sangharakkhita.

From the *Aṭṭhasālinī*, pp. 267f.

IV *The Social Significance of the Roots*

16. FROM THE KĀLĀMA SUTTA

'What do you think, Kālāmas? When greed, hatred and delusion arise in a man, is it for his benefit or harm?' – 'For his harm, venerable sir.' – 'Kālāmas, a person who is greedy, hating and deluded, overpowered by greed, hatred and delusion, his thoughts controlled by them, will take life, take what is not given, indulge in sexual misconduct, and tell lies; he will also prompt others to do likewise. Will that conduce to his harm and his suffering for a long time?' – 'Yes, venerable sir.'

'What do you think, Kālāmas? Are these things wholesome or unwholesome?' – 'Unwholesome, venerable sir.' – 'Blamable or blameless?' – 'Blamable, venerable sir.' – 'Censured or praised by the wise?' – 'Censured, venerable sir.' – 'Undertaken and practised, do these things lead to harm and suffering, or not? Or how is it in this case?' – 'Undertaken and practised, these things lead to harm and to suffering. So does it appear to us in this case.'

'Therefore, Kālāmas, did we say: Do not go upon repeated hearing (of orally transmitted religious tradition), nor upon a linear succession (of teachers), nor upon hearsay, nor upon the authority of scriptures, nor upon speculative and logical grounds, nor upon thought-out theories, nor on preference for views pondered upon, nor upon another's seeming competence, nor on the consideration that "The monk is our teacher."

'But when you yourselves know: "These things are unwholesome, blamable, censured by the wise and if undertaken and practised they will lead to harm and suffering," then give them up.'

Anguttara Nikāya, 3: 65.

17. WHY GIVE UP THE ROOTS OF EVIL?

Once a wandering ascetic, Channa by name, visited the venerable Ānanda and spoke to him as follows:

'You, friend Ānanda, teach the giving up of greed, hatred and delusion, and we, too, teach it. But, friend Ānanda, what disadvantage have you seen in greed, hatred and delusion that you teach that they ought to be given up?'

'Friend, a person who is greedy, hating and deluded, overpowered by greed, hatred and delusion, his thoughts controlled by them, aims at his own harm, aims at others' harm, aims at the harm of both, and he suffers pain and grief in his mind. But when greed, hatred and delusion are given up, he will not aim at his own harm, nor at the harm of others, nor at the harm of both, and he will not suffer pain and grief in his mind.

'A person who is greedy, hating and deluded, overpowered by greed, hatred and delusion, his thoughts controlled by them, leads an evil way of life in deeds, words and thoughts; he does not know his own true advantage, nor that of others, nor that of both. But when greed, hatred and delusion are given up, he will not lead an evil way of life in deeds, words and thoughts: and he will understand his own true advantage, that of others, and that of both.

'Greed, hatred and delusion, friend, make one blind, unseeing and ignorant; they destroy wisdom, are bound up with distress, and do not lead to Nibbāna.

'Because we have seen these disadvantages in greed, hatred and delusion, therefore, friend, do we teach that they ought to be given up.

'This Noble Eightfold Path, namely: right understanding, right thought, right speech, right action, right livelihood, right effort, right mindfulness and right concentration – this, friend, is the path, this is the way to the giving up of greed, hatred and delusion.'

Anguttara Nikāya, 3: 71.

18. THE VISIBLE TEACHING

'People speak of the "visible teaching". In how far, Lord, is the teaching visible here and now, of immediate result, inviting to come and see, onward-leading, to be directly experienced by the wise?'

'A person who is greedy, hating and deluded, over-powered by greed, hatred and delusion, aims at his own harm, at others' harm, at the harm of both, and he suffers pain and grief in his mind. He also leads an evil way of life in deeds, words and thoughts, and he does not know his own true advantage, that of others and that of both.

'But when greed, hatred and delusion are given up, he will not aim at his own harm, at others' harm, at the harm of both, and he will not suffer pain and grief in his mind. He will not lead an evil life and he will understand his own true advantage, that of others and that of both.

'In that sense is the teaching visible here and now, of immediate result, inviting to come and see, onward-leading, to be directly experienced by the wise.'

Anguttara Nikāya, 3: 53

Comment

The description of the teaching (Dhamma) as being 'visible here and now' and so forth, is the same as in the traditional text of homage to the Dhamma.

The Dhamma taught by the Buddha is the Four Noble Truths. If that Dhamma is here identified with the teaching on the unwholesome roots and their abandonment, we may understand the connection thus: the presence of greed, hate and delusion corresponds to the truths of suffering and its origin, their abandonment to the truths of the path and its goal, Nibbāna, the cessation of suffering.

When, through earnest effort in practising the Dhamma, one succeeds in weakening the evil roots, the truth of the teaching becomes clearly visible. The Dhamma indeed yields immediate results. Having accepted its invitation to 'come and see', one has tested it and seen its benefits for oneself. Encouraged by these partial results, one will be led onwards towards the goal – the final eradication of greed, hatred and delusion. But the experience has to be personal – gone through by each one himself, alone, through wisdom and energy devoted to the work of liberation.

19. FOUR TYPES OF PEOPLE

There are four types of people in the world. One who works for his own good, but not for the good of others; one who works for the good of others, but not for his own good; one who works neither for his own good nor for the good of others; and one who works for his own good as well as for the good of others.

And which is the person who works for his own good, but not for the good of others? It is he who strives for the abolishing of greed, hatred and delusion in himself, but does not encourage others to abolish greed, hatred and delusion.

And which is the person who works for the good of others, but not for his own good? It is he who encourages others to abolish greed, hatred and delusion, but does not strive for the abolishing of greed, hatred and delusion in himself.

And which is the person who works neither for his own good nor for the good of others? It is he who neither strives for the abolishing of greed, hatred and delusion in himself, nor encourages others to abolish greed, hatred and delusion.

And which is the person who works for his own good as well as for the good of others? It is he who strives for the abolishing of greed, hatred and delusion in himself, and also encourages others to abolish greed, hatred and delusion.

Anguttara Nikāya, 4: 76

20. THE ROOTS OF VIOLENCE AND OPPRESSION

There are, O monks, three roots of the unwholesome: greed, hatred and delusion.

Greed, hatred and delusion of every kind are unwholesome. Whatever kamma a greedy, hating and deluded person heaps up, by deeds, words or thoughts, that, too, is unwholesome.[14] Whatever suffering such a person, overpowered by greed, hatred and delusion, his thoughts con-

trolled by them, inflicts under false pretexts[15] upon another –
by killing, imprisonment, confiscation of property, false
accusations or expulsion, being prompted in this by the
thought, 'I have power and I want power' – all this is
unwholesome too. In this manner, there arise in him many
evil unwholesome states of mind, born of and originating
from greed, hatred and delusion, caused and conditioned by
greed, hatred and delusion.

Anguttara Nikāya, 3: 69

Comment

As our text vividly shows, the three roots of evil have dreadful
repercussions on society, as causes of cruelty and the infliction
of suffering. The Buddha speaks of the three as motives for the
unrestrained use of power, and the examples given in the text
make it clear that he refers to political power: a ruler's abuse of
power whether in time of war against his country's enemy, or in
peacetime towards its own population. During his lifetime, the
Buddha must have observed many cases of violence and
oppression. He also must have known that the false pretexts
justifying such abuses of power are used in war as well as in
peace. False propaganda against a country's enemy, and slander
of the chosen victims in the ruler's own country, obviously
existed even 2500 years ago. In fact, all those instances of
violence and oppression mentioned by the Buddha have quite a
familiar ring today. And of course, the driving forces behind
them are still the same: greed, hatred and delusion. In modern
history, however, the central role has shifted towards delusion,
which runs beneath various aggressive ideologies of a religious,
political or racial character.

The Buddha may have been recalling his life as a prince at his
father's court when he spoke those moving verses opening the
sutta called 'The Use of Violence' (Aṭṭa-daṇḍa Sutta):

The use of violence breeds terror:
See the nation embroiled in strife!
How this has moved my heart,
How I was stirred, I shall now tell.

Seeing the crowds in frantic movement,
Like swarms of fish when the pond dries up;
Seeing how people fight each other,
By fear and horror I was struck.

Sutta Nipāta, vv. 935–936

Only rarely did the Buddha speak about those darker sides of contemporary society, but these few texts show that he was a keen and compassionate observer.

Generally, all three roots of evil operate in those acts of violence and oppression which our text mentions. But in specific cases any of the three might be dominant, though an element of delusion, or ignorance, will always be present. In war, rulers might be motivated chiefly by greed for territory, wealth, economic dominance or political supremacy; but to make the war popular among their own people, they will employ hate-propaganda to whip up their will to fight. Delusion was a prominent motive in the religious wars of the past, and in our present time it still crops up in ideological wars and revolutions, as well as in religious, political and racial persecutions within a country. In all these cases, delusion produces hate, with greed too often lurking in the background. Oppressive regimes, in their acts directed against sections of their own people, share the same motives. The interaction of the roots is sometimes quite complex, as they grow in strength by feeding each other.

The Buddha understood well the psychology of the mighty, which basically has not changed through the millenia. All those wrongful acts, from killing down to expulsion of innocent victims, are committed out of the lust for power – the enjoyment of power, the wish to secure it and the drive to expand its range. This power craze is, of course, an obsessive delusion intricately bound up with authority. It threatens to overcome all those who exercise authority over others, from the old-style monarchs to the modern dictator. Even the petty bureaucrat does not escape: he too delights in wielding his own little share of power and displaying his stamp of authority.

V   The Removal of the Unwholesome Roots

21.   THE TRIPLE GEM AND THE ABANDONING OF THE EVIL ROOTS

Once the venerable Ānanda was staying in Kosambi, at Ghosita's monastery. At that time a certain householder, a lay

devotee of the Ājīvaka ascetics, went to see the venerable
Ānanda. Having arrived, he saluted him and sat down at one
side. So seated, he said this to the venerable Ānanda:

'How is it, revered Ānanda: Whose doctrine is *well-
proclaimed*? Who are those who live *well-conducted* in the
world? Who are *the blessed ones* in the world?'[16]

'Now, householder, I shall ask you a question on this
matter, and you may answer as you think fit. What do you
think, householder: as to those who teach a doctrine for the
abandoning of greed, hatred and delusion, is their doctrine
well-proclaimed or not? Or what do you think about this?'

'I think their doctrine is well-proclaimed, revered sir.'

'Then, householder, what do you think: those whose
conduct is directed to the abandoning of greed, hatred and
delusion, do they live well-conducted in this world or not?
Or what do you think about this?'

'I think they are well-conducted, revered sir.'

'And further, householder, what do you think: those in
whom greed, hatred and delusion are abandoned, cut off at
the root, made (barren) like a palm-stump, brought to non-
existence, no longer liable to arise in the future again – are
they the blessed ones in the world or not? Or what do you
think about this?'

'Yes, I do think, revered sir, that these are the blessed ones
in the world.'

'So householder, you have admitted this: Well-proclaimed
is the creed of those who teach a doctrine for the abandoning
of greed, hatred and delusion. Those are well-conducted
whose conduct is directed to the abandoning of greed, hatred
and delusion. And the blessed ones are those who have
abandoned greed, hatred and delusion and have totally
destroyed it in themselves.'

'Wonderful, revered sir! Marvellous, revered sir! There
was no extolling of your creed, nor a disparaging of another's
creed. Just by keeping to the subject matter, the doctrine was
explained by you. Only facts were spoken of and no selfish
reference was brought in.

'It is excellent, revered sir, very excellent. It is as if one were
to set aright what was overturned, reveal what was hidden,
point the way to those who have lost it, hold up a light in the
darkness so that those who have eyes may see what is visible.

Thus was the teaching in diverse ways explained by the worthy Ānanda.

'I now go for refuge to that Exalted One, to his teaching and to the Order of monks. May master Ānanda accept me as a lay follower from this day onwards as long as life shall last. May he regard me as one who has thus taken refuge.'

Anguttara Nikāya, 3: 71

Comment

This text introduces us to an unnamed lay follower of the Ājīvakas, a sect of naked ascetics contemporary with the Buddha. The questioner must have been a person of sensitivity, and was obviously disgusted with the self-advertisement he may have found in his own sect and among other contemporary religious teachers. So he wanted to test a disciple of the Buddha to see if they too indulged in self-praise. He even laid a trap for the venerable Ānanda, by phrasing his questions in terms of the well-known Buddhist formula of homage to the Triple Gem. Perhaps he expected that the venerable Ānanda would answer thus: 'These are the very words we use, and we claim these achievements for *our* doctrine, for *our* monks and for *our* Buddha.' But the venerable Ānanda's reply, being free from self-praise and blame of others, came as a happy surprise to him. And as the questioner was perceptive, he immediately grasped the profound significance of the venerable Ānanda's words connecting the Three Gems with the abandonment of the unwholesome roots. Moved to admiration for both the speaker and his teaching, the inquirer declared on the spot his dedication to the Triple Gem.

This dialogue between a non-Buddhist and a Buddhist monk suggests that the teaching on the three roots can be immediately convincing to anyone with an open mind and heart. It offers an eminently practical, non-creedal approach to the very core of the Dhamma, even for those reluctant to accept its other tenets. It is for this reason that the awareness of those three roots and their significance is elsewhere called a directly 'visible teaching' (Text 18) and a doctrine that can be grasped without recourse to faith, tradition or ideologies (Text 29). It can be easily seen that greed, hatred and delusion are at the root of all individual and social conflict. Those who still hesitate to accept the Buddha's teaching on the truths of suffering and its origin in their entire range of validity may not be ready to admit that *all* degrees and varieties of greed, hatred and delusion are roots of suffering. Yet even if they only understand the more extreme forms of those three states to be the root causes of evil and unhappiness, such understanding, practically applied, will be immensely beneficial to themselves and to society.

From such an initial understanding and application, it may not be too difficult for an honest searching mind to proceed to the conclusion that even the very subtle tendencies towards greed, hatred and delusion are harmful – seeds from which their most destructive forms may grow. But the Dhamma is a gradual teaching: the extension of that initial understanding should be left to the natural growth of the individual's own insight and experience without being forced upon him. This was the very attitude which the Enlightened One himself observed in his way of teaching.

Following the example of the venerable Ānanda, it will be profitable also in the present day if, for various levels of understanding, the practical message of the Dhamma is formulated in terms of the wholesome and unwholesome roots. In its simplicity as well as its profundity, this teaching carries the distinct seal of Enlightenment. It is a teaching that will directly affect everyday life, and will also reach to the very depth of existence, showing the way to transcend all suffering.

22. IT CAN BE DONE

Abandon what is unwholesome, O monks! One *can* abandon the unwholesome, O monks! If it were not possible, I would not ask you to do so.

If this abandoning of the unwholesome would bring harm and suffering, I would not ask you to abandon it. But as the abandoning of the unwholesome brings benefit and happiness, therefore I say, 'Abandon what is unwholesome!'

Cultivate what is wholesome, O monks! One *can* cultivate the wholesome, O monks! If it were not possible, I would not ask you to do so.

If this cultivation of the wholesome would bring harm and suffering, I would not ask you to cultivate it. But as the cultivation of the wholesome brings benefit and happiness, therefore I say, 'Cultivate what is wholesome!'

Anguttara Nikāya, 2: 19

Comment

This text proclaims, in simple and memorable words, man's potential for achieving the good, thus invalidating the common charge that Buddhism is pessimistic. But since man also has, as we know only too well, a strong potential for evil, there is as little ground for unreserved optimism about him and his future. Which of his potentialities becomes actual – that for good or that for evil – depends on his own choice. What makes a person a full human being is facing choices and making use of them. The range of man's choices and his prior awareness of them expand with the growth of his mindfulness and wisdom, and as mindfulness and wisdom grow, those forces that seem to 'condition' and even to compel his choices into a wrong direction become weakened.

These hope-inspiring words of the Buddha about man's positive potential will be grasped in their tremendous significance and their full range, if we remember that the words *wholesome* and *unwholesome* are not limited to a narrow moral application. The wholesome that can be cultivated comprises everything beneficial, including those qualities of mind and heart which are indispensable for reaching the highest goal of final liberation. The unwholesome that can be abandoned includes even the finest traces of greed, hatred and delusion. It is, indeed, a bold and heartening assurance – a veritable 'lion's roar' – when the Buddha said, with such wide implications, that what is beneficial can be cultivated and what is harmful can be abandoned.

23. THE ARISING AND NON-ARISING OF THE ROOTS

There may be outsiders, O monks, who will ask you:

'Now, friends, what is the cause and condition whereby unarisen greed arises and arisen greed becomes stronger and more powerful?' 'An attractive object', they should be told. In him who gives unwise attention to an attractive object, unarisen greed will arise, and greed that has already arisen will become stronger and more powerful.

'Now, friends, what is the cause and condition whereby unarisen hatred arises and arisen hatred becomes stronger and more powerful?' 'A repulsive object', they should be told. In him who gives unwise attention to a repulsive object, unarisen hatred will arise, and hatred that has already arisen will grow stronger and more powerful.

'Now, friends, what is the cause and condition whereby unarisen delusion arises and arisen delusion becomes stronger and more powerful?' 'Unwise attention', they should be told. In him who gives unwise attention, unarisen delusion will arise, and delusion that has already arisen will grow stronger and more powerful.

'Now, friends, what is the cause and condition for unarisen greed not to arise and for the abandoning of greed that has arisen?' 'A (meditation) object of impurity', they should be told. In him who gives wise attention to a (meditation) object of impurity, unarisen greed will not arise and greed that has arisen will be abandoned.

'Now, friends, what is the cause and condition for unarisen hatred not to arise and for the abandoning of hatred that has arisen?' 'Loving-kindness that is a freeing of the mind', they should be told. In him who gives wise attention to loving-kindness that is a freeing of the mind, unarisen hatred will not arise and hatred that has arisen will be abandoned.

'Now, friends, what is the cause and condition for unarisen delusion not to arise and for the abandoning of delusion that has arisen?' 'Wise attention', they should be told. In him who gives wise attention, unarisen delusion will not arise and delusion that has arisen will be abandoned.'

Anguttara Nikāya, 3: 68

Comment

This text shows the decisive role *attention* plays in the origination and eradication of the unwholesome roots. In the discourse 'All Taints' (Sabbāsava Sutta, Majjhima Nikāya 2) it is said: 'The uninstructed common man . . . does not know the things worthy of attention nor those unworthy of attention. Hence he fails to give attention to what is worthy of it and directs his attention to what is unworthy of it.' And of the well-instructed disciple the same discourse says that he knows what is worthy of attention and what is not, and that he acts accordingly.

The commentary to that discourse makes a very illuminating remark: 'There is nothing definite in the nature of the things (or objects) themselves that makes them worthy or unworthy of attention; but there is such definiteness in the *manner* (*ākāra*) of attention. A manner of attention that provides a basis for the arising of what is unwholesome or evil (*akusala*), that kind of attention should not be given (to the respective object); but the kind of attention that is the basis for the arising of the good and wholesome (*kusala*), that manner of attention should be given.'

It is this latter type of attention that in our present text is called 'wise attention' (*yoniso manasikāra*). The former kind is 'unwise attention' (*ayoniso manasikāra*), which elsewhere in the commentaries is said to be the proximate cause of delusion.

Things pleasant or unpleasant – that is, those potentially attractive or repulsive – are given to us as facts of common experience, but there is nothing compelling in their own nature that determines our reaction to them. It is our own deliberate attitude towards them, the 'manner of attention', which decides whether we will react with greed to the pleasant and with aversion to the unpleasant, or whether our attention will be governed instead by right mindfulness and right understanding, resulting in right action. In some cases, it will also be possible and advisable to withdraw or divert attention altogether from an object; and this is one of the methods recommended by the Buddha for the removal of unwholesome thoughts. (See Text 24 and Comment.)

Our freedom of choice is present in our very first reaction to a given experience, that is, in the way we attend to it. But only if we direct *wise* attention to the object perceived can we make use of our potential freedom of choice for our own true benefit. The range of freedom can be further widened if we train ourselves to raise that wise attention to the level of right mindfulness.

24. FIVE METHODS FOR REMOVING UNWHOLESOME THOUGHTS

A monk who is intent on the higher consciousness (of meditation) should from time to time give attention to five items. What five?

1. When, owing to an object to which the monk has given (wrong) attention, there arise in him evil unwholesome thoughts connected with desire,[17] with hatred and with delusion, then that monk should give his attention to a different object, to one connected with what is wholesome. When he is doing so, those evil unwholesome thoughts connected with desire, hatred and delusion are abandoned in him and subside. With their abandonment, his mind becomes

inwardly steady and settled, unified and concentrated. . . .

2. If, when giving attention to an object that is wholesome, there still arise in him evil unwholesome thoughts connected with desire, with hatred and with delusion, then the monk should reflect upon the danger in these thoughts thus: 'Truly, for such and such reasons these thoughts are unwholesome, they are reprehensible and result in suffering!' When he is reflecting in this way, those evil unwholesome thoughts are abandoned in him and subside. With their abandonment, his mind becomes inwardly steady and settled, unified and concentrated. . . .

3. If, when reflecting upon the danger in these thoughts, there still arise in him evil unwholesome thoughts connected with desire, with hatred and with delusion, he should try not to be mindful of them, not to give attention to them. When he is not giving attention to them, those evil unwholesome thoughts will be abandoned in him and subside. With their abandonment, his mind becomes inwardly steady and settled, unified and concentrated. . . .

4. If, when he is not giving attention to these thoughts, there still arise in him evil unwholesome thoughts connected with desire, with hatred and with delusion, he should give attention to the removal of the source of these thoughts.[18] When he is doing so, those evil unwholesome thoughts are abandoned in him and subside. With their abandonment, his mind becomes inwardly steady and settled, unified and concentrated. . . .

5. If, while he is giving attention to the removal of the source of these thoughts, these evil unwholesome thoughts still arise in him, he should, with teeth clenched and the tongue pressed against the palate, restrain, subdue and suppress mind by mind.[19] When he is doing so, those evil unwholesome thoughts are abandoned in him and subside. With their abandonment, his mind becomes inwardly steady and settled, unified and concentrated. . . .

When those evil unwholesome thoughts connected with desire, hate and delusion, which have arisen owing to (wrong) attention given to an object, have been abandoned in a monk and have subsided (due to his applying these five methods), and when (due to that) his mind has become steady and settled, unified and concentrated, – then that monk is called a master of the pathways of thoughts: he will think the thoughts he wants to think and will not think those he does not want to think. He has cut off craving, severed the fetter (to existence) and with the full penetration of conceit, he has made an end of suffering.

Majjhima Nikāya 20 (Vitakkasaṇṭhāna Sutta)[20]

Comment

This *Discourse on the Removal of Unwholesome Thoughts* was addressed by the Buddha to monks devoted to meditation, especially to the attainment of the meditative absorptions (*jhāna*), which constitute the higher consciousness (*adhicitta*) mentioned in the sutta. But the five methods for stopping unwholesome thoughts are not restricted to those engaged in strict meditative practice. They are also helpful when desire, aversion and delusion arise during less intensive contemplations undertaken by monks or lay people. Even in situations of ordinary life, when one is confronted with an onrush of unwholesome thoughts, these methods will prove effective, provided one can muster the presence of mind needed to promptly apply them. In applying them, one will be practising right effort, the sixth factor of the Noble Eightfold Path. For the attempt to overcome arisen unwholesome thoughts is one of the four great efforts (*sammappadhāna*), constituting the path factor of right effort.

By the *first* method one tries to replace harmful thoughts by their beneficial opposites. The discourse gives the simile of a carpenter removing a coarse peg with the help of a fine peg. The commentary explains as follows: when an unwholesome thought of desire for a living being arises, one should counter it by thinking of the impurity of the body; if there is desire for an inanimate object, one should consider its impermanence and its ownerless nature. In the case of aversion against a living being, one should direct thoughts of loving-kindness and friendliness towards that being; one should remove resentment against inanimate things or against adverse situations by thinking of their impermanence and impersonal nature. When deluded or confused thoughts arise, one should make an effort to clarify them and discern things as they are.

The sutta statement deals with the case of countering undesirable thoughts immediately on their arising. For sustained success in substantially reducing and finally abolishing them, one should strengthen the wholesome roots opposed to them whenever one meets the opportunity to do so. Non-greed should be enhanced by selflessness, generosity and acts of renunciation; non-hate by patience and compassion; non-delusion by cultivating clarity of thought and a penetrative understanding of reality.

The *second* method for removing unwholesome thoughts is that of evoking repugnance and a sense of danger with regard to them. The simile in the discourse is that of a well-dressed young man or woman who feels horrified, humiliated and disgusted when the carcass of an animal is slung around his or her neck. Calling to mind the unworthiness of evil thoughts will produce a sense of shame (*hiri*) and abhorrence. The awareness that these unwholesome thoughts are harmful and dangerous will produce a deterring 'dread of consequences' (*ottappa*). This method of evoking repugnance may also serve as an aid for returning to the first method of 'replacement by good thoughts', unless one has now become able to check the intruding thoughts through the second method. This method can be very effective when encounters in ordinary life call for quick restraint of the mind.

By the *third* method one tries to ignore undesirable thoughts by diverting one's attention to other thoughts or activities. Here the simile is that of closing one's eyes at a disagreeable sight or looking in another direction. If this method is applied during a session of meditation, it may require a temporary interruption of the meditation. For a diverting occupation, the commentary gives as examples recitation, reading or looking through the contents of one's bag (or pocket). Reciting or reading may be helpful outside meditative practice, too. Until those troublesome thoughts have subsided, one might also take up some little work that requires attention.

The *fourth* method is illustrated in the discourse by a man who runs fast and then asks himself: 'Why should I run?' and he slows down; he then continues that process of calming his activity by successively standing still, sitting and lying down. This simile suggests that this method involves a sublimating and refining of the coarse unwholesome thoughts. But as this sublimation is a slow and gradual process, it may not be applicable to a meditative situation when a quicker remedial action is required. The commentarial interpretation seems, therefore, to be preferable: one traces unwholesome thoughts back to the thoughts or the situation which caused them to arise and then tries to remove that thought source from one's mind. This may often be easier than confronting directly the full-grown end-result. It will also help to divert the mind (according to the third method) from those unwholesome thoughts, which at this stage may be hard to dislodge. We may thus describe the fourth method as 'tracing the thought source'. But from the longer view of a continued endeavour to eliminate the harmful thoughts, interpreting this method as sublimation and gradual refinement need not be excluded. Such refinement can reduce the intensity and the immoral quality of the three unwholesome roots and even divert their energy into wholesome channels.

The *fifth* and last method is that of vigorous suppression. This method is to be applied when unwholesome thoughts have gained such a strength that they threaten to become unmanageable and to bring about situations of grave peril, practically and morally. The discourse illustrates this method by a strong-bodied man forcing down a weaker person by sheer physical strength.

If the application of these five methods is not neglected but is kept alive in meditative practice as well as in ordinary circumstances, one can expect a marked and progressive weakening of the three unwholesome roots, culminating in the perfect mastery of thoughts promised at the end of the sutta.

25. FOR ONE'S OWN SAKE

For one's own sake, monks, vigilant mindfulness should be made the mind's guard and this for four reasons:

'May my mind not harbour lust for anything inducing lust!' – for this reason vigilant mindfulness should be made the mind's guard, for one's own sake.

'May my mind not harbour hatred toward anything inducing hatred!' – for this reason vigilant mindfulness should be made the mind's guard, for one's own sake.

'May my mind not harbour delusion concerning anything inducing delusion!' – for this reason vigilant mindfulness should be made the mind's guard, for one's own sake.

'May my mind not be infatuated by anything inducing infatuation!' – for this reason vigilant mindfulness should be made the mind's guard, for one's own sake.

When now, monks, a monk's mind does not harbour lust for lust-inducing things, because he is free from lust;

when his mind does not harbour hatred toward hate-inducing things, because he is free from hatred;

when his mind does not harbour delusion concerning anything inducing delusion, because he is free from delusion;

when his mind is not infatuated by anything inducing infatuation, because he is free from infatuation – then such a monk will not waver, shake or tremble, he will not succumb to fear, nor will he adopt the views of other recluses.[21]

Anguttara Nikāya, 4: 17

26. THE NOBLE POWER

Monks, it is good for a monk if, from time to time:

he perceives the repulsive in the unrepulsive,

if he perceives the unrepulsive in the repulsive,

if he perceives the repulsive in both the unrepulsive and the repulsive,

if he perceives the unrepulsive in both the repulsive and the unrepulsive,

if he avoids both the repulsive and the unrepulsive (aspects), and dwells in equanimity, mindful and clearly comprehending.

But with what motive should a monk perceive the repulsive in the unrepulsive? 'May no lust arise in me for lust-inducing objects!' – it is with such a motive that he should perceive in this way.

With what motive should he perceive the unrepulsive in the repulsive? 'May no hatred arise in me towards hate-inducing objects!' – it is with such a motive that he should perceive in this way.

With what motive should he perceive the repulsive in the unrepulsive as well as in the repulsive? 'May no lust arise in me for lust-inducing objects nor hatred towards hate-inducing objects!' – it is with such a motive that he should perceive in this way.

With what motive should he perceive the unrepulsive in the repulsive as well as in the unrepulsive? 'May no hatred arise in me towards hate-inducing objects nor lust for lust-inducing objects!' – it is with such a motive that he should perceive in this way.

With what motive should he avoid both the repulsive and the unrepulsive, and dwell in equanimity, mindful and clearly comprehending? 'May lust for lust-inducing objects, hatred towards hate-inducing objects, and delusion towards deluding objects never arise in me anywhere in any way!' – it is with such a motive that he should avoid both the repulsive and the unrepulsive, and dwell in equanimity, mindful and clearly comprehending.

Anguttara Nikāya, 5: 144

Comment

This fivefold method of mastering perception is called in Pāli *ariya iddhi*, a term which may be rendered as noble power, noble success or noble magic; or, alternatively, as the power, success or magic of the noble ones (*ariya*). In its perfection, this arduous practice can be ascribed only to Arahats as several suttas and commentaries indicate. But, as our text shows at the beginning, the Buddha recommended this training to the monks in general, including those in whom the three unwholesome roots were still active. It is eradication of these roots which is said to be the motivation for taking up this practice.

For applying this fivefold power, the following directions have been given in the canon and commentaries.[22]

1. To perceive the repulsive in the unrepulsive, one pervades attractive living beings with the contemplation of the body's impurity; towards attractive inanimate objects one applies the contemplation of impermanence.

2. To perceive the unrepulsive in the repulsive, one pervades repulsive living beings with loving-kindness and views repulsive inanimate objects as consisting of the four elements; but living beings too ought to be contemplated by way of the elements.

3. To perceive the repulsive in both the unrepulsive and the repulsive, one pervades both with the contemplation of impurity and applies to them the contemplation of impermanence. Or, if one has first judged a being to be attractive and later repulsive, one now regards it as unrepulsive throughout, i.e. from the viewpoint of impurity and impermanence.[23]

4. To perceive the unrepulsive in both the repulsive and the unrepulsive, one pervades both with loving-kindness and views both as bare elements. Or, if one has first judged a being to be repulsive and later attractive, one now regards it as unrepulsive throughout; i.e. from the viewpoint of loving-kindness and as consisting of elements.

5. Avoiding both aspects, one applies the six-factored equanimity of which it is said: 'On perceiving (any of the six sense objects, including mental objects), he is neither glad nor sad, but keeps to equanimity and is mindful and clearly comprehending.' He does not lust after a desirable object nor does he hate an undesirable one; and where others thoughtlessly allow delusion to arise, he does not give room to delusion. He remains equanimous towards the six objects, being equipped with the six-factored equanimity which does not abandon the pure natural state of the mind.

These five methods of applying the noble power have several applications. They are first for use during meditation, when images of repulsive and unrepulsive beings or things arise in the mind. At such a time one can overcome the attraction or aversion by dwelling on the counteractive ideas – such as loving-kindness or analysis into elements – as long as required to dispel the defilements. Second, these methods can be used in the encounters of everyday life when the counteractive ideas must be tersely formulated and rapidly applied. This will require previous familiarity with them and alertness of mind. In encounters with repulsive people one may also think of their good qualities and of their common human nature, with its failings and sufferings. When meeting a physically attractive person, one may vividly visualize that person's body as subject to ageing and decay.

These five modes of perception, as perfected in the Arahat, reveal the high-point of the mind's sovereign mastery over the world of feelings and emotions. They show a state where the response to provocative objects, usually so habitually fixed, can be chosen at will. This approach differs from that used in the contemplation of feelings as shown below (Text 31). In the latter the feeling-values of experience are accepted as they are given, but by applying bare attention to them, one 'stops short' at the feelings themselves without allowing them to grow into the passionate reactions of lust or aversion. However, in this method of the noble power, the meditator does not take the feeling-values for granted; he does not accept them as they present themselves. His response is to reverse the feeling-value (mode 1, 2), to equalize the response to the repulsive and the unrepulsive (mode 3, 4) and to transcend both by mindful equanimity (mode 5).

These fives modes thus constitute a subtle 'magic of transformation' by which pleasant and unpleasant feelings, as they habitually arise, can be changed at will or replaced by equanimity. A mind that has gone through this training has passed the most severe test, indeed. Through that training, it obtains an increasing control over emotive reactions, and internal independence from the influence of habits and passions. It is said in the Satipaṭṭhāna Sutta, 'He dwells independent and clings to nothing.' These words conclude a statement recurring after each of the exercises given in the sutta. In the light of the above observations, it is significant that they also occur after the section on contemplation of feelings found in that sutta.

According to our text, the purpose for cultivating the noble power is the eradication of greed, hatred and delusion. In a mind disciplined in this radical training, the root defilements cannot find a fertile soil for growth. The training also provides the experiential basis for comprehending the true nature of feelings as being relative and subjective. This the five modes of the noble power demonstrate in a convincing way. The relativity of feelings and of the emotions roused by them was succinctly expressed by Āryadeva (2nd century CE):

By the same thing lust is incited in one, hate in the other, delusion in the next. Hence sense objects have no inherent value.

Catuḥ-Śataka, 8: 177

Perfection in applying this noble power is the domain only of the truly noble ones, the Arahats, whose mastery of mind and strength of will are equal to the task of exercising it effortlessly. But also on much lower levels, an earnest endeavour to develop this noble power will be of great benefit. In the text here commented upon, the Buddha does not restrict the cultivation of the noble power to Arahats, but begins his exposition with the words: 'It is good for a monk . . .'. We may add: not only for a monk. Prior practice of right mindfulness (satipaṭṭhāna), however, will be indispensable. Of particular importance is the contemplation of feelings, by which one learns to distinguish between the feeling linked with a perception and the subsequent emotional reaction to it.

VI Removal through Mindfulness and Insight

27. TO BE ABANDONED BY SEEING

Which are the things, O monks, that can neither be abandoned by bodily acts nor by speech, but can be abandoned by wisely seeing them? Greed can neither be abandoned by bodily acts nor by speech; but it can be abandoned by wisely seeing it. Hatred can neither be abandoned by bodily acts nor by speech; but it can be abandoned by wisely seeing it. Delusion can neither be abandoned by bodily acts nor by speech; but it can be abandoned by wisely seeing it.

Anguttara Nikāya, 101: 23

Comment

'Wisely seeing', according to the commentary, refers here to the wisdom pertaining to the paths of emancipation along with the insight that culminates in the paths. From this explanation it follows that the term *abandoning* has to be understood here in its strict sense, as final and total elimination, effected by realization of the paths of emancipation (stream-entry, etc.).

Nevertheless, a weakening of the unwholesome roots can be effected also by body and speech, through curbing more and more their outward manifestations in deeds and words, motivated by greed, hatred and delusion.

The phrase 'wisely seeing' may serve to emphasize the crucial importance of mindfully observing the presence or absence of the unwholesome roots within one's own mind flux. This repeated confrontation with them prepares the way to liberating insight.

28. FROM THE SATIPAṬṬHĀNA SUTTA

And how, monks, does a monk dwell practising mind-contemplation on the mind?

Herein a monk knows the mind with lust as with lust; the mind without lust as without lust; the mind with hatred as with hatred; the mind without hatred as without hatred; the mind with delusion as with delusion; the mind without delusion as without delusion. . . .

Thus he dwells practising mind-contemplation on the mind, internally, or externally, or both internally and externally. He dwells contemplating the states of origination in the mind, or he dwells contemplating the states of dissolution in the mind, or he dwells contemplating the states of both origination and dissolution in the mind. Or his mindfulness that 'there is mind' is established in him to the extent necessary for knowledge and awareness. He dwells detached, clinging to nothing in the world.

Majjhima Nikāya 10

29. BEYOND FAITH

'Is there a way, O monks, by which a monk without recourse to faith, to cherished opinions, to tradition, to specious reasoning, or to preference for his preconceived views, may declare the final knowledge (of Arahatship), thus: "Rebirth has ceased, the holy life has been lived, completed is the task, and nothing remains after this"?

'There is such a way, O monks. And what is it?

'Herein, monks, a monk has seen a form with his eyes, and if greed, hatred and delusion are in him, he knows "There is in me greed, hatred and delusion"; and if greed, hatred and delusion are absent in him, he knows "There is no greed, hatred and delusion in me."

'Further, monks, a monk has heard a sound, smelled an odour, tasted a flavour, felt a tactile sensation or cognized a mental object, and if greed, hatred and delusion are in him, he knows "There is in me greed, hatred and delusion"; and if greed, hatred and delusion are absent in him, he knows "There is no greed, hatred and delusion in me."

'And if he thus knows, O monks, are these ideas such as to be known by recourse to faith, to cherished opinions, to tradition, to specious reasoning or to preference for one's preconceived views?'

'Certainly not, Lord.'

'Are these not rather ideas to be known after wisely realizing them by experience?'

'That is so, Lord.'

'This, monks, is a way by which a monk, without recourse

to faith, to cherished opinions, to tradition, to specious reasoning or to preference for his preconceived views, may declare final knowledge (of Arahatship), thus: "Rebirth has ceased, the holy life has been lived, completed is the task and nothing more remains after this".'

Saṁyutta Nikāya, 47: 12

30. THE VISIBLE TEACHING[24]

Once the venerable Upavāna went to the Exalted One, saluted him respectfully and sat down at one side. Thus seated he addressed the Exalted One as follows:
'People speak of the "visible teaching". In how far, Lord, is the teaching visible here and now, of immediate result, inviting to come and see, onward-leading, to be directly experienced by the wise?'

'Herein, Upavāna, a monk, having seen a form with his eyes, experiences the form and experiences desire for the form.[25] Of the desire for forms present in him, he knows: "There is in me a desire for forms." If a monk, having seen a form with his eyes, experiencing the form and experiencing desire for the form, knows that desire for forms is present in him – in so far, Upavāna, is the teaching visible here and now, of immediate result, inviting to come and see, onward-leading, to be directly experienced by the wise.

'It is similar if a monk experiences desire when he hears a sound with his ears, smells an odour with his nose, tastes a flavour with his tongue, feels a tangible with his body or cognizes an idea with his mind. If he knows in each case that desire is present in him – in so far, Upavāna, is the teaching visible here and now, of immediate result, inviting to come and see, onward-leading, to be directly experienced by the wise.

'Further, Upavāna, a monk, having seen a form with his eyes, experiences the form without experiencing desire for the form. Of the absent desire for form he knows: "There is in me no desire for forms." If a monk, having seen a form with his eyes, experiencing the form without experiencing desire for the form, knows that desire for forms is not present in him – in so far, too, Upavāna, is the teaching visible here and now, of immediate result, inviting to come and see, onward-leading, to be directly experienced by the wise.

'It is similar if a monk does not experience desire when he hears a sound with his ears, smells an odour with his nose, tastes a flavour with his tongue, feels a tangible with his body or cognizes an idea with his mind. If he knows in each case that desire is not present in him – in so far, Upavāna, is the teaching visible here and now, of immediate result, inviting to come and see, onward-leading, to be directly experienced by the wise.'

Saṁyutta Nikāya, 35: 70

Comment on Texts 28–30

When thoughts connected with greed (desire, attraction), hatred (anger, aversion) or delusion (prejudices, false views) arise in an untrained mind, generally one reacts to them in one of two ways: either one allows oneself to be carried away by them or one tries to repress them. The first type of reaction is a full identification with the unwholesome roots; the second extreme is the attempt to ignore their presence, shirking a confrontation with them. In this latter case, one regards the defiled thoughts as a disreputable part of one's mind, harmful to one's self-esteem, and thence blots them out from one's awareness.

The approach through *bare attention*, as indicated in the above texts, is a middle way that avoids these two extremes. It involves neither passive submission nor anxious recoil, but a full awareness of the unwholesome thoughts while holding to the mental post of detached observation. These thoughts will then be seen simply as psychological events, as impersonal and conditioned mental processes, as 'mere phenomena rolling on' (*suddhadhammā pavattanti*). When thus objectified, they will no longer initiate emotional reactions by way of attachment, aversion or fear. Bare attention empties these thoughts of self-reference, and prevents the identification with them as a fictive ego. Thus the confrontation even with one's imperfections may give rise to a clear realization of egolessness. From that, again, there may emerge the state of mind described in the Sati-paṭṭhāna Sutta: 'He dwells detached, clinging to nothing.' It will now be understood why, in Texts 18 and 30, it is said that even the awareness of the unwholesome in oneself can make the teaching 'visible here and now'.

This application of detached awareness can be said to belong to the first method of Text 24, replacing the arisen unwholesome thoughts by the wholesome ones of right mindfulness. Even if one does not fully succeed with this method, a sober, factual awareness of the inherent danger, according to the second method, may prove to be effective. If not, one may then be obliged to use the stronger emotional impact of repugnance to eliminate them.

31. REMOVAL THROUGH THE CONTEMPLATION OF FEELINGS

In the case of pleasant feelings, O monks, the underlying tendency to lust should be given up; in the case of painful feelings the underlying tendency to resistance (aversion) should be given up; in the case of neutral feelings, the underlying tendency to ignorance should be given up.

If a monk has given up the tendency to lust in regard to pleasant feelings, the tendency to resistance in regard to painful feelings and the tendency to ignorance in regard to neutral feelings, then he is called one who is free of unwholesome tendencies, one who has the right outlook. He has cut off craving, severed the fetter to existence, and, through the full penetration of conceit, he has made an end of suffering.[26]

If one feels joy, but knows not feeling's nature,
Bent towards greed, one will not find deliverance.

If one feels pain, but knows not feeling's nature,
Bent towards hate, one will not find deliverance.

And even neutral feeling which as peaceful
The Lord of Wisdom has proclaimed,
If, in attachment, one should cling to it,
One will not be free from the round of ill.

But if a monk is ardent and does not neglect
To practise mindfulness and comprehension clear,
The nature of all feelings will he penetrate.

And having done so, in this very life
He will be free from cankers and all taints.
Mature in knowledge, firm in Dhamma's ways,
When once his life span ends, his body breaks,
All measure and concepts he will transcend.

Saṁyutta Nikāya, 36: 3

Comment

In these three 'underlying tendencies' (*anusaya*), we encounter the three unwholesome roots under different names. These tendencies are defilements which, by repeated occurrence, have become habitual responses to situations provoking greed, hate and delusion, and hence tend to appear again and again. They may also be called inherent propensities of the mind. Underlying the stream of consciousness in a state of latency, they are always ready to spring up when a stimulus incites them, manifesting themselves as unwholesome deeds, words or thoughts. By having grown into underlying tendencies, the three roots obtain a most tenacious hold on the mind. Even moral conduct (*sīla*) and concentration (*samādhi*), by themselves, cannot prevail against the tendencies; at best they can only check their outward manifestations. To uproot the tendencies at the level of depth, what is required is insight-wisdom (*vipassanā-paññā*), aided by virtue and concentration. The insight-wisdom needed to fully uproot the three must have the strength acquired at the two final stages of emancipation, non-return and Arahatship.[27]

The non-returner eliminates completely the tendency to resistance or aversion, i.e. the root 'hatred'; the tendency to lust, i.e. the root 'greed', he eliminates as far as it extends to desire for the five outer sense pleasures.

The Arahat eliminates the remaining tendency to lust, the desire for fine-material and immaterial existence, and also all tendencies to ignorance, the root 'delusion'.

Though not able to effect a final elimination of the underlying tendencies, moral restraint in bodily and verbal acts helps to reduce the active formation of *new* unwholesome tendencies, and concentration helps to control the *mental* source of such tendencies, at least temporarily. Insight-wisdom attained on levels lower than the noble paths and fruitions will provide the basis for gradual progress towards the full maturation of liberating wisdom.

The type of insight practice which is particularly efficacious in weakening and removing the underlying tendencies is the Satipaṭṭhāna method called the contemplation of feelings (*vedanānupassanā*). It is the uncontrolled reaction to feelings that produces and nourishes the tendencies. According to Buddhist psychology, the feelings one passively undergoes in sense experience are morally neutral. They are *results* of kamma, not creators of kamma. It is the reaction to feelings following the passive sense encounters that determines the wholesome or unwholesome quality of the responsive active states of consciousness. In the contemplation of feelings, one distinctly realizes that a pleasant feeling is not identical with lust and need not be followed by it; that an unpleasant feeling is not identical with aversion and need not be followed by it; that a neutral feeling is not identical with ignorant deluded thoughts and need not be followed by them. In that practice, the meditator learns to stop at the bare experience of pleasant, painful and neutral feelings. By doing so, he makes a definite start in cutting through the chain of dependent origination at that decisive point where feeling becomes the condition for craving (*vedanā paccayā taṇhā*). It will thus become the meditator's indubitable experience that the causal sequence of feeling and craving is not a necesary one, and that the Buddha's words of encouragement are true: 'One *can* abandon the unwholesome! If it were not possible, I would not ask you to do so.' (See Text 22.)

VII *The Goal*

32. THE VISIBLE NIBBĀNA

When greed, hatred and delusion are abandoned, one neither aims at one's own harm, nor at the harm of others, nor at the harm of both, and one will not suffer pain and grief in one's mind. In that sense is Nibbāna visible here and now.

If one experiences the complete elimination of greed, the complete elimination of hatred, the complete elimination of delusion, in that sense is Nibbāna visible here and now, of immediate result, inviting to come and see, onward-leading, to be directly experienced by the wise.

Anguttara Nikāya, 3: 56

33. WHAT IS NIBBĀNA?

A wandering ascetic, Jambukhādaka by name, approached the venerable Sāriputta and asked him the following question:

'One speaks about "Nibbāna,''. Now, what is that Nibbāna, friend?'

'It is the elimination of greed, the elimination of hatred, the elimination of delusion – this, friend, is called Nibbāna.'

'But is there a way, is there a path, friend, for the realization of that Nibbāna?'

'Yes, friend, there is such a way, there is a path for the realization of that Nibbāna. It is the Noble Eightfold Path, namely right understanding, right thought, right speech, right action, right livelihood, right effort, right mindfulness and right concentration.'

Samyutta Nikāya, 38: 1

34. TWO ASPECTS OF NIBBĀNA

This was said by the Blessed one, spoken by the Holy One, and thus I have heard:

There are, O monks, two aspects of Nibbāna: the Nibbāna-element with the groups of existence still remaining (sa-upādisesa-nibbānadhātu), and the Nibbāna-element with no groups remaining (anupādisesa-nibbānadhātu).

What is now the Nibbāna-element with the groups of existence still remaining? In that case, O monks, a monk is an Arahat: he is taint-free, has fulfilled the holy life, accomplished his task, thrown off the burden, attained his goal, cast off the fetters of existence and is liberated through right wisdom. But there still remain with him (until his death) the five sense-organs that have not yet disappeared and through which he still experiences what is pleasant and unpleasant, as well as bodily ease and pain. The extinction of greed, hatred and delusion in him, this is called the Nibbāna-element with the groups of existence still remaining.

And what is the Nibbāna-element with no groups of existence remaining? In that case, O monks, a monk is an Arahat . . . liberated through right wisdom. In him, all those feelings, no longer relished, will even here (at his death) come to extinction. This is called the Nibbāna-element with no groups of existence remaining.

Itivuttaka 44
(Adapted from the translation by
Nyanatiloka Mahāthera.)

35. THE HAPPINESS OF LIBERATION

He, the Arahat, knows this:

'Once there was greed, and that was evil; now that is no more, and so it is well. Once there was hatred, and that was evil; now that is no more, and so it is well. Once there was delusion, and that was evil; now that is no more, and so it is well.'

Thus the Arahat lives, even during his lifetime, free of craving's hunger, stilled and cooled (of passion's heat), feeling happy, with his heart become holy.

Anguttara Nikāya, 3: 66

Notes

1. See *The Wheel of Birth and Death*, Bhikkhu Khantipalo, (WHEEL No. 147/149), p. 16.

2. Mundane (*lokiya*) are all those states of consciousness – arising in the worldling as well as in noble ones (*ariya*) – which are not associated with the supramundane paths and fruitions of stream-entry, etc. The supramundane (*lokuttara*) type of the wholesome signifies the four paths and the four fruitions of the stream-enterer, once-returner, non-returner and the Arahat.

3. Comy.: absence of knowledge concerning (the truth of) suffering, etc.

4. The Buddhist scriptures speak of five 'heinous offences' – parricide, matricide, killing an Arahat, wounding a Buddha and maliciously causing a schism in the Saṅgha.

5. On 'wrong views with fixed result' (*niyata-micchā-diṭṭhi*), see *Apannaka Sutta*, (WHEEL No. 98/99), p. 23.

6. Māra: the personification of the forces antagonistic to enlightenment.

7. The term 'embodied group' (*sakkāya*) refers to the transient personality consisting of the five aggregates: body, feeling, perception, mental formations and consciousness.

8. Literally, 'leading to the piercing' (*nibbedha-gāmini*). This refers to the piercing, or destroying, of the mass of defilements.

9. The 'holy realm' is Nibbāna.

10. 'Through perfect knowledge' (*sammad-aññāya*). *Aññā* is the highest knowledge, or gnosis, attained by Arahatship.

11. The former die and fall away from their heaven because of anger, the latter because of their negligence. See the Brahmajāla Sutta (Dīgha 7).

12. By way of rebirth.

13. For a fuller repudiation of this thesis in the Buddha's own time, see *The Snake Simile* (Majjhima Nikāya 22), tr. by Nyanaponika, (WHEEL No. 48/49), pp. 13, 16, 39.

14. The verb *abhisankharoti*, 'heaps up', refers to kammic accumulation through the volitional kamma-formations (*sankhāra*), which are here of an

unwholesome character. The commentary emphasizes the fact that greed, hate and delusion are not only unwholesome in themselves, but also roots of future unwholesome evil conditions.

15. *Asatā*; lit.: falsely, untruthfully.

16. The words used here, 'well-proclaimed' (*svākkhāta*), 'well-conducted' (*supaṭipanna*) and 'blessed ones' (*sugata*) are key words in the well-known formula of homage to the Dhamma, Sangha and the Buddha (in our text, in this sequence). The term *sugata*, 'well-farer', was perhaps pre-Buddhist usage for a saintly person and was later on increasingly applied to the Buddha as one of his epithets. In Medieval India, the Buddhists were known as *Saugata*, the followers of the Sugata.

17. Here, the Pāli term used is *chanda*, not *rāga* (lust) or *lobha* (greed).

18. This rendering follows the sutta's commentary which explains the word *sankhāra* (in the phrase *vitakka-sankhāra-saṇṭhāna*) by condition, cause or root. An alternative rendering of this phrase would be 'quieting the thought formations'.

19. That is, he has restrained the unwholesome state of mind by a wholesome state of mind, i.e. by his efforts to remove those unwholesome thoughts.

20. For a complete translation, including the commentary, see *The Removal of Distracting Thoughts*, tr. by Soma Thera, (WHEEL No.21).

21. That is, other religious or philosophical ideas.

22. Compiled from the Paṭisambhidā Magga and commentaries to the Dīgha Nikāya and Anguttara Nikāya.

23. 'Owing to a change in one's own attitude towards a person or due to a change in character (or behaviour) of that person'. Sub. Comy. to Majjhima Nikāya.

24. See also Text 18.

25. Though this text refers only to desire (*rāga*, 'lust'), the statements in it are also valid for a reaction to the six-fold sense perception by hatred and delusion.

26. 'Conceit' refers in particular to 'self-conceit' (*asmi-māna*), on both the intellectual and emotional levels.

27. See *Manual of Insight*, Ledi Sayadaw, (WHEEL No. 31/32), pp. 81 ff.

The Four Nutriments
Of Life

Monks, when a monk becomes entirely dispassionate towards one thing, when his lust for it entirely fades away, when he is entirely liberated from it, when he sees the complete ending of it, then he is one who, after fully comprehending the goal, makes an end of suffering here and now.

What one thing? 'All beings subsist by nutriment' – when a monk becomes entirely dispassionate towards this one thing (nutriment), when his lust for it entirely fades away, when he is entirely liberated from it, and when he sees the complete ending of it, then, O monks, he is one who, after fully comprehending the goal, makes an end of suffering here and now.

Anguttara Nikāya, 10: 27

The Four Nutriments of Life

'All beings subsist on nutriment' (*sabbe sattā āhāraṭṭhitakā*) – this, states the Buddha, is the one single fact about life that, above all, deserves to be remembered, contemplated and understood. If understood widely and deeply enough, this saying of the Buddha reveals a truth that leads to the root of all existence and also to the uprooting of that root. Here, too, the Buddha proves to be one who, as an ancient text says, 'has seen things through down to the root' (Sutta Nipāta, v. 1043).

In Pāli, as in English, the word 'nutriment'[1] is used in ordinary discourse to signify physical food. But in the Buddha's teaching the idea of nutriment is given a wider meaning, being applied to all the primary supports of life – mental as well as biological. This fact the Buddha expresses by declaring that there are *four* kinds of nutriment: edible food, sense-impression, volition and consciousness, which are called nutriments in the sense that they nourish, support and sustain the individual life-continuity.

Despite a difference in modes, the same basic laws govern the process of nutrition in all its forms, whether physical or mental, as is clear from certain common facts shared by every form of nutrition. First, it is hunger that stands behind the entire process of nutrition, wielding its whip relentlessly. The body, from birth to death, craves ceaselessly for material food; and mind hungers as eagerly for its own kind of nourishment, for ever new sense-impressions and for an ever expanding universe of ideas. Craving (*taṇhā*) is thus the principal condition of any 'in-take' or 'up-take' (*upādāna*),[2] that is, of nutriment in its widest sense. This is the first factor common to all types of nutriment, be they physical or mental.

The second common factor is the process of the *assimilation* of food. In the process of eating and digesting, what was external becomes internal; what was foreign matter becomes 'one's own' and is identified with one's personality. The common saying, 'Man is what he eats', applies as much to mental as to physical nourishment. Like the body, our mind also feeds on 'external' material: on sense-impressions and variegated experiences; on the contents of the store-house of knowledge accumulated by the race; and on the precipitate derived from all these sources. Our memories, when they become objects of mind, are as much 'external' to the present thought-moment as the ideas read in a book. What cannot be absorbed by the system is discarded. Thus, in the mind as well as in the body, there is a constant process of grasping and rejecting, assimilating and dissimilating, identifying with oneself and alienating. If we look closely at this process of nutrition, physical and mental, we shall notice that it is not only the eater who consumes the food, but also that in the course of assimilation, the food devours the eater. There is thus between them a process of mutual absorption. We know how much people can be changed, for better or worse, by ideas they have absorbed and which finally absorb and consume *them*.

These laws governing physical and mental nutriment are sufficient to convince a thoughtful observer how illusory is the conception of an abiding self or substance. The process of nutrition thus vindicates the Anattā doctrine, the Buddha's deeply revolutionizing teaching of no-self.

As the German Buddhist writer, Paul Dahlke, says: 'Individualized life is neither a metaphysical 'I'-identity (pure spirit, pure subject, according to the soul-theory of the religions) nor a mere physical process (pure body, pure object, according to scientific materialism), but a nutrimental process and as such it is neither something which is in and by itself nor something caused by another, but something that is *maintaining* itself: and all these so-called higher faculties of thinking and feeling are different forms of eating, of maintaining oneself.'

But besides vindicating the Anattā doctrine, the process of nutrition is likewise a convincing teacher of the two other characteristics of life, impermanence and suffering. Impermanence (*anicca*) is at the very root of the nutritive process, which cries for constant replenishment of the food consumed. As long as we live, the bottomless gaping hole has to be filled again and again. It is no different with our mental hunger, which craves for change and variety in its own diet. This repetitive monotony of the process of nutrition kept going by the urge to preserve life, this is enough to reveal *dukkha*, the suffering of life, the tiresomeness of the tedious round of eating and being hungry again. Hence a medieval Jewish sage was moved to say, 'I am fed up with being hungry again and again, and I hunger after final satiety.'[3]

Suffering is thus inherent in the very function of eating, but it is usually hidden from us by our habituation to this most elementary feature of routine life. Reflection is required to strip away the deception and reveal the concrete suffering and pain involved in the search for and acquisition of food. We can then understand the mute suffering in the animal world where 'devouring each other is the law', the terror of animals butchered for food, the violence of man's fight for land and his wars for 'world markets', the pangs of hunger among the poor and the cries of the starving children. And though the resources for feeding humanity have grown considerably in our days, man has still not controlled famine, even where it would be in his power to do so. Moreover, all progress in the field of food-production today threatens to be dwarfed by the rapid growth of the world's population. This problem looms large on the horizon of present-day humanity and may well become desperate if the disparity between available food and increasing population reaches a critical point. Should that critical point be reached, we do not know what dire consequences may follow, unless a united mankind can solve the problem by concerted action and peaceful means.

Hence, also for mankind's future, what the Dhamma teachers of old said remains true: that the search for food is an ever-present source of suffering. As such it can stir our sense of urgency when we consider, in the light of 'nutriment', our own nature, our incessant needs and our situation in a world where the need to eat is life's constant companion.

This contemplation of the suffering connected with nutriment leads to a corresponding formulation of the Four Noble Truths. The four nutriments of life stand for the first truth of suffering; the craving for the four nutriments is the origin of suffering, the second truth; the stopping of that craving, the cessation of the continued process of grasping for material amd mental food, is the end of suffering, the third truth; and the Noble Eightfold Path, the fourth noble truth, is the way to that cessation (see Majjhima Nikāya 9).

It is because the process of nutrition, material and mental, demonstrates the conditioned nature of all existence that we find it reveals those salient features of the Dhamma – the three characteristics of impermanence, suffering and not-self, and the Four Noble Truths.

The most important and revealing of the Buddha's discourses on nutriment is the Discourse on Son's Flesh, translated below. The commentator, Ācariya Buddhaghosa, explains the compelling reason for this seemingly harsh discourse: At the time, the community of monks received abundant support by way of almsfood and other requisites. Considering this, the Master asked himself:

'Will the monks be able to eat the almsfood and still keep to that mindfulness and clear comprehension which lays hold (of the true nature) of nutriment? Will they be detached, and free of desire and greed?, And he saw that there were some young monks, recently ordained, who ate the almsfood without due reflection. Seeing this, he thought: 'When I practised the perfections (*pāramī*) for four incalculable periods and a hundred thousand aeons, I did not do so for the sake of the requisites, such as robes, almsfood etc., but for the sake of the highest fruition of Arahatship. Also, these monks who took ordination under me did not become ordained for the sake of these requisites, but for the sake of attaining Arahatship. And now they take the unessential for the essential, the worthless for what is worthy! I shall place before them a mirror of the Dhamma for their self-control and restraint, so that, contemplating it again and again, the monks of the future will make use of their material requisites only after due reflection.'

The Buddha then spoke the Discourse on Son's Flesh, extending his concern to all four of 'the nutriments of life'. Each of these he illustrates with a pithy, even startling, simile, and careful consideration of these will open for us profound insights into the Dhamma revealed in the apparently drab function of bodily and mental nutrition.

I. EDIBLE FOOD (*kabaḷinkārāhāra*)

Simile: A couple, foodless in the midst of a desert, eat their little child to enable them to reach their destination.

Ever since emerging on this planet, man, like the husband and wife in the Buddha's simile, has traversed the desert of life where food is the most urgent concern. And again, as in that story, the stilling of his hunger has often been a heart-rending business – if not for the sometimes quite callous 'eater', then for his prey and for a sensitive observer. Often, in his search for food, man has destroyed what is commonly dearest to him, be it relatives and friends or the ideals of his youth. True, this is only *one* aspect of life, which is not entirely a desert as it contains a good number of oases where travellers can rest and enjoy themselves. But in doing so, they are prone to forget the surrounding sands, which often encroach upon and bury their tiny oasis.

The couple in the Buddha's story, coming near starvation, eat their own beloved child: a gruesome, seemingly fantastic story indeed! But knowing from the records of history that, at times of famine, war or shipwreck, men *did* resort to cannibalism, we have to admit that what our story tells us may sometimes have substantially happened. In his incessant search for food, or for better food and greater control of food resources – how often has man killed, cruelly crushed or exploited his fellow creatures, even those close to him by common blood or common race! And is there not a close kinship between *all* that lives? These last words are not merely a sentimental phrase (as they are mostly used), but also point to a hard and cruel fact. Are we not akin to the voracious greed, the cruel rage and the destructive stupidity which we encounter in life and of which we become victim or perpetrator in the struggle for food or power? If we were not akin to them, *could* we encounter them in one way or another? For an unfathomable time, caught in the ever-turning wheel of life, we have been *everything*: the prey and the devourer of all, parent and child of all. This we should consider when contemplating the nutriment of edible food and the Buddha's simile.

If we wish to eat and live, we have to kill or tacitly accept that others do the killing for us. When speaking of the latter, we do not refer merely to the butcher or the fisherman. For the strict vegetarian's sake, too, living beings have to die. The farmer's ploughshare brings cities of worms and insects to destruction. The protection of vegetables and grains means the death of countless 'pests' which, like ourselves, are also living beings in search of food. A growing population's need for more arable land deprives animals of their living space and, in the course of history, has caused many species to be eliminated. It is a world of killing in which we live, and in this world we play our own part. We should face this horrible fact and in our reflection on edible food keep it vividly in our awareness. To do so will stir us to effort to escape from this murderous world by bringing to an end our craving for the four nutriments.

In one short lifetime, how many trainloads of food have passed in and out of our puny bodies! How many people have had to labour in the production, preparation and distribution of food to keep unbroken the 'traffic line' running straight through our alimentary canal! It is a grotesque picture to visualize.

There is yet another aspect of that 'life-giving' function of eating to consider. Let us think of a silo, or a storehouse or a feedbag. After it has been emptied, generally a few grains or other tiny morsels of food remain behind. Similarly, in our bodies there will always be left small remnants of food that are neither assimilated nor expelled. These remain and putrefy, and some physiologists say that it is this putrefaction of residual food that, in the absence of other causes, ultimately brings about the ageing and death of the organism. If they are right, then food is not only life-giving but also death-bestowing. Thus it appears that we have in this life of ours the choice between death by starvation and death by putrefaction: 'The food devours the eater!' This close connection between nutriment and death is very poignantly expressed in Greek myth, according to which Demeter is the goddess of corn (that is, food) as well as of death. Bachofen, that great explorer and interpreter of classic myth, has expressed its significance very succinctly: 'She feeds man as a prey to herself.'

People, as far as they give any thought to the humdrum act of eating, take very different attitudes towards food. Some, tired with the dull routine of eating dull food, make a 'fine art' of it and become gourmands. To them the Buddha says: 'All nutriment is miserable, even divine food.' Others, keenly aware of the importance of food for good health, devise various ideas about 'pure food'. We have here the dietetic rules of several religions, and the belief of ancient and modern sects in man's 'purification by nutriment' (āhāra-parisuddhi). Such sects existed already in the Buddha's time, and the Buddha knew of their beliefs and rejected them. Others, again, have tried to solve the problem of the body's dependence on food by reducing nourishment below sustenance level and by long periods of fasting. This harsh and futile method of self-mortification the Buddha had also tried and rejected before his Enlightenment, as he vividly describes in the Great Discourse on the Lion's Roar (Mahāsīhanāda Sutta, Majjhima Nikāya 12). Following his Enlightenment, the Buddha never recommended periods of fasting beyond the abstention from solid food after noon, enjoined upon bhikkhus, and upon lay people during their periodic observance of the eight or ten precepts. What he advised, as a teacher of the middle way, was moderation in eating, non-attachment to the taste of food, and wise reflection on nutriment.

2. SENSE-IMPRESSION (*phassa*)

Simile: A skinned cow, wherever she stands, is ceaselessly attacked by the insects and other creatures living in her vicinity.

Like a skinned cow, man is helplessly exposed to the constant excitation and irritation of the sense-impressions crowding upon him from all sides through the six senses – eye, ear, nose, tongue, body and mind. The Pāli word *phassa*, rendered here by sense-impression, means literally 'touch' or 'contact'. However, what is meant is not a physical impact, but mental contact with the objects occurring through the six senses, including the mind. Together with attention (*manasikāra*), sense-impression is the mind's first and simplest response to the stimulus exercised by sense data and ideas. Buddhist psychology treats it as a constituent factor in each and every state of mind, the lowest and the highest, occurring also in dreams and in subliminal states of consciousness.

Sense-impression, as a nutriment, is a basic sustaining condition of life. What it particularly nourishes or conditions are feelings (*vedanā*). Feelings live on the multitude of constantly occurring sense-impressions and assimilate them as pleasant, unpleasant or indifferent. This relationship has also a place in the formula of dependent origination: 'Conditioned by sense-impression is feeling' (*phassa-paccayā vedanā*). Craving thrives on unguarded feelings, and as long as there is craving for sense-impressions, there will be an unlimited supply of that foodstuff to be digested by feeling. Throughout our lives, in rapid alternation, forms, sounds, smells, flavours, bodily impacts and ideas impinge upon us in an unending stream. It was the poignant awareness of that constant bombardment that induced the Buddha to choose for sense-impression the simile of a skinned cow whose raw flesh is the target of swarms of insects causing her intensely painful feelings. According to the Buddha, for one not yet free from attachment any type of feeling is bound to cause suffering and conflict. Painful feeling is suffering in itself; pleasant feeling brings suffering through its transiency and its unsatisfying and unsatisfactory nature; worldly indifferent feeling produces suffering through its inherent dullness and boredom. Sense-impression, as the constant feeder of these feelings, thus becomes the cause of this threefold suffering.

A monk of old, yearning to see still more vidily the burning and irritating nature of sense-impressions, was moved to exclaim:

When shall I with calm endowed
Wisely see as caught in raging blaze
The countless forms, sounds, scents, and tastes,
And contacts and mental things?

Theragāthā v. 1099, Tālaputa

Though we are amply aware of the host of painful impressions impinging on our senses, generally we are quite willing to pay this price for our pleasures. In fact, we seem to prefer any sort of sensation to none at all, unless the pain aroused threatens to pass beyond the tolerance level. What is at the psychological root of this situation is our hunger for ever new experiences. If that hunger is not regularly satisfied, it leaves us empty, starved and helpless. Thence our need for change and novelty, and our longing for constant contact with life. So habitual does this contact become that for most people solitude is dreaded as an unbearable deprivation.

The nutriment sense-impression feeds the 'world as enjoyment'; it feeds the craving for existence (bhava-taṇhā). This habitual craving can be broken only if we cease to identify ourselves with the stream of impressions, if we learn to dispense with automatic active responses and to stand back as an observer. Then the feeling that is nourished by sense-impression will cease to turn into craving, and at this point the dependent origination of suffering will be severed.

3. VOLITIONAL THOUGHT (manosañcetanā)

Simile: Two strong men grab another man by the arms and drag him towards a pit of glowing embers.

Volitional thought here means chiefly kamma, i.e. rebirth-producing and life-affirming action. The two strong men in the simile represent the dragging forces of our kammic actions – our good but deluded actions and our evil actions. It is our kammic proclivities, our life-affirming volitions, our plans and ambitions, that drag us irresistibly to that deep pit of saṁsāra with its glowing embers of intense suffering. Hence it is said that volitional thought, in the sense of kamma, is the nutriment for rebirth on the three planes of existence.

The nutriment, volitional thought, manifests itself in man's incessant urge to plan and to aspire, to struggle and to conquer, to build and to destroy, to do and to undo, to invent and to discover, to form and to transform, to organize and to create. This urge has sent him into the depths of the ocean and into the vastness of space. It has made him the most vicious of predatory animals and also enabled him to reach the lofty heights of genius in creative art and thought.

The restlessness at the root of all that lust for activity, and of the creative urge as well, is the constant hunger for the four nutriments of life. We crave for them in a variety of forms and on different levels of coarseness and sublimity. It is volitional thought that has to go foraging to provide us with the nutriment for which we crave. This becomes an incessant task, for any satisfaction we gain is of short duration, eventually yielding to new hunger and thence to a new search for nutriment.

In volitional thought, the world appears as will, power and creative force. Nourished by this powerful nutriment, the process of world-building and world-destruction goes on until saṁsāra is seen in its true nature – as a pit of glowing embers, the bottomless depth of which we can never fill no matter how often we plunge into it in the various guises we assume in our migrations from life to life.

4.   CONSCIOUSNESS (*viññāṇa*)

Simile: A criminal is struck with a hundred spears three times a day – morning, noon and evening – and lives to experience the pain.

Every day, at all times of the day, conscious awareness opens us up to the impact of the world of objects, the punitive results of our past cravings and delusions which pierce our protective skins with their sharp shafts.

This shockingly harsh image of consciousness as a punishment reminds us of one of Franz Kafka's main motifs so often appearing in his work – the hidden, unknown, intangible and seemingly quite amoral guilt of man inherent in his very existence, for which he is inscrutably punished and which punishment, in the depth of his being, he accepts as just (see *The Trial*, *The Castle*, and 'In the Penal Colony').

The desire for conscious awareness has the same character as that for sense impressions: the craving to be alive, to *feel* alive in the constant encounter with the world present to consciousness. But there is a still more important meaning to be derived from the description of consciousness as a nutriment. For consciousness in this context is explained primarily as *rebirth-consciousness*; and this, though it occurs for only a single moment, 'feeds' the entire mind-body process (*māma-rūpa*) throughout the whole present existence, from birth to death. It is the arising of such moments of rebirth-consciousness at the beginning of each successive life that continues the interminable chain of births, deaths and suffering. Growth or proliferation is a characteristic feature of all consciousness. Though any given rebirth-consciousness is directly linked only with the immediately preceding life, it has behind it the inexhaustible store-house of the beginningless past, a vast granary containing countless potential seeds of life. Fed from the dark unfathomable recesses of the past, consciousness lurks like an octopus with not eight but a thousand arms, ready to grasp and take hold wherever it finds a chance, and there to procreate a fresh breed of beings each with its own set of grasping tentacles.

The writer once visited large subterranean caverns which had long passages and high-roofed temple-like halls with huge stalactites and stalagmites resembling the lofty columns of a cathedral. For the convenience of the numerous visitors to the caverns, electric light had been installed, and where the bulbs were low enough one could see around them a small spread of lichen, the only trace of organic life amidst the barren rocks. Life springs up wherever it gains the slightest opportunity through favouring conditions like warmth, moisture and light. In the spectator's mind this little harmless proliferation of primitive plant life assumed the menacing features of a beast of prey that, having lurked long under the cover of darkness, at last got the chance for its hungry leap.

Life is always ready to spring up and its most prolific

manifestation is consciousness. Seen from our limited view-point, it is consciousness that contributes most to the 'expand-ing universe' of saṁsāra. Hence the Enlightened One warned: 'Do not be an augmentor of worlds!' It is by our insatiable and greedy feeding on consciousness and the other nutriments that the world 'grows'; and the potentialities for its growth are endless. The end of the world of consciousness also cannot be reached by walking. Seen from that world-wide perspective, consciousness appears as the feeder and procreator of in-numerable beings all of whom undergo the daily ordeal of life's piercing spears. Such a visualization of the reach of con-sciousness will strip away the magician's enchanting illusions with which the Buddha compared the aggregate of conscious-ness. Undeceived by these deceptions, one will move in-creasingly towards revulsion, turning away and dispassion.

Looking back at the Buddha's similes for the four nutriments, we are struck by the fact that all four evoke pictures of extreme suffering and danger, unusual situations of grave agony. Considering that the daily process of nutrition, physical and mental, is such a humdrum function in life, those extraordinary similes arouse great surprise, even a deep inner disturbance. And they were meant to be disquietening. They are meant to break through the unthinking complacency with which we perform and view these so common functions: eating, per-ceiving, willing and cognizing.

The contemplations on the four nutriments, as presented on these pages, cut at the very roots of the attachment to life. To pursue these contemplations radically and methodically will be a grave step, advisable only for those who are determined to strive for the final cessation of craving and are thus willing to face all consequences which that path of practice may have for the direction of their present life and thought.

But apart from such full commitment, serious and repeated thought given to this teaching of the four nutriments will be beneficial to any earnest follower of the Buddha. To those who feel it premature for themselves to aim straight at the cessation of craving, the Dhamma has enough teachings to soothe the wounds received in the battle of life, and to encourage and help a steady progress on the path. Amidst the harshness of life, a gentle guidance will often be welcome. Yet, when there is only such gentleness, when the winds of fate blow softly and pleasantly, there is a danger that we will settle down to a comfortable routine and forget our precarious situation in this world. Hence there is a need for us to face such stern teachings as those on the nutriments. To do so will keep us alert and will strengthen our mental fibre so we can fearlessly meet the unveiled truth about the world in which we live.

The contemplation on the four nutriments of life has much to teach us. From that contemplation, we can learn 'not to recoil from the real and not to be carried away by the unreal'. We can learn that it is suffering only which is nourished and sustained by the four nutriments, that *only suffering arises where anything arises and only suffering ceases where anything ceases*. And another statement of the Master will gain fresh significance and increasing weight: '*This only do I teach: suffering and its end.*'

The Discourse on Son's Flesh (Saṁyutta Nikāya, 12:63)

'There are, O monks, four nutriments for the sustenance of beings born, and for the support of beings seeking birth. What are the four?

'First, edible food, coarse and fine; second, sense-impression; third, volitional thought; fourth, consciousness.

'How, O monks, should the nutriment *edible food* be considered? Suppose a couple, husband and wife, have set out on a journey through the desert, carrying only limited provisions. They have with them their only son, dearly beloved by them. Now, while these two travelled through the desert, their limited stock of provisions ran out and came to an end, but there was still a stretch of desert not yet crossed. Then the two thought: "Our small stock of provisions has run out, it has come to an end; and there is still a stretch of desert that is not yet crossed. Should we not kill our only son, so dearly beloved, prepare dried and roasted meat, and eating our son's flesh, cross in that way the remaining part of the desert, lest all three of us perish?"

'And these two, husband and wife, killed their only son, so dearly beloved by them, prepared dried and roasted meat, and eating their son's flesh, crossed in that way the remaining part of the desert. And while eating their son's flesh, they beat their breast and cried: "Where are you, our only beloved son? Where are you, our only beloved son?"

'What do you think, O monks? Will they eat the food for pleasure, for enjoyment, for comeliness' sake, for the body's embellishment?'

'Certainly not, O Lord.'

'Will they not rather eat the food merely for the sake of crossing the desert?'

'So it is, O Lord.'

'In the same manner, I say, O monks, should edible food be considered. If, O monks, the nutriment edible food is comprehended, the lust for the five sense-objects is thereby comprehended. And if lust for the five sense-objects is comprehended, there is no fetter by which enchained a noble disciple might come to this world again.[4]

'And how, O monks, should the nutriment *sense-impression* be considered? Suppose, O monks, there is a skinned cow. If it stands close to a wall, then the creatures living in the wall will nibble at it; if it stands near a tree, then the creatures living in the tree will nibble at it; if it stands in the water, the creatures living in the water will nibble at it; if it stands in the open air, the creatures living in the air will nibble at it. Wherever that skinned cow stands, the creatures living there will nibble at it.

'In that manner, I say, O monks, should the nutriment sense-impression be considered. If the nutriment sense-impression is comprehended, the three kinds of feeling[5] are thereby comprehended. And if the three kinds of feeling are comprehended, there is, I say, no further work left for the noble disciple to do.[6]

'And how, O monks, should the nutriment *volitional thought* be considered? Suppose, O monks, there is a pit of glowing embers filled to cover a man's height, with embers glowing without flames and smoke. Now a man comes that way, one who loves life and does not wish to die, who wishes for happiness and detests suffering. Then two strong men seize both his arms and drag him to the pit of glowing embers. Then, O monks, that man would wish to be far away from the pit, he would long to be far away from it, he would incline to be far away from it. And why? Because the man knows: "If I fall into that pit of glowing embers, I shall meet death or deadly pain."

'In that manner, I say, O monks, should the nutriment volitional thought be considered. If the nutriment volitional thought is comprehended, the three kinds of craving[7] are thereby comprehended. And if the three kinds of craving are comprehended, there is, I say, no further work left for the noble disciple to do.

'And how, O monks, should the nutriment *consciousness* be considered? Suppose, O monks, people have seized a criminal, a robber, and brought him before the king saying: "This is a criminal, a robber, O Majesty! Mete out to him the punishment you think fit!" Then the king would tell them: "Go, and in the morning strike this man with a hundred spears!" And they strike him in the morning with a hundred spears. At noon the king would ask his men: "How is that man?" – "He is still alive, Your Majesty." – "Then go and strike him again at noontime with a hundred spears!" So they do, and in the evening the king asks them again: "How is that man?" – "He is still alive." – "Then go and in the evening strike him again with a hundred spears!" And so they do.

'What do you think, O monks? Will that man, struck with three hundred spears during a day, suffer pain and torment owing to that?'

'Even if he were to be struck only by a single spear, he would suffer pain and torment owing to that. How much more if he is struck by three hundred spears!'

'In that manner, I say, O monks, should the nutriment consciousness be considered. If the nutriment consciousness is comprehended, mind-and-matter is thereby comprehended. And if mind-and-matter is comprehended, there is, I say, no further work left for the noble disciple to do.'

Notes

1. *Āhāra*: from the verb *āharati*, to take up, to take upon oneself; to bring, carry, fetch.
2. Both Pāli words *āhāra* (nutriment) and *upādāna* (clinging) have the same original meaning of 'taking up' or 'seizing'.
3. Abraham ben Chisdai, in '*Ben-hamelekh we-hanasir*' ('The Prince and the Ascetic'). This is an old Hebrew version of the 'Barlaam and Joasaph' story which unwittingly carried the main features of the Buddha's life story through a major part of the medieval world. The Hebrew version has several distinct traces not only of the Buddha's life story, but also of Buddhist ideas, like the one quoted above.

4. That is, he has become a non-returner (*anāgāmi*) by eradicating the fetter of sensual desire (*kāmarāga-saṁyojana*) which, according to Comy. forms a unit with those other fetters given up at this stage, i.e. personality belief, sceptical doubt, attachment to rites and rituals, ill-will.

5. Pleasant, unpleasant and neutral feeling.

6. This refers to the attainment of Arahatship.

7. Sensual craving, craving for (eternal) existence, craving for self-annihilation.

The Threefold Refuge

In all Buddhist lands the followers of the Buddha profess their allegiance to him and his liberating doctrine by the ancient, simple, and yet so touching formula of *going for refuge* to the Triple Gem.

The 'going for refuge', as this figurative expression itself suggests, should be a conscious act, not the mere profession of a theoretical belief or a habitual rite of traditional piety. The protecting refuge *exists*, but we have to go to it by our own effort. It will not come to us by itself, while we stay put. The Buddha, as he repeatedly declared, is only the teacher, 'pointing out the way'. Therefore, the going for refuge, expressive of Buddhist faith (*saddhā*), is in the first place a conscious act of *will* and determination directed towards the goal of liberation. Hereby the conception of faith as a mere passive waiting for 'saving grace' is rejected.

In the Pāli commentaries there is a remarkable statement that the expression 'going for refuge' is meant to convey, in addition, the idea of 'knowing' and 'understanding'. This points to the second aspect of going for refuge – namely as a conscious act of *understanding*. Hereby unthinking credulity and blind faith based on external authority are rejected.

The commentator emphasizes this aspect by describing the going for refuge as a state of mind that does not rely on others (*aparapaccaya*). On many occasions the Master warned his disciples not to accept teachings out of mere trust in him, but only after personal experience, practice and reflection. Here it may suffice to recall the famous sermon to the Kālāmas: 'Do not go by hearsay, nor by tradition, nor by people's tales, nor by the authority of scriptures. Do not go by reasoning, nor by logic and methodical investigations, nor by approval of speculative views, nor moved by reverence, nor by the thought: "The recluse is my teacher!" ' (Anguttara Nikāya, 3: 65).

It is a threefold knowledge that is implied in the act of going for refuge. It is a knowledge answering the following questions: Is this world of ours really such a place of danger and misery that there is a need for taking refuge? Does such a refuge actually exist? And what is its nature?

There are many who do not see any need for a refuge. Being well pleased with themselves and with the petty, momentary happiness of their lives, they are fully convinced that 'all is well with the world'. They do not wish, or are not able, to look beyond their narrow horizons. For them neither the Buddha nor any other great religious teacher has yet appeared. But the majority of men know very well, by their own bitter experience, the hard and cruel face of the world which is only temporarily hidden by a friendly mask. There are others who, sufficiently aware of a fellow being's actual existence, add to that personal experience by observation of other lives. And there is a still smaller number of people who are able to reflect wisely on both experience and observation. Particularly to those latter ones 'whose eyes are less covered by dust', life will appear as a vast ocean of suffering of unfathomable depth, on the surface of which beings swim about for a little while, or navigate in their fragile nutshells of which they are very proud.

True, there are spells of calm on the waters when it is pleasant to float upon a smooth sea, or to prove and to enjoy the strength of one's body by a long swim. But those with open eyes and minds are not deceived by these short moments of respite: they know the overpowering fierceness of a storm-swept sea, its dangerous currents and whirlpools, the demons and monsters of the deep. They know that, even under the most favourable conditions, the feeble strength of man will soon be exhausted by the impact of life's elemental forces. The vicissitudes of life give no chance of maintaining permanently, during the unlimited sequence of transformations, even the lowest degree of happiness, even the lowest standard of moral worth. There is nothing to gain by traversing ever anew the infinite expanse of life's ocean, in any of its regions. There is only the same senseless repetition of the ups and downs, of ebb and tide. Faced by the ever-present perils of life and by its essential monotony, there will be only the one cry for refuge in a heart and mind that has truly grasped its situation within the world. A refuge is the one great need of all life and 'going to it' the one sane act demanded by that situation.

But, granting its necessity, does a refuge from the world's ills actually exist? The Buddhist affirms it and proves by that affirmation to be anything but a pessimist. The refuge to which he turns his steps is the triad of the Buddha, his doctrine and the Order of noble disciples. Being what is most precious and most pure, it has been called 'the Triple Gem'. But the fact that it provides the final refuge and not only a temporary shelter, those who take refuge can prove only to themselves, by actually attaining to the refuge through their own inner realization.

The Triple Gem has objective existence as an impersonal idea or ideal as long as it is known and cherished. Even in that mode it is doubtlessly a persisting and active source of benefit for the world. But it is transformed from an impersonal idea to a personal refuge only to the extent that it is realized in one's own mind and manifested in one's own life. Therefore, the existence of the Triple Gem in its characteristic nature as a refuge cannot be proved to others. Each must find this refuge in himself by his own efforts. The refuge becomes and grows by the process of going to it.

By effort, earnestness and self-control
Let the wise man make for himself an island
Which no flood can overwhelm.

Dhammapada, v. 25

The refuge exists for us only so far as something within ourselves responds and corresponds to it. Therefore the Sixth Zen Patriarch said:

Let each of us take refuge in the Three Gems within our mind!

With regard to the first refuge, in the Buddha, the Master himself said, shortly after his Enlightenment:

Like me they will be conquerors
Who have attained to the defilements' end.

Majjhima Nikāya 26 (Ariyapariyesana Sutta)

Concerning the second refuge, in the Dhamma, the Buddha said shortly before his decease:

Be islands for yourselves, be refuges for yourselves! Take no other refuge! Let the Dhamma be your island, let the Dhamma be your refuge! Take no other refuge!

Dīgha Nikāya 16 (Mahāparinibbāna Sutta)

In the commentarial literature it is said, in reference to another passage, but applicable to the one just quoted:

The Dhamma is called 'self' (*attā*), because, in the case of a wise one, the Dhamma is not different from himself and because it pertains to his personal existence.

Ṭīkā to Mahāsatipaṭṭhāna Sutta

The third refuge, the Saṅgha, being the Order of noble disciples, is the great and inspiring model for emulation. The actual foundation of that refuge is the capacity inherent in all beings to become one of the eight noble beings who form the Saṅgha of the refuge.[1]

We turn now to the third subject of the knowledge implied in taking refuge, the ultimate nature of the Threefold Refuge.

We have seen that the refuge becomes attainable only by way of the living roots, by the actual foundations it has within the average mind. Like the lotus it arises within the waters of worldly existence; there it develops and from there it takes its nourishment. But what is still immersed in the ocean of worldliness and suffering cannot be the ultimate refuge, the place of safety and bliss. It must not only assuage, but must also ultimately transcend the world of danger, fear and ill, like the lotus that rises above the surface of the water and remains unsullied by it. Therefore, the consummate refuge meant in the traditional formula is of supramundane nature – *lokuttara*, world-transcending.

Thus the first refuge is not the Recluse Gotama, but the Buddha as the personification of world-transcending Enlightenment. In the Vīmaṁsaka Sutta it is said of the noble disciple: 'He believes in the Enlightenment of the Exalted One' (Majjhima Nikāya 47).

The Dhamma of the second refuge is not the faint, fragmentary, or even distorted picture of the doctrine as mirrored in the mind of an unliberated worldling. It is the supramundane path and its consummation in Nibbāna. The commentator underlines the supramundane nature of the second refuge by saying that the Dhamma, as an object of learning, is included in the refuge only in so far as it is a formulation of the consummate knowledge acquired on the path to liberation.

The Saṅgha of the third refuge is not the all-inclusive congregation of monks, having all the weaknesses of its single members and sharing in the shortcomings attached to any human institution. It is rather the Order of noble disciples who are united by the invisible tie of common attainment to the four stages of liberation. In other words, it too is of supramundane nature: the assurance of possible progress to the world-transcending heights of a mind made holy and pure.

By this threefold knowledge about the need, existence and nature of the refuge, the going for refuge becomes a conscious act of *understanding*.

This knowledge and understanding forms the firm basis of the third, the emotional aspect of taking refuge, which has three facets: confidence, devotion and love. The knowledge of the existence of a refuge provides the basis for a firm and justified confidence, for the calmness of inner assurance and the strength of conviction. The knowledge of the need for a refuge instills unswerving devotion to it. And the understanding of its sublime nature fills the heart with love towards the highest that can be conceived. Confidence is the firmness in faith; devotion is the patient endurance in loyal service and effort; and love adds the element of ardour, warmth and joy. In the sense of these three constituents, the going for refuge is also a conscious act of wise *faith*.

We may now define the going for refuge as *a conscious act of will directed towards liberation, based upon knowledge and inspired by faith*; or briefly: *a conscious act of determination, understanding and devotion*.

These three aspects of taking refuge have their counterparts in the volitional, rational and emotional sides of the human mind. Thus for a harmonious development of character the cultivation of all three is required.

Will, understanding and faith support each other in their common task. Will, transformed into purposive action, frees faith from the barrenness and dangers of emotional self-indulgence; it prevents intellectual understanding from stopping short at mere theoretical appreciation. Will harnesses the energies of both emotion and intellect to actual application. Understanding gives direction and method to will; it provides a check to the exuberance of faith and gives to it its true content. Faith keeps will from slackening, and is the vitalizing and purposive factor in intellectual understanding.

The presence of these three aspects is the distinguishing feature of true Buddhist faith. In the conception of faith, as found in other world religions, the emotional aspect tends to be overstressed at the expense of will and understanding. Against such an over-emphasis on emotional faith, Buddhism moves from the very beginning of its spiritual training towards wholeness and completeness, towards a harmonious development of mental faculties. Therefore, the act of going for refuge in its true sense is accomplished only if there is connected with it at least a minimal degree of purposeful will and genuine understanding. Only in that case will faith have the quality of a 'seed' attributed to it by the Buddha, a seed productive of further growth. The element of will in that seed of faith will grow until maturing into the irrepressible desire for liberation (*muñcitukamyatā-ñāṇa*), one of the advanced stages of insight (*vipassanā*). The element of initial understanding in true faith will grow into the penetrative wisdom that finally transforms the assurance of faith into the inner certitude conferred by realization.

Taking refuge by way of thoughtless recital of the formula is a degradation of that venerable ancient practice. It deprives it of its true significance and efficacy. 'Going for refuge' should be the expression of a genuine inner urge, in the same way as, in ordinary life, one may be urged by the awareness of a great danger to seek without delay the refuge of a place of safety.

When taking refuge, one should always keep in mind the implications of this act, as outlined above. This will be, at the same time, a beneficial training in right mindfulness. One should always ask oneself how the presently undertaken act of going for refuge can be translated into terms of will and understanding. Seeing that the house of our life is ablaze, it will not do merely to worship the safety and freedom that beckons outside, without making an actual move to reach it. The first step in that direction of safety and freedom is taking refuge in the right way, as a conscious act of determination, understanding and devotion.

The commentarial literature preserves a precious document of ancient Buddhist practice showing the thoughtful and discriminating way in which the devotees of old took refuge in the Triple Gem. The document mentions four different methods of going for refuge, each represented by the utterance of its own specific formula, each entailing a different degree of commitment. Ranked in ascending order, the four begin with homage by prostration, evolve through the acceptance of discipleship and the acceptance of the Triple Gem as the guiding ideal, and culminate in complete self-surrender. The formulas all commence with the words 'From today onwards . . .', which mark the day of the first utterance as initiating a new period in the life of the devotee and stress that the act is a definite and personal dedication as distinguished from an impersonal ritual. The three lower formulas conclude with the words 'Thus may you know me!', a call to witness, giving to those declarations the strong emphasis and solemnity of a vow. Both the beginning and end of these modes of refuge echo the earliest expression of commitment reported in the suttas: 'I go for refuge to the Lord Gotama, the Dhamma and the Order of monks! May the Lord Gotama know of me as a lay follower! From today onwards, as long as life lasts, I have taken refuge!'

From the formulas it is clear that the ancient devotees who coined and used them were highly sensitive to the deep significance of going for refuge. They perceived this apparently simple act as a most momentous step decisive for life, entailing sacred responsibilities. By means of their fourfold distinction demanding a definite personal choice, they safeguard the process of taking refuge from degenerating into a routine habit and enable it to accommodate a growing intensity and earnestness of dedication. The structure of the gradation shows that the ancients were aware that the going for refuge is actually consummated only by complete self-surrender to the Triple Gem, without any reservations. In the lesser modes of the act, there is still something of the presumed self that is kept back; it is a going for refuge with reservations. Nevertheless, these lesser modes are definite steps towards the highest, and should be consciously cultivated. As in any harmonious mental development, here too the higher level does not exclude the lower but absorbs it into its wider compass. In trying to obtain a clearer picture of those four modes, we shall therefore start from the lowest level and work up to the highest.

I. The first mode of going for refuge is *homage by prostration* (*paṇipāta*), expressed by the formula: 'From today onwards I shall give respectful greeting, devoted attendance and salutation only to the Buddha, the Dhamma and the Saṅgha. Thus may you know me!' Homage is the mental attitude, and the bodily and verbal expression, of reverence, resulting from the recognition and appreciation of something higher than oneself. It breaks through the first and hardest shell of pride and self-contented ignorance that knows of nothing better than one's own petty self. When encountering something higher, animals and undeveloped men, whether 'primitive' or 'civilized', usually react by distrust, fear, flight, attack, resentment, hostility or persecution; for they can view that higher form of life only as something different, alien, and therefore suspect. It is the sign of a truly developed human mind that it meets the higher with due respect, with admiration, and the wish to emulate. Recognition and appreciation of something higher is therefore the preliminary condition of spiritual growth, and the true respect resulting from it forms the basis of moral education as well.

For this reason, in man's relation to the highest, the Triple Gem, true homage comes first. As a way of taking refuge, homage is the spontaneous expression of the deep veneration felt when becoming aware of the existence and significance of the supreme refuge. It is the emotional reaction in gratitude, devotion and joy when feeling the full weight of the tremendous fact that there is actually a refuge from this universe of suffering. Thus, in the commentary this mode of taking refuge is illustrated not by the habitual act of worship by confirmed devotees, but by the highly emotional conversion of an aged brahmin who, deeply stirred, prostrates himself before the Exalted One, embracing and kissing his feet.

Homage represents the emotional side of taking refuge, being its aspect as a conscious act of faith. Through its single-heartedness and humility, the act of doing homage by body, speech and mind, prepares the disciple emotionally for complete self-surrender. It is an indispensable step to it, but, being deficient with regard to understanding and determination, it requires supplementation by the following two stages.

II. While homage is still a distant and one-sided relationship to the Supreme, the devotee still being in the outer court of the sanctuary, the next step – *the acceptance of discipleship* (*sissabhāv'ūpagamana*) – ushers him through the door. The disciple declares: 'From today onward I am a disciple of the Buddha, the Dhamma and the Saṅgha. Thus may you know me!', and through that declaration goes for refuge to supreme wisdom, opening himself to its permeating influence.

The respect and humility acquired earlier by true homage has earned for the disciple the right of entry into the sanctuary of wisdom. Only if approached in that reverential attitude will the guru, the spiritual teacher of the East, impart his knowledge, as these qualities are the first indication that the disciple is ready to receive.

If refuge is taken in the sense of discipleship, life becomes a constant act of learning, of adapting the mind to the standards set by the Buddha, the Dhamma and the Saṅgha. It is the character of the wise man that he is always willing and anxious to learn. The process of learning establishes a mutual relationship between teacher, teaching and pupil, such that a gradual and partial identification takes place and the pupil can absorb the teacher's wisdom and make it his own.

The acceptance of discipleship represents the rational side of taking refuge, which is here a conscious act of understanding. It supplies the full and satisfying reasons for the act of homage, and in that way adds to the strength and loyalty of devotion. But man is not always a devotee or learner. There remains much in life that cannot be mastered easily by faith and understanding alone. It requires a strong will and determination, as well as the skill of long experience, to change the course of the manifold habitual activities of life into the direction of the refuge. This task of gradually making the refuge the centre of one's life is performed by the third mode of taking refuge.

III. At the third level, the disciple *accepts the Triple Gem as his guiding ideal* (tapparāyaṇatā), avowing 'From today onward the Buddha is my guiding ideal, and so too the Dhamma and the Saṅgha. Thus may you know me!' In taking this form of refuge, the disciple pledges himself to subordinate, step by step, all the essential activities of his life to the ideals embodied in the Triple Gem. He vows to apply his strength to the task of impressing this sacred threefold seal upon his personal life and upon his environment, too, as far as he can overcome its resistance. The Threefold Refuge in its aspect as the guiding ideal, the determining factor of life, calls for complete dedication in the sphere of external activities.

But this dedication to the service of the Triple Gem is not yet the highest form of taking refuge. There still exists in the disciple's mind a difference between the noble objective and the person working for it. The delusive ego has been retained: it rejoices at the success of the work and grieves when it fails. In a subtle way, instead of the Triple Gem, the work itself becomes the refuge. If identification of self and work is not complete, the ego, as it were, hides in the work and evades the call for full surrender to the true refuge. Progress beyond this step is possible only if the service of the guiding ideal is done in a highly detached way, without looking for any reward.

IV. This detached attitude towards work will be one of the many fruits of the last step: complete *self-surrender* to the Triple Gem (*attasanniyyatanā*). This form of refuge taken by the worldling leaves no room for reservations. Yet also, in a sense, it demands nothing; for if true understanding has told us before that nothing can be gained in saṁsāra, which is the objective aspect of self, then nothing can be lost by the surrender of self, which is the subjective aspect of saṁsāra. However, though this surrender of self is only the surrender of a delusion, it is a very hard sacrifice as all of us know. But if we ever wish to be free of the bonds of saṁsāra, at one time or another this self-surrender must be done, and thus it may as well be done today as tomorrow.

The highest prize is won only by the highest stake, by the sacrifice of that illusive self that has assumed so much power that it requires the highest effort to break it. In taking refuge by way of self-surrender, the disciple will follow in his own modest way the example of the Exalted One who, in the last great struggle before his Enlightenment, addressed his inner opponent, personified as Māra, with the following words: 'It's muñja grass I wear! Shame on life! I would rather die in battle than live on as a vanquished one!' (Sutta Nipāta, v. 440). Muñja grass was the crest of those ancient Indian warriors who entered battle with the vow 'to do or die'. It should be the symbol of the spiritual warrior too. If any reservations, regrets or reluctance are retained, there will be merely a half-hearted attempt instead of that single-minded effort which alone can bring victory.

If the grave step of taking refuge by self-surrender has once been taken, a feeling of lightness, unconcernedness and fearlessness will enter the heart of the disciple. A self that has been renounced cannot and need not have any fear for a life that has been surrendered and that is now kept only on trust for the definite purpose of being used for the highest realization. Therefore, in the early days of the Dhamma, when those of determined mind entered the 'field of spiritual action', taking up a subject of meditation to be cultivated up to Arahatship, they would start their work by taking the vow of self-surrender, as advised in the following passage of the *Visuddhimagga* (Chapter III, sect. 123–127):

Having approached his Noble Friend (i.e. the meditation master) the meditator should first surrender himself to the Buddha, the Exalted One, or to his teacher, and then, possessed of a strong desire and a high resolve, he should ask for the subject of meditation. His surrender of self to the Buddha should be as follows: 'This personal existence of mine, I offer to thee, O Exalted One!' For one who, without such a surrender of self, lives in lonely places will be unable to stand firm against fearful objects that approach him. He may return to the village, and, associated with lay folk, might take up a search that is wrongful and come to distress. But to one who has surrendered his self, no fear arises even when approached by fearful objects. Only gladness will arise in him when he reflects: 'Hast thou not, O wise man, on that earlier day surrendered thyself to the Buddha?'

And again, in surrendering himself to his teacher, he should say, 'This personal existence of mine, Reverend Sir, I offer to thee!' For without such a surrender of self, he will be unruly, stubborn, unwilling to accept advice; he will go about at his own will without asking the teacher's leave. And the teacher will favour him with neither material nor with spiritual help and will not instruct him in difficult books. Not receiving this twofold favour, he will become unvirtuous, or return to lay life.

This way of taking refuge by self-surrender is, of course, still far from the complete abolition of egotism and self-delusion, but it is a powerful means to that end. It may mark the transition from the worldly or mundane refuge to which it still belongs, to the supramundane refuge at which it aims.

The refuge by self-surrender is given in the commentarial text by the following formula:

'From today onward I surrender myself to the Buddha, the Dhamma and the Saṅgha. To the Exalted One I am giving my self, to the Dhamma I am giving my self, to the Saṅgha I am giving my self. I am giving them my life. Until my life ends, I take refuge in the Buddha. The Buddha is my refuge, my shelter, my protection, and so too the Dhamma and the Saṅgha.'

Even in its external form, this mode of refuge differs from the preceding three in that it lacks the concluding call to witness,

'Thus may you know me!' From this we may conclude that this gravest of all vows was to be taken in the secrecy of one's heart, as befits the sacredness of the resolve. Here the presence of a witness as a kind of moral support for keeping the vow should no more be required; such a requirement would only prove that it is premature to take this step. Any public avowal would only detract from the supreme dignity of the vow, and would render its observance more difficult by making the disciple too self-conscious or even proud. Needless to say, a deliberate parading of the vow would defeat its very purpose, by re-instating the self that was to be surrendered.

The longer formula of self-surrender enlarging upon the short sentence in the *Visuddhimagga* has been rendered here into a Western language for the first time. Its Pāli original also seems to have evoked little attention in our day. If we reproduce that formula here, we do so in the hope that it will be received with the reverence due to that precious document of ancient devotion, hallowed by the efforts and achievements of those who may have practised in accordance with it. We add the earnest request that it not be made use of lightly for the purpose of ordinary devotion, and that the vow not be taken rashly on the spur of a moment's enthusiasm. This solemn pledge should be taken only after having tested one's strength and perseverance for a long time by minor observances and renunciations. We should beware of making those highest things of the spirit cheap and common by approaching them in too facile a way, by talking too glibly about them, or by taking them into our hands and dropping them again when interest fades or our feeble fingers get tired. Therefore, if we are not sure of our strength, we should not take upon ourselves the severe demands of self-surrender, but take our refuge by way of those lesser modes. For these will likewise prove to be powerful helpers to high spiritual achievements.

In making an intelligent use of that fourfold devotional road of the ancients, we shall preserve the most popular religious practice in the Buddhist world, the going for refuge, from becoming stale and ineffective. We shall be able to turn it into a strong, life-giving current of devotion that will carry us one day to the Isle of Final Peace, to Nibbāna, where refugee and refuge are merged into one.

Notes

1. See *Aṭṭha-ariya puggalā*: 'the eight noble beings' in Glossary.

The Four Sublime
States

Introduction

Four sublime states of mind have been taught by the Buddha:

Love or *Loving-kindness* (*mettā*)
Compassion (*karuṇā*)
Sympathetic Joy (*muditā*)
Equanimity (*upekkhā*)

In Pāli, the language of the Buddhist scriptures, these four are known under the name of *Brahma-vihāra*. This term may be rendered by: excellent, lofty or sublime states of mind; or alternatively, by: Brahma-like, god-like or divine abodes.

These four attitudes are said to be *excellent* or *sublime* because they are the right or ideal way of conduct towards living beings (*sattesu sammā paṭipatti*). They provide, in fact, the answer to all situations arising from social contact. They are the great removers of tension, the great peace-makers in social conflict, and the great healers of wounds suffered in the struggle of existence. They level social barriers, build harmonious communities, awaken slumbering magnanimity long forgotten, revive joy and hope long abandoned, and promote human brotherhood against the forces of egotism.

The Brahma-vihāras are incompatible with a hating state of mind, and in that they are akin to Brahmā, the divine but transient ruler of the higher heavens in the traditional Buddhist picture of the universe. In contrast to many other conceptions of deities, East and West, who by their own devotees are said to show anger, wrath, jealousy and 'righteous indignation', Brahmā is free from hate; and one who assiduously develops these four sublime states, by conduct and meditation, is said to become an equal of Brahmā (*brahma-samo*). If they become the dominant influence in his mind, he will be reborn in congenial worlds, the realms of Brahmā. Therefore, these states of mind are called *God-like, Brahma-like*.

They are called *abodes* (*vihāra*) because they should become the mind's constant dwelling-places where we feel 'at home'; they should not remain merely places of rare and short visits, soon forgotten. In other words, our minds should become thoroughly saturated by them. They should become our inseparable companions, and we should be mindful of them in all our common activities. As the Mettā Sutta, the Song of Loving-kindness, says:

When standing, walking, sitting, lying down,
Whenever he feels free of tiredness,
Let him establish well this mindfulness –
This, it is said, is the Divine Abode.

These four – love, compassion, sympathetic joy and equanimity – are also known as the *boundless states* (*appamaññā*), because, in their perfection and their true nature, they should not be narrowed by any limitation as to the range of beings towards whom they are extended. They should be non-exclusive and impartial, not bound by selective preferences or prejudices. A mind that has attained to that boundlessness of the Brahma-vihāras will not harbour any national, racial, religious or class hatred.

But unless rooted in a strong natural affinity with such a mental attitude, it will certainly not be easy for us to effect that boundless application by a deliberate effort of will and to avoid consistently any kind or degree of partiality. To achieve that, in most cases, we shall have to use these four qualities not only as principles of conduct and objects of reflection, but also as subjects of methodical meditation. That meditation is called *Brahma-vihāra-bhāvanā*, the meditative development of the sublime states. The practical aim is to achieve, with the help of these sublime states, those high stages of mental concentration called *jhāna*, 'meditative absorption'. The meditations on love, compassion and sympathetic joy may each produce the attainment of the first three absorptions, while the meditation on equanimity will lead to the fourth jhāna only, in which equanimity is the most significant factor.

Generally speaking, persistent meditative practice will have two crowning effects: first, it will make these four qualities sink deep into the heart so that they become spontaneous attitudes not easily overthrown; second, it will bring out and secure their *boundless* extension, the unfolding of their all-embracing range.

In fact, the detailed instructions given in the Buddhist scriptures for the practice of these four meditations are clearly intended to unfold gradually the boundlessness of the sublime states. They systematically break down all barriers restricting their application to particular individuals or places.

In the meditative exercises, the selection of people to whom the thought of love, compassion or sympathetic joy is directed, proceeds from the easier to the more difficult. For instance, when meditating on loving-kindness, one starts with an aspiration for one's own well-being, using it as a point of reference for gradual extension: 'Just as I wish to be happy and free from suffering, so may *that* being, may *all* beings be happy and free from suffering!' Then one extends the thought of loving-kindness to a person for whom one has a loving respect, as, for instance, a teacher; then to dearly beloved people, to indifferent ones, and finally to enemies, if any, or those disliked. Since this meditation is concerned with the welfare of the living, one should not choose people who have died; one should also avoid choosing people towards whom one may have feelings of sexual attraction. After one has been able to cope with the hardest task, to direct one's thoughts of loving-kindness to disagreeable people, one should now 'break down the barriers' (*sīmā-sambheda*). Without making any discrimination between those four types of people, one should extend one's loving-kindness to them equally. At that point of the practice one will have come to the higher stages of concentration: with the appearance of the mental reflex-image (*paṭibhāganimitta*), 'access concentration' (*upacāra samādhi*) will have been reached, and further progress will lead to the full concentration (*appanā*) of the first jhāna, then the higher jhānas.

For spatial expansion, the practice starts with those in one's immediate environment such as one's family, then extends to the neighbouring houses, to the whole street, the town, country, other countries and the entire world. In 'pervasion of the directions', one's thought of loving-kindness is directed first to the east, then to the west, north, south, the intermediate directions, the zenith and nadir.

The same principles of practice apply to the meditative development of compassion, sympathetic joy and equanimity, with due variations in the selection of people. Details of the practice will be found in the texts (see *Visuddhimagga*, Chapter IX).

The ultimate aim of attaining these Brahmavihāra-jhānas is to produce a state of mind that can serve as a firm basis for the liberating insight into the true nature of all phenomena, as being impermanent, liable to suffering and unsubstantial. A mind that has achieved meditative absorption induced by the sublime states will be pure, tranquil, firm, collected and free of coarse selfishness. It will thus be well prepared for the final work of deliverance which can be completed only by insight.

The preceding remarks show that there are two ways of developing the sublime states: first by practical conduct and an appropriate direction of thought; and second by methodical meditation aiming at the absorptions. Each will prove helpful to the other. Methodical meditative practice will help love, compassion, joy and equanimity to become spontaneous. It will help make the mind firmer and calmer in withstanding the numerous irritations in life that challenge us to maintain these four qualities in thoughts, words and deeds.

On the other hand, if one's practical conduct is increasingly governed by these sublime states, the mind will harbour less resentment, tension and irritability, the reverberations of which often subtly intrude into the hours of meditation, forming there the 'hindrance of restlessness'. Our everyday life and thought has a strong influence on the meditative mind; only if the gap between them is persistently narrowed will there be a chance for steady meditative progress and for achieving the highest aim of our practice.

Meditative development of the sublime states will be aided by repeated reflection upon their qualities, the benefits they bestow and the dangers from their opposites. As the Buddha says, 'What a person considers and reflects upon for a long time, to that his mind will bend and incline.'

The Basic Passage on the Four Sublime States
from the Discourses of the Buddha

I

Here, monks, a disciple dwells pervading one direction with his heart filled with loving-kindness, likewise the second, the third, and the fourth direction; so above, below and around; he dwells pervading the entire world everywhere and equally with his heart filled with loving-kindness, abundant, grown great, measureless, free from enmity and free from distress.

II

Here, monks, a disciple dwells pervading one direction with his heart filled with compassion, likewise the second, the third and the fourth direction; so above, below and around; he dwells pervading the entire world everywhere and equally with his heart filled with compassion, abundant, grown great, measureless, free from enmity and free from distress.

III

Here, monks, a disciple dwells pervading one direction with his heart filled with sympathetic joy, likewise the second, the third and the fourth direction; so above, below and around; he dwells pervading the entire world everywhere and equally with his heart filled with sympathetic joy, abundant, grown great, measureless, free from enmity and free from distress.

IV

Here, monks, a disciple dwells pervading one direction with his heart filled with equanimity, likewise the second, the third and the fourth direction; so above, below and around; he dwells pervading the entire world everywhere and equally with his heart filled with equanimity, abundant, grown great, measureless, free from enmity and free from distress.

Dīgha Nikāya 13

Contemplations on The Four Sublime States

I

LOVE (Mettā)

Love, without desire to possess, knowing well that in the

ultimate sense there is no possession and no possessor: this is the highest *love*.

Love, without speaking and thinking of 'I', knowing well that this so-called 'I' is a mere delusion.

Love, without selecting and excluding, knowing well that to do so means to create love's own contrasts: dislike, aversion and hatred.

Love, embracing all beings: small and great, far and near, be it on earth, in the water or in the air.

Love, embracing impartially all sentient beings, and not only those who are useful, pleasing or amusing to us.

Love, embracing all beings, be they noble-minded or low-minded, good or evil. The noble and the good are embraced because *love* is flowing to them spontaneously. The low-minded and evil-minded are included because they are those who are most in need of *love*. In many of them the seed of goodness may have died merely because warmth was lacking for its growth, because it perished from cold in a loveless world.

Love, embracing all beings, knowing well that we all are fellow wayfarers through this round of existence – that we all are overcome by the same law of suffering.

Love, but not the sensuous fire that burns, scorches and tortures, that inflicts more wounds than it cures – flaring up now, at the next moment being extinguished, leaving behind more coldness and loneliness than was felt before.

Rather, *love* that lies like a soft but firm hand on the ailing beings, ever unchanged in its sympathy, without wavering, unconcerned with any response it meets. *Love* that is comforting coolness to those who burn with the fire of suffering and passion; that is life-giving warmth to those abandoned in the cold desert of loneliness, to those who are shivering in the frost of a loveless world; to those whose hearts have become as if empty and dry by the repeated calls for help, by deepest despair.

Love, that is a sublime nobility of heart and intellect which knows, understands and is ready to help.

Love, that *is* strength and *gives* strength: this is the highest *love*.

Love, which by the Enlightened One was named 'the liberation of the heart', 'the most sublime beauty': this is the highest *love*.

And what is the highest manifestation of *love*?

To show to the world the path leading to the end of suffering, the path pointed out, trodden, and realized to perfection by Him, the Exalted One, the Buddha.

II

COMPASSION (Karuṇā)

The world suffers. But most men have their eyes and ears closed. They do not see the unbroken stream of tears flowing through life; they do not hear the cry of distress continually pervading the world. Their own little grief or joy bars their sight, deafens their ears. Bound by selfishness, their hearts turn stiff and narrow. Being stiff and narrow, how should they be able to strive for any higher goal, to realize that only release from selfish craving will effect their own freedom from suffering?

It is *compassion* that removes the heavy bar, opens the door to freedom, makes the narrow heart as wide as the world. *Compassion* takes away from the heart the inert weight, the paralysing heaviness; it gives wings to those who cling to the lowlands of self.

Through *compassion* the fact of suffering remains vividly present to our mind, even at times when we personally are free from it. It gives us the rich experience of suffering, thus strengthening us to meet it prepared, when it does befall us.

Compassion reconciles us to our own destiny by showing us the life of others, often much harder than ours.

Behold the endless caravan of beings, men and beasts, burdened with sorrow and pain! The burden of every one of them, we also have carried in bygone times during the unfathomable sequence of repeated births. Behold this, and open your heart to *compassion*!

And this misery may well be our own destiny again! He who is without *compassion* now, will one day cry for it. If sympathy with others is lacking, it will have to be acquired through one's own long and painful experience. This is the great law of life. Knowing this, keep guard over yourself!

Beings, sunk in ignorance, lost in delusion, hasten from one state of suffering to another, not knowing the real cause, not knowing the escape from it. This insight into the general law of suffering is the real foundation of our *compassion*, not any isolated fact of suffering.

Hence our *compassion* will also include those who at the moment may be happy, but act with an evil and deluded mind. In their present deeds we shall foresee their future state of distress, and *compassion* will arise.

The *compassion* of the wise man does not render him a victim of suffering. His thoughts, words and deeds are full of pity. But his heart does not waver; unchanged it remains, serene and calm. How else should he be able to help?

May such *compassion* arise in our hearts! *Compassion* that is sublime nobility of heart and intellect which knows, understands and is ready to help.

Compassion that *is* strength and *gives* strength: this is highest *compassion*.

And what is the highest manifestation of *compassion*?

To show to the world the path leading to the end of suffering, the path pointed out, trodden and realized to perfection by Him, the Exalted One, the Buddha.

III

SYMPATHETIC JOY (Muditā)

Not only to compassion, but also to *joy with others* open your heart!

Small, indeed, is the share of happiness and joy allotted to beings! Whenever a little happiness comes to them, then you may rejoice that at least one ray of joy has pierced through the darkness of their lives, and dispelled the grey and gloomy mist that enwraps their hearts.

Your life will gain in joy by sharing the happiness of others as if it were yours. Did you never observe how in moments of happiness men's features change and become bright with joy? Did you never notice how joy rouses men to noble aspirations and deeds, exceeding their normal capacity? Did not such experience fill your own heart with joyful bliss? It is in your power to increase such experience of *sympathetic joy*, by producing happiness in others, by bringing them joy and solace.

Let us teach real joy to men! Many have unlearned it. Life, though full of woe, holds also sources of happiness and joy, unknown to most. Let us teach people to seek and to find real joy within themselves and to rejoice with the joy of others! Let us teach them to unfold their joy to ever sublimer heights!

Noble and sublime joy is not foreign to the Teaching of the Enlightened One. Wrongly the Buddha's Teaching is sometimes considered to be a doctrine diffusing melancholy. Far from it: the Dhamma leads step by step to an ever purer and loftier happiness.

Noble and sublime joy is a helper on the path to the extinction of suffering. Not he who is depressed by grief, but one possessed of joy finds that serene calmness leading to a contemplative state of mind. And only a mind serene and collected is able to gain the liberating wisdom.

The more sublime and noble the joy of others is, the more justified will be our own *sympathetic joy*. A cause for our *joy with others* is their noble life securing them happiness here and in lives hereafter. A still nobler cause for our *joy with others* is their faith in the Dhamma, their understanding of the Dhamma, their following the Dhamma. Let us give them the *help* of the Dhamma! Let us strive to become more and more able ourselves to render such help!

Sympathetic joy means a sublime nobility of heart and intellect which knows, understands and is ready to help.

Sympathetic joy that *is* strength and *gives* strength: this is the highest joy.

And what is the highest manifestation of *sympathetic joy*?

To show to the world the path leading to the end of suffering, the path pointed out, trodden, and realized to perfection by Him, the Exalted One, the Buddha.

IV

EQUANIMITY (Upekkhā)

Equanimity is a perfect, unshakable balance of mind, rooted in insight.

Looking at the world around us, and looking into our own heart, we see clearly how difficult it is to attain and maintain balance of mind.

Looking into life we notice how it continually moves between contrasts: rise and fall, success and failure, loss and gain, honour and blame. We feel how our heart responds to all this with happiness and sorrow, delight and despair, disappointment and satisfaction, hope and fear. These waves of emotion carry us up and fling us down; and no sooner do we find rest, than we are in the power of a new wave again. How can we expect to get a footing on the crest of the waves? How shall we erect the building of our lives in the midst of this ever restless ocean of existence, if not on the Island of Equanimity.

A world where that little share of happiness allotted to beings is mostly secured after many disappointments, failures and defeats;

a world where only the courage to start anew, again and again, promises success;

a world where scanty joy grows amidst sickness, separation and death;

a world where beings who were a short while ago connected with us by *sympathetic joy*, are at the next moment in want of our *compassion* – such a world needs *equanimity*.

But the kind of equanimity required has to be based on vigilant presence of mind, not on indifferent dullness. It has to be the result of hard, deliberate training, not the casual outcome of a passing mood. But equanimity would not deserve its name if it had to be produced by exertion again and again. In such a case it would surely be weakened and finally defeated by the vicissitudes of life. True equanimity, however, should be able to meet all these severe tests and to regenerate its strength from sources within. It will possess this power of resistance and self-renewal only if it is rooted in insight.

What, now, is the nature of that insight? It is the clear understanding of how all these vicissitudes of life originate, and of our own true nature. We have to understand that the various experiences we undergo result from our kamma – our actions in thought, word and deed – performed in this life and in earlier lives. Kamma is the womb from which we spring (*kamma-yoni*), and whether we like it or not, we are the inalienable 'owners' of our deeds (*kamma-ssakā*). But as soon as we have performed any action, our control over it is lost: it forever remains with us and inevitably returns to us as our due heritage (*kamma-dāyādā*). Nothing that happens to us comes from an 'outer' hostile world foreign to ourselves; everything is the outcome of our own mind and deeds. Because this knowledge frees us from fear, it is the first basis of equanimity. When, in everything that befalls us we only meet ourselves, why should we fear?

If, however, fear or uncertainty should arise, we know the refuge where it can be allayed: our good deeds (*kamma-paṭisaraṇā*). By taking this refuge, confidence and courage will grow within us – confidence in the protecting power of our good deeds done in the past; courage to perform more good deeds right now, despite the discouraging hardships of our present life. For we know that noble and selfless deeds provide the best defence against the hard blows of destiny, that it is never too late but always the right time for good actions. If that refuge, in doing good and avoiding evil, becomes firmly established within us, one day we shall feel assured: 'More and more ceases the misery and evil rooted in the past. And this present life – I try to make it spotless and pure. What else can the future bring than increase of the good?' And from that certainty our minds will become serene, and we shall gain the strength of patience and equanimity to bear with all our present adversities. Then our deeds will be our friends (*kamma-bandhu*).

Likewise, all the various events of our lives, being the result of our deeds, will also be our friends, even if they bring us sorrow and pain. Our deeds return to us in a guise that often makes them unrecognizable. Sometimes our actions return to us in the way that others treat us, sometimes as a thorough upheaval in our lives; often the results are against our expectations or contrary to our wills. Such experiences point out to us consequences of our deeds we did not foresee; they render visible half-conscious motives of our former actions which we tried to hide even from ourselves, covering them up with various pretexts. If we learn to see things from this angle, and to read the messages conveyed by our own experience, then suffering, too, will be our friend. It will be a stern friend, but a truthful and well-meaning one who teaches us the most difficult subject, knowledge about ourselves, and warns us against abysses towards which we are moving blindly. By looking at suffering as our teacher and friend, we shall better succeed in enduring it with equanimity. Consequently, the teaching of kamma will give us a powerful impulse for freeing ourselves from kamma, from those deeds which again and again throw us into the suffering of repeated births. Disgust will arise at our own craving, at our own delusion, at our own propensity to create situations which try our strength, our resistance and our equanimity.

The second insight on which equanimity should be based is the Buddha's teaching of no-self (*anattā*). This doctrine shows that in the ultimate sense deeds are not performed by any self, nor do their results affect any self. Further, it shows that if there is no self, we cannot speak of 'my own'. It is the delusion of a self that creates suffering and hinders or disturbs equanimity. If this or that quality of ours is blamed, one thinks: '*I* am blamed' and equanimity is shaken. If this or that work does not succeed, one thinks: '*My* work has failed' and equanimity is shaken. If wealth or loved ones are lost, one thinks: 'What is *mine* has gone' and equanimity is shaken.

To establish equanimity as an unshakable state of mind, one has to give up all possessive *thoughts of 'mine'*, beginning with little things from which it is easy to detach oneself, and gradually working up to possessions and aims to which one's whole heart clings. One also has to give up the counterpart to such thoughts, all egoistic *thoughts of 'self'*, beginning with a small section of one's personality, with qualities of minor importance, with small weaknesses one clearly sees, and gradually working up to those emotions and aversions which one regards as the centre of one's being. Thus detachment should be practised.

To the degree we forsake thoughts of 'mine' or 'self' equanimity will enter our hearts. For how can anything we realize to be foreign and void of a self cause us agitation due to lust, hatred or grief? Thus the teaching of no-self will be our guide on the path to deliverance, to perfect *equanimity*.

Equanimity is the crown and culmination of the four sublime states. But this should not be understood to mean that equanimity is the negation of love, compassion and sympathetic joy, or that it leaves them behind as inferior. Far from that, equanimity includes and pervades them fully, just as they fully pervade perfect equanimity.

How, then, do these four sublime states pervade and suffuse each other?

Unbounded *love* guards *compassion* against turning into partiality, prevents it from making discriminations by selecting and excluding and thus protects it from falling into partiality or aversion against the excluded side.

Love imparts to *equanimity* its selflessness, its boundless nature and even its fervour. For fervour, too, transformed and controlled, is part of perfect *equanimity*, strengthening its power of keen penetration and wise restraint.

Compassion prevents *love* and *sympathetic joy* from forgetting that, while both are enjoying or giving temporary and limited happiness, there still exist at that time most dreadful states of suffering in the world. It reminds them that their happiness coexists with measureless misery, perhaps at the next doorstep. It is a reminder to *love* and *sympathetic joy* that there is more suffering in the world than they are able to mitigate; that, after the effect of such mitigation has vanished, sorrow and pain are sure to arise anew until suffering is uprooted entirely at the attainment of Nibbāna. *Compassion* does not allow that *love* and *sympathetic joy* shut themselves up against the wide world by confining themselves to a narrow sector of it. *Compassion* prevents *love* and *sympathetic joy* from turning into states of self-satisfied complacency within a jealously-guarded petty happiness. *Compassion* stirs and urges *love* to widen its sphere; it stirs and urges *sympathetic joy* to search for fresh nourishment. Thus it helps both of them to grow into truly boundless states (*appamaññā*).

Compassion guards *equanimity* from falling into a cold indifference, and keeps it from indolent or selfish isolation. Until *equanimity* has reached perfection, *compassion* urges it to enter again and again the battlefield of the world, in order to be able to stand the test, by hardening and strengthening itself.

Sympathetic joy holds *compassion* back from becoming overwhelmed by the sight of the world's suffering, from being absorbed by it to the exclusion of everything else. *Sympathetic joy* relieves the tension of mind, soothes the painful burning of the compassionate heart. It keeps *compassion* away from melancholic brooding without purpose, from a futile sentimentality that merely weakens and consumes the strength of mind and heart. *Sympathetic joy* develops compassion into active sympathy.

Sympathetic joy gives to *equanimity* the mild serenity that softens its stern appearance. It is the divine smile on the face of the Enlightened One, a smile that persists in spite of his deep knowledge of the world's suffering, a smile that gives solace and hope, fearlessness and confidence: 'Wide open are the doors to Deliverance', thus it speaks.

Equanimity rooted in insight is the guiding and restraining power for the other three sublime states. It points out to them the direction they have to take, and sees to it that this direction is followed. *Equanimity* guards *love* and *compassion* from being dissipated in vain quests and from going astray in the labyrinths of uncontrolled emotion. *Equanimity*, being a vigilant self-control for the sake of the final goal, does not allow *sympathetic joy* to rest content with humble results, forgetting the real aims we have to strive for.

Equanimity, which means 'even-mindedness', gives to *love* an even, unchanging firmness and loyalty. It endows it with the great virtue of patience. *Equanimity* furnishes *compassion* with an even, unwavering courage and fearlessness, enabling it to face the awesome abyss of misery and despair which confront boundless *compassion* again and again. To the active side of *compassion*, *equanimity* is the calm and firm hand led by wisdom – indispensable to those who want to practise the difficult art of helping others. And here again *equanimity* means patience, the patient devotion to the work of *compassion*.

In these and other ways equanimity may be said to be the crown and culmination of the other three sublime states. The first three, if unconnected with equanimity and insight, may dwindle away due to the lack of a stabilizing factor. Isolated virtues, if unsupported by other qualities which give them either the needed firmness or pliancy, often deteriorate into their own characteristic defects. For instance, loving-kindness, without energy and insight, may easily decline to a mere sentimental goodness of weak and unreliable nature. Moreover, such isolated virtues may often carry us in a direction contrary to our original aims and contrary to the welfare of others, too. It is the firm and balanced character of a person that knits isolated virtues into an organic and harmonious whole, within which the single qualities exhibit their best manifestations and avoid the pitfalls of their respective weaknesses. And this is the very function of equanimity, the way it contributes to an ideal relationship between all four sublime states.

Equanimity is a perfect, unshakable balance of mind, rooted in insight. But in its perfection and unshakable nature equanimity is not dull, heartless and frigid. Its perfection is not due to an emotional 'emptiness', but to a 'fullness' of understanding, to its being complete in itself. Its unshakable nature is not the immovability of a dead, cold stone, but the manifestation of the highest strength.

In what way, now, is *equanimity* perfect and unshakable?

Whatever causes stagnation is here destroyed, what dams up is removed, what obstructs is destroyed. Vanished are the whirls of emotion and the meanderings of intellect. Unhindered goes the calm and majestic stream of consciousness, pure and radiant. Watchful mindfulness (*sati*) has harmonized the warmth of faith (*saddhā*) with the penetrative keenness of wisdom (*paññā*); it has balanced strength of will (*viriya*) with calmness of mind (*samādhi*); and these five inner faculties (*indriya*) have grown into inner forces (*bala*) that cannot be lost again. They cannot be lost because they do not lose themselves any more in the labyrinths of the world (*samsāra*), in the endless diffuseness of life (*papañca*). These inner forces emanate from the mind and act upon the world, but being guarded by mindfulness, they nowhere bind themselves, and they return unchanged. Love, compassion and sympathetic joy continue to emanate from the mind and act upon the world, but being guarded by *equanimity*, they cling nowhere, and return unweakened and unsullied.

Thus within the Arahat, the Liberated One, nothing is lessened by giving, and he does not become poorer by bestowing upon others the riches of his heart and mind. The Arahat is like the clear, well-cut crystal which, being without stains, fully absorbs all the rays of light and sends them out again, intensified by its concentrative power. The rays cannot stain the crystal with their various colours. They cannot pierce its hardness, nor disturb its harmonious structure. In its genuine purity and strength, the crystal remains unchanged. 'Just as all the streams of the world enter the great ocean, and all the waters of the sky rain into it, but no increase or decrease of the great ocean is to be seen' – even so is the nature of *holy equanimity*.

Holy equanimity, or – as we may likewise express it – the Arahat endowed with holy equanimity, is the inner centre of the world. But this inner centre should be well distinguished from the numberless apparent centres of limited spheres; that is, their so-called 'personalities', governing laws, and so on. All of these are only apparent centres, because they cease to be centres whenever their spheres, obeying the laws of impermanence, undergo a total change of their structure; and consequently the centre of their gravity, material or mental, will shift. But the inner centre of the Arahat's equanimity is unshakable, because it is immutable. It is immutable because it clings to nothing.

Says the Master:

For one who clings, motion exists; but for one who clings not, there is no motion. Where no motion is, there is stillness. Where stillness is, there is no craving. Where no craving is, there is neither coming nor going. Where no coming nor going is, there is neither arising nor passing away. Where neither arising nor passing away is, there is neither this world nor a world beyond, nor a state between. This, verily, is the end of suffering.

Udāna 74

Anattā and Nibbāna

Introduction

> This world, Kaccāna, usually leans upon a duality: upon (the belief in) existence or non-existence. . . . Avoiding these two extremes, the Perfect One shows the doctrine in the middle: Dependent on ignorance are the kamma-formations. . . . By the cessation of ignorance, kamma-formations cease. . . .
>
> Saṁyutta Nikāya, 12: 15

The above saying of the Buddha speaks of the duality of existence (*atthitā*) and non-existence (*natthitā*). These two terms refer to the theories of eternalism (*sassata-diṭṭhi*) and annihilationism (*uccheda-diṭṭhi*), the basic misconceptions of actuality that in various forms repeatedly reappear in the history of human thought.

Eternalism is the belief in a permanent substance or entity, whether conceived as a multitude of individual souls or selves, created or not, as a monistic world-soul, a deity of any description or a combination of any of these notions. *Annihilationism*, on the other hand, asserts the temporary existence of separate selves or personalities, which are entirely destroyed or dissolved after death. Accordingly, the two key words of the text quoted above refer (1) to the absolute, i.e. eternal, existence of any assumed substance or entity, and (2) to the ultimate, absolute annihilation of separate entities conceived as impermanent, i.e. their non-existence after the end of their lifespan. These two extreme views stand and fall with the assumption of something static of either permanent or impermanent nature. They will lose their basis entirely if life is seen in its true nature, as a continuous flux of material and mental processes arising from their appropriate conditions – a process which will cease only when these conditions are removed. This will explain why our text introduces here the formula of dependent origination (*paṭicca-samuppāda*), and its reversal, dependent cessation.

Dependent *origination*, being an unbroken process, excludes the assumption of an absolute non-existence, or naught, terminating individual existence; the qualifying *dependent* indicates that there is also no absolute, independent existence, no static being *per se*, but only an evanescent arising of phenomena dependent on likewise evanescent conditions.

Dependent *cessation* excludes the belief in absolute and permanent existence. It shows, as well, that there is no automatic lapse into non-existence, for the cessation of relative existence too is a conditioned occurrence.

Thus these teachings of dependent origination and dependent cessation are a true doctrine in the middle, transcending the extremes of existence and non-existence.

Thinking by way of such conceptual contrasts as existence and non-existence has, however, a powerful hold on man. The hold is so powerful because this way of thinking is perpetually nourished by several strong roots deeply embedded in the human mind. The strongest of them is the practical and theoretical assumption of an ego or self. It is the powerful wish for a preservation and perpetuation of the personality, or a refined version of it, that lies behind all the numerous varieties of eternalistic belief. But even with people who have discarded eternalistic creeds or theories, the instinctive belief in the uniqueness and importance of their particular personalities is still so strong that they take death, the end of the personality, to mean complete annihilation or non-existence. Thus the belief in a self is responsible not only for eternalism, but also for the annihilationist view, either in its popular unphilosophical form which regards death as the utter end or in materialistic theories elaborating the same position.

There are other contributory roots of these notions of existence and non-existence closely connected with the main root of ego-belief. There is, for instance, a *linguistic* root, consisting in the basic structure of language (subject and predicate, noun and adjective) and its tendency to simplify affirmative and negative statements for the sake of easy communication and orientation. The structural features of language and linguistic habits of simplified statements have exercised a subtle but strong influence on our way of thinking, making us inclined to assume that 'there must be a thing if there is a word for it'.

These one-sided views may also spring from *emotional*

reasons, expressive of basic attitudes to life. They may reflect the moods of optimism and pessimism, hope and despair, the wish to feel secure through metaphysical support, or the desire to live without inhibitions in a materialistically conceived universe. The theoretical views of eternalism or annihilationism held by an individual may well change during his lifetime, together with the corresponding moods or emotional needs. There is also an *intellectual* root: the speculative and theorizing propensity of the mind. Certain thinkers, people of the theorizing type (*diṭṭhicarita*) in Buddhist psychology, are prone to create various elaborate philosophical systems in which, with great ingenuity, they play off against each other the pairs of conceptual opposites. The great satisfaction this gives to those engaged in such thought-constructions further reinforces the adherence to them.

From these brief remarks, one will be able to appreciate the strength and variety of the forces which induce man to think, feel and speak in the way of these opposites: absolute existence or absolute non-existence. Thus the Buddha had good reason for saying in our introductory passage, that men *usually* lean upon a duality. We need not be surprised that even Nibbāna, the Buddhist goal of deliverance, has been wrongly interpreted in the sense of these extremes. But rigid concepts of existence and non-existence cannot do justice to the dynamic nature of actuality. Still less do they apply to Nibbāna, which the Buddha declared to be supramundane (*lokuttara*) and beyond conceptual thinking (*atakkāvacara*).

In the early days, when knowledge of Buddhist teachings had just reached the West, most writers and scholars (with a few exceptions like Schopenhauer and Max Mueller) took Nibbāna to be pure and simple *non-existence*. Consequently, Western writers too readily described Buddhism as a nihilistic doctrine teaching annihilation as its highest goal, a view these writers condemned as philosophically absurd and ethically reprehensible. Similar statements still sometimes appear in prejudiced non-Buddhist literature. The pendular reaction to that view was the conception of Nibbāna as *existence*. It was now interpreted in the light of already familiar religious and philosophical notions as pure being, pure consciousness, pure self or some other metaphysical concept.

But even Buddhist thought could not always keep clear of a lopsided interpretation of Nibbāna. This happened even in early times: the sect of the Sautrāntikas had a rather negativistic view of Nibbāna, while the Mahāyānistic conceptions of Buddha-fields (*Buddhaksetra*), Primordial (*Ādi-*) Buddha, Tathāgata-garbha, etc., favoured a positive-metaphysical interpretation. It is, therefore, not surprising that modern Buddhist writers also sometimes advocate these extremes. In Buddhist countries of the East, however, there is now not a single Buddhist school or sect known to the writer that favours a nihilistic interpret-ation of Nibbāna. Contrary to erroneous opinions, voiced mainly by uninformed or prejudiced Western authors, The-ravāda Buddhism is definitely averse to the view that Nibbāna is mere extinction. This statement will be substantiated in the first main section of this essay.

For reasons mentioned earlier, it is not always easy to steer clear of those two opposite views of existence and non-existence, and to keep closely to the middle path shown by the Buddha, the teaching of dependent origination and dependent cessation. Until that way of thinking in terms of conditionality has been fully absorbed into the mind, constant watchfulness will be required to avoid slipping unaware into either eternalism or annihilationism, or coming too close to them. When discussing these questions, there is the danger one will be carried away by one's own arguments and counter one extreme by endorsing its opposite. Therefore, in the treatment of that problem, great caution and self-criticism is required lest one lose sight of the middle path.

The primary purpose of this treatise is to offer material for clearly demarcating the Buddha's doctrine of Nibbāna from both misinterpretations. Its intention is not to encourage speculations on the nature of Nibbāna, which are bound to be futile and may even be detrimental to the endeavour to attain it. The canonical texts elucidating the Four Noble Truths say that Nibbāna, the third truth, is to be realized (*sacchikātabbaṁ*); it is not to be understood (as the first truth), nor to be developed (as the fourth truth). We must also emphasize that the material presented here should not be used in a one-sided manner as an argument in favour of either extreme against the other. Each of the two main sections of this treatise requires the other for its qualification and completion. It is hoped that the material from canonical and commentarial sources collected in these pages, by clarifying the position of Theravāda, will at least reduce the points of conflict between the opposing interpretations.

I   *The Nihilistic-negative Extreme*

SECTION I

We shall first consider the basic work of post-canonical
Theravāda literature, *The Path of Purification* (*Visuddhimagga*),
compiled in the 5th century AC by the great commentator,
Bhadantācariya Buddhaghosa. This monumental work furnishes a comprehensive and systematic exposition of the
principal Buddhist doctrines. It is derived from the Pāli Canon
and ancient commentarial literature which partly incorporates
material that may well go back to the earliest times of the
teaching.

In this work, in Chapter XVI on the Faculties and Truths, in
the section dealing with the third noble truth, we find a lengthy
disquisition on Nibbāna. It is striking that the polemic part of it
is exclusively directed against what we have called the
'nihilistic-negative extreme' in the interpretation of Nibbāna.
We cannot be sure about the reason for that limitation, since no
explicit statement is given. It is, however, possible that the
Venerable Buddhaghosa (or perhaps the traditional material he
used) was keen that the Theravāda teachings on that subject
should be well distinguished from those of a prominent
contemporary sect, the Sautrāntikas, which in other respects
was close to the general standpoint of Theravāda. The
Sautrāntikas belonged to that group of schools which we
suggest should be called Sāvakayāna, following the *early*
Mahāyānist nomenclature, instead of the derogatory
'Hīnayāna'. The Theravādins obviously did not want to be
included in the accusation of nihilism which the Mahāyānists
raised against the Sautrāntikas. This might have been the
external reason for the *Visuddhimagga*'s emphasis on the rejection of the nihilistic conception of Nibbāna.

As to the positive-metaphysical view, the Venerable
Buddhaghosa perhaps thought it sufficiently covered by the
numerous passages in the *Visuddhimagga* dealing with the
rejection of the eternity-view and of a transcendental self.
However that may be, even nowadays Buddhism, and
Theravāda in particular, is quite often wrongly accused of
nihilism. It is therefore apposite to summarize here the
arguments found in the *Visuddhimagga*, followed (in Section 2)

by additions from the commentary to that work.[1] Many passages from the suttas relevant to a rejection of nihilism are quoted in both these extracts, making it unnecessary to deal with them separately.

In the aforementioned chapter of the *Visuddhimagga*, the argument proper is preceded by a definition of Nibbāna. The definition uses three categories usually employed in commentarial literature for the purpose of elucidation.

> Nibbāna has peace as its *characteristic*. Its *function* is not to die; or its function is to comfort. It is *manifested* as the signless [without the 'signs', or marks, of greed, hatred and delusion]; or it is manifested as non-diversification.

In the argument proper, the Venerable Buddhaghosa first rejects the view that Nibbāna is non-existent, holding it must exist as it can be realized by practising the path. The adversary, however, while admitting that Nibbāna is not non-existent, still insists on a negative understanding of the nature of Nibbāna. He argues first that Nibbāna should be understood simply as the absence of all the factors of existence, i.e. the five aggregates. Buddhaghosa counters this by replying that Nibbāna can be attained during an individual's lifetime, while his aggregates are still present. The adversary then proposes that Nibbāna consists solely in the destruction of all defilements, quoting in support of his contention the sutta passage: 'That, friend, which is the destruction of greed, hate and delusion – that is Nibbāna' (Saṃyutta Nikāya, 38: 1). Buddhaghosa rejects this view too, pointing out that it leads to certain undesirable consequences: it would make Nibbāna temporal, since the destruction of the defilements is an event that occurs in time; and it makes Nibbāna conditioned, since the actual destruction of the defilements occurs through conditions. He points out that Nibbāna is called the destruction of greed, hate and delusion in a metaphorical sense: because the unconditioned reality, Nibbāna, is the basis or support for the complete destruction of those defilements.

Venerable Buddhaghosa next deals with the negative terminology the Buddha uses to describe Nibbāna. He explains that such terminology is used because of Nibbāna's extreme subtlety. The opponent argues that since Nibbāna is attained by following the path, it cannot be uncreated. Buddhaghosa answers that Nibbāna is only reached by the path, but not produced by it; thus it is uncreated, without beginning, and free from aging and death. He then goes on to discuss the nature of Nibbāna more explicitly:

> . . . The Buddha's goal is one and has no plurality. But this (single goal, Nibbāna) is firstly called 'with result of past clinging left' (sa-upādisesa) since it is made known together with the (aggregates resulting from past) clinging still remaining (during the Arahant's life), being thus made known in terms of the stilling of defilements and the remaining (result of past) clinging that are present in one who has reached it by means of development. But secondly, it is called 'without result of past clinging left' (anupādisesa) since after the last consciousness of the Arahant, who has abandoned arousing (future aggregates) and so prevented kamma from giving result in a future (existence), there is no further arising of aggregates of existence, and those already arisen have disappeared. So the (result of past) clinging that remained is non-existent, and it is in terms of this non-existence, in the sense that 'there is no (result of past) clinging here' that that (same goal) is called 'without result of past clinging left'. (See Itivuttaka 44.)

Because it can be arrived at by distinction of knowledge that succeeds through untiring perseverance,[2] and because it is the word of the Omniscient One,[3] Nibbāna is not non-existent as regards its nature in the ultimate sense (paramatthena nāvij-jamānaṁ sabhāvato nibbānaṁ); for this is said: 'Bhikkhus, there is an unborn, an unbecome, an unmade, an unformed' (Udāna 73; Itivuttaka.45).

SECTION 2

Taking up the last quotation, the commentary to the Visuddhimagga (Paramattha-mañjūsā)[4], written by Ācariya Dhammapāla (6th century), says:

> ★ By these words the Master proclaimed the actual existence of Nibbāna in the ultimate sense. But he did not proclaim it as a mere injunction of his [i.e. as a creedal dogma], saying 'I am the Lord and Master of the Dhamma'; but, in his compassion for those to whom intellectual understanding is the highest that is attainable, he also stated it as a reasoned conclusion in the continuation of the passage quoted above (Udāna 73):

'If, bhikkhus, there were not the unborn, etc., an escape from what is born, etc., could not be perceived. But because, bhikkhus, there is an unborn, etc., an escape from what is born, etc., can be perceived.' This is the meaning: if the unformed element (Nibbāna), having the nature of being unborn, etc., did not exist, no escape from the formed or conditioned, i.e. the five aggregates, could be perceived in this world; their final coming-to-rest (i.e. cessation) could not be perceived, could not be found or apprehended, would not be possible. But if right understanding and the other path factors, each performing its own function, take Nibbāna as object, then they will completely destroy the defilements. Therefore one can perceive here a getting-away, an escape from the suffering of existence in its entirety.

Now in the ultimate sense the existingness of the Nibbāna-element has been demonstrated by the Fully Enlightened One, compassionate for the whole world, by many sutta passages such as 'Dhammas without condition', 'Unformed dhammas' (see *Dhammasaṅgaṇī*, Abhidhamma Piṭaka); 'Bhikkhus, there is that sphere (*āyatana*) where neither earth . . .' (Udāna 71); 'This state is very hard to see, that is to say, the stilling of all formations, the relinquishing of all substance of becoming' (Dīgha 14; M.26); 'Bhikkhus, I shall teach you the unformed and the way leading to the unformed' (Saṃyutta Nikāya, 43: 12) and so on, and in this sutta, 'Bhikkhus, there, is an unborn . . .' (Udāna 73) . . . The words 'Bhikkhus, there is an unborn, an unmade, an unformed' and so on, which demonstrate the existingness of Nibbāna in the ultimate sense, are not misleading because they are spoken by the Omniscient One, like the words 'All formations are impermanent, all formations are painful, all *dhammas* (states) are not self' (Dhammapada, vv. 277–9; Aṅguttara Nikāya, 3: 134, etc.).

* If Nibbāna were mere non-existence, it could not be described by terms such as 'profound [deep, hard to see, hard to comprehend, peaceful, lofty, inaccessible to ratiocination, subtle, to be known by the wise]', etc.; or as 'the unformed, [the cankerless, the true, the other shore]', etc.[5]; or as 'kammically neutral, without condition, unincluded [within the three realms of existence]', etc.[6]

SECTION 3

The references to sutta-texts, quoted in the extracts from the *Visuddhimagga* and its commentary, make it quite clear that the Buddha declared Nibbāna to be an attainable entity and did not conceive it as the mere fact of extinction or cessation. All negatively formulated statements on Nibbāna should be understood in the light of the sutta passages quoted here, and do not admit an interpretation contradictory to these texts. Any forced or far-fetched interpretation of them will be contrary to the whole straightforward way of the Buddha's exposition.

If we have spoken above of Nibbāna as an 'entity' it should be taken just as a word-label meant to exclude 'non-existence'. It is used in the same restricted sense of a linguistic convention as the emphatic words in the Udāna: 'There *is* an unborn . . .'; 'There *is* that sphere where neither earth . . .'. It is not meant to convey the meaning of 'existence' in the usual sense, which should be kept limited to 'the five aggregates or any one of them'. Nibbāna is indescribable in the strictest sense (*avacanīya*).

Our extracts from such an authoritative work as the *Visuddhimagga* show how emphatically the Theravāda tradition rejects a nihilistic conception of its highest ideal, Nibbāna. This fact may perhaps help to remove one of the points of controversy among modern writers and Buddhist schools: the prejudice that Theravāda, or even the Pāli Canon, advocates 'annihilation' as its highest goal.

There is, however, another principal point of difference in the interpretation of Buddhism, and of the Pāli Canon in particular, which is likewise closely connected with the conception of Nibbāna. It is the question of the range of validity, or application, of the Anattā doctrine, i.e. the doctrine of impersonality. This doctrine, we maintain, applies not only to the world of conditioned phenomena, but also to Nibbāna. As far as the denial of its application to the latter falls under the heading of the 'positive-metaphysical extreme', it will be treated in the following sections.

II *The Positive-metaphysical Extreme*

SECTION 4

In India, a country so deeply religious and philosophically so creative, the far greater danger to the preservation of the

Dhamma's character as a 'middle way' came from the other extreme. It consisted in identifying, or connecting, the concept of Nibbāna with any of the numerous theistic, pantheistic or other speculative ideas of a positive-metaphysical type, chiefly with various conceptions of an abiding self. According to the penetrative analysis in the Brahmajāla Sutta (Dīgha Nikāya 1), all the diverse metaphysical and theological views concerning the nature of the self, the world and a divine ground from which they might come, arise from either of two sources: (1) from a limited and misinterpreted meditative experience (in which we may also include supposed revelations, prophetic inspirations, etc.), and (2) from bare reasoning (speculative philosophy and theology). But behind all these metaphysical and theological notions, there looms, as the driving force, the powerful urge in man to preserve, in some way, his belief in an abiding personality which he can invest with all his longings for permanence, security and eternal happiness. It is therefore not surprising that a number of present-day interpreters of Buddhism – perhaps through the force of that powerful, instinctive urge for self-preservation and the influence of long-cherished and widely-held views – advocate a positive-metaphysical interpretation of Nibbāna and Anattā. Some of these sincerely believe themselves to be genuine Buddhists, and possess a genuine devotion towards the Buddha and a fair appreciation of other aspects of his teaching. We shall now look at these views.

In the spirit of the middle way, the following refutation of the positive-metaphysical extreme is also meant to guard against any metaphysical conclusions which may be wrongly derived from our rejection of nihilism in the first part of this essay. In the reverse, that first section may serve to counter an excessive 'defence-reaction' against the metaphysical views to be treated now.

The positive-metaphysical extreme in the interpretation of Nibbāna consists in the identification, or metaphysical association, of a refined or purified self with what, in the context of the respective view, is held to be Nibbāna. Two main types of the metaphysical view can be distinguished, as the preceding paragraph already implies.

(1) The assumption of a universal and unitary (non-dual and non-pluristic) principle with which a purified self, one thought to be liberated from the empirical personality, either merges, or

is assumed to be basically one. These views might differ in details, according to their being influenced either by Theosophy, Vedānta or Mahāyāna (the latter, with varying degrees of justification).

(2) The assumption that the transcendental 'selves' of the Arahats, freed from the aggregates, enter Nibbāna, which is regarded as their 'eternal home' and as 'the only state adequate to them'. Nibbāna itself is admitted to be not-self (*anattā*), while the Holy Ones (Arahats) are supposed to retain 'in Nibbāna' some kind of individuality, in a way unexplained and unexplainable. This view is, to our knowledge, advocated in such a way only by the German author Dr. Georg Grimm and his followers.

SECTION 5

(a) Common to both views is the assumption of an eternal self supposed to exist beyond the five aggregates that make up personality and existence in its entirety. The supposition that the Buddha should have taught anything like that is clearly and sufficiently refuted by the following saying alone:

Any ascetics or brāhmans who conceive manifold (things or ideas) as the self, all conceive the five aggregates (as the self) or any one of them.

Samyutta Nikāya, 22: 47

This textual passage also excludes any misinterpretation of the standard formulation of the Anattā doctrine: 'This does not belong to me, this I am not, this is not my self.' Some writers believe that this formula permits the conclusion that the Buddha supposed a self to exist outside, or beyond, the five aggregates to which the formula usually refers. This wrong deduction is disposed of by the statement of the Buddha quoted above which clearly says that all the manifold conceptions of a self can have reference only to the five aggregates – either collectively or selectively. How else could any idea of a self or a personality be formed, if not from the material of the five aggregates and from a misconception about them? On what else could notions about a self be based? This fact about the only possible way ideas of a self can be formed was expressed by the Buddha himself in the continuation of the text quoted above:

There is, bhikkhus, an uninstructed worldling. . . . He regards corporeality as self, or the self as possessing corporeality, or the corporeality as being within the self, or the self within corporeality [similarly with the four mental aggregates].[7] In this way he arrives at that very conception 'I am'.

Further it was said: 'If there are corporeality, feeling, perception, formations and consciousness, on account of them and dependent on them arises the belief in individuality . . . and speculations about a self' (Saṃyutta Nikāya, 22: 154, 155).

(b) If the words 'I', 'ego', 'personality' and 'self' should have meaning at all, any form of an ego-conception, even the most abstract and diluted one, must necessarily be connected with the idea of particularity or separateness with a differentiation from what is regarded as *not* 'ego'. But from what could that particularity or differentiation be derived if not from the only available data of experience, the physical and mental phenomena comprised by the five aggregates?

In the Majjhima Nikāya sutta called 'The Simile of the Snake' (No. 22), it is said: 'If, monks, there is a self, will there also be what belongs to self?' – 'Yes, Lord.' – 'If there is what belongs to self, will there also be "My self"?' 'Yes, Lord.' – 'But since a self and self's belongings cannot truly be found, is this not a perfectly foolish doctrine: "This is the world, this the self. Permanent, abiding, eternal, immutable shall I be after death, persisting in eternal identity"?' – 'It is, Lord, a perfectly foolish doctrine?'[8]

The first sentence of that text expresses, in a manner as simple as it is emphatic, the fact pointed out before: that the assumption of a self requires also something belonging to a self (*attaniya*), i.e. properties by which that self receives its distinguishing characteristics. To speak of a self devoid of such differentiating attributes, having therefore nothing to characterize it and to give meaningful contents to the word, will be entirely senseless and in contradiction to the accepted usage of these terms 'self', 'ego', etc. But this very thing is done by those who advocate the first of the two main-types of the 'positive-metaphysical extreme': that is, the assumption of a 'great universal self or over-self' (*mahātman*) supposed to merge with, or be basically identical with, a universal and undifferentiated (*nirguṇa*) metaphysical principle which is sometimes equated with Nibbāna. Those who hold these views are sometimes found to make the bold claim that the Buddha wanted to deny only a separate self and that in none of his utterances did he reject the existence of a transcendental self. What has been said before in this section may serve as an answer to these beliefs.

Those views which we have assigned to the second category take an opposite view. They insist on the separate existence of liberated, transcendental selves within the Nibbāna-element. However, their advocates leave quite a number of issues unexplained. They do not indicate how they arrive at the idea of separateness without reference to the world of experience; and they fail to show what that separateness actually consists in and how it can be said to persist in the Nibbāna-element, which, by definition, is undifferentiated (*nippapañca*), the very reverse of separateness.

Both varieties of individuality-belief wish to combine various conceptions of self with the Buddhist teaching of Nibbāna. They are, at the very outset, refuted by the philosophically very significant statement in the discourse on the 'Simile of the Snake', implying that I and mine, owner and property, substance and attribute, subject and predication are inseparable and correlative terms, which, however, lack reality in the ultimate sense.

SECTION 6

The two main-types of a positive-metaphysical interpretation of Nibbāna can be easily included in a considerable number of false views mentioned, classified and rejected by the Buddha. A selection of applicable classifications will be presented in what follows. This material, additional to the fundamental remarks in the preceding section, will furnish an abundance of documentation for the fact that not a single eternalistic conception of self and Nibbāna, of any conceivable form, is reconcilable with the teachings of the Buddha as found in their oldest available presentation in the Pāli Canon.

(a) In the Saṁyutta Nikāya (22: 86) we read: 'Do you think, Anurādha, that the Perfect One (*tathāgata*) is apart from corporeality (*aññatra rūpā*) . . . apart from consciousness?'[9] – 'Certainly not, O Lord.' – 'Do you think that the Perfect One is someone without corporeality (*arūpī*) . . . someone without consciousness?'[10] – 'Certainly not, O Lord.' – 'Since the Perfect One, Anurādha, cannot, truly and really, be found by you even during lifetime, is it befitting to declare: "He who is the Perfect One, the highest being . . . that Perfect One can be made known outside of these four possibilities: The Perfect One exists after death . . . does not exist . . . exists in some way and in another way not . . . can neither be said to exist nor not to exist"?' – 'Certainly not, O Lord.'

This text applies to both main-types of view which assume a self beyond the aggregates. It should be mentioned here that the commentary paraphrases the words 'the Perfect One' (tathāgata) by 'living being' (satta). That is probably meant to show that the statements in the text are valid not only for the conventional term 'the Perfect One' but also for any other terms designating an individuality.

(b) Since the concept of a self is necessarily linked with that of an ownership of qualities and possessions (see 5 b), both main-types come under the following headings of the twenty kinds of individuality-belief (sakkāya-diṭṭhi; see 5 a).

He regards the self as possessing corporeality . . . as possessing feeling . . . perception . . . formations . . . consciousness.'

This applies, in particular, to the second main-type advocated by Dr. Georg Grimm, who expressly speaks of the five aggregates as 'attributions' ('Beilegungen') of the self. It does not make any difference here that these 'attributions' are regarded by Grimm as 'incommensurate' to the self and as capable of being discarded. What matters is the fact that such a relationship between the self and the aggregates is assumed, and this justifies the inclusion of that view in the aforementioned type of individuality belief.

(c) From the 'Discourse on the Root Cause' (Mūla-pariyāya Sutta; Majjhima Nikāya 1) the following categories apply to both types: 'He thinks (himself) different from (or beyond) the four material elements, the heavenly worlds, the uncorporeal spheres; from anything seen, heard, (differently) sensed and cognized; from the whole universe (sabbato).' To the second type are applicable the views: 'He thinks (himself) in Nibbāna (nibbānasmiṁ) or as different from nibbāna (nibbānato maññati).' That is, he believes the liberated self which is supposed to enter the Nibbāna element to be different from it.

(d) In the sutta 'All Cankers' (*Sabbāsava Sutta*; Majjhima Nikāya 2) the following instances of unwise and superficial thinking (*ayoniso manasikāra*) are mentioned and rejected:

Six theories about the self from which the following are applicable here: 'I have a self' and 'By the self I know the self.'[11]

Sixteen kinds of doubt about the existence and nature of the self, with reference to the past, present and future, e.g. 'Am I or am I not?', 'What am I?', 'Shall I be or not?', 'What shall I be?'

Hereby any type of speculation about an alleged self is rejected.

(e) In the Brahmajāla Sutta (Dīgha Nikāya 1) the theories about a self are specified as to their details. Those, however, who advocate the two main-types of the positive-metaphysical extreme, with which we are here concerned, generally avoid or reject detailed statements on the nature of Nibbāna and the self. But if they assume an eternal and transcendental self, it must be conceived as being passive, motionless and immutable. For any active relationship to the world would involve an abandonment of the transcendental state assumed. Therefore both main-types fall under the eternalist view, characterized and rejected in the Brahmajāla Sutta as follows: 'Eternal are self and world, barren, motionless like a mountain peak, steadfast like a pillar'.

(f) The rejection of any belief in a self (as abiding or temporarily identical), and of the extremes of existence and not-existence, cannot be better concluded than by quoting the continuation of the saying that forms the motto of this treatise:

For him, Kaccāna, who considers, according to reality and with true wisdom, the origination of (and in) the world, there is not what in the world (is called) 'non-existence' (*natthitā*). For him, Kaccāna, who considers, according to reality and with true wisdom, the cessation of (and in) the world, there is not what in the world (is called) 'existence' (*atthitā*). This world, Kaccāna, is generally fettered by propensities, cling-ings and biases. But concerning these propensities, clingings, fixed mental attitudes, biases and deep-rooted inclinations, he (the man of right understanding) does not come near, does not cling, does not have the mental attitude: 'I have a self' (*n'adhiṭṭhāti attā me'ti*). He has no doubt or uncertainty that it is suffering, indeed, that arises, and suffering that ceases. Herein his knowledge does not rely on others. In so far, Kaccāna, is one a man of right understanding.

Saṁyutta Nikāya, 12: 15

III *Transcending the Extremes*

If we examine the utterances on Nibbāna in the Pāli Canon, we find that it is described (or better: paraphrased) in both positive and negative terms. Statements of a positive nature include designations like 'the profound, the true, the pure, the permanent, the marvellous,' etc. (Saṁyutta Nikāya, 43); and such texts as those quoted above (see Section 2), 'There is that sphere . . .'; 'There is an unborn . . .', etc. Statements in the form of negative terms include such definitions of Nibbāna as 'the destruction of greed, hate and delusion' and as 'cessation of existence' (*bhava-nirodha*). If the Buddhist conception of Nibbāna is to be understood correctly, one will have to give full weight to the significance of both types of utterance. If one were to quote only one type as a vindication of one's own one-sided opinion, the result would be a lop-sided view.

To the utterances of positive character we may ascribe the following purposes: (1) to exclude the nihilistic extreme; (2) to allay the fears of those who are still without an adequate grasp of the truths of suffering and *anattā*, and thus shrink back from the final cessation of suffering, i.e. of rebirth, as if recoiling from a fall into a bottomless abyss; (3) to show Nibbāna as a goal capable of attainment and truly desirable.

The emphatic 'There is' that opens the two well-known texts on Nibbāna in the Udāna, leaves no doubt that Nibbāna is not conceived as bare extinction or as a camouflage for an absolute zero. But, on the other hand, as a precaution against a metaphysical misinterpretation of that solemn enunciation '*There is . . . (atthi)*', we have that likewise emphatic rejection of the extremes of existence (*atthitā*) and non–existence (*natthitā*).

But even those utterances on Nibbāna which are phrased positively, include mostly negative terms too:

'There is that sphere where there is neither earth . . . neither this world nor the next, neither coming nor going.'

'There is an *un*born, an *un*become . . .'.

'I shall teach you the unformed . . . the profound . . . and the way to it. What now is the unformed . . . the profound? It is the destruction of greed, the destruction of hatred, the destruction of delusion.'

These texts, combining positive and negative statements, illustrate our earlier remark that both the positive and the negative utterances on Nibbāna require mutual qualification, as a precaution against sliding into an extremist position.

Negative utterances are meant to emphasize the supra-mundane and ineffable nature of Nibbāna, which eludes adequate description in positive terms. Our language is basically unsuited for such description, since it is necessarily related to the world of our experience from which its structure and terms are derived. Therefore the positive statements in the suttas cannot be more than allusions or metaphors (*pariyāya desanā*). They make use of emotional values intelligible to us to characterize experiences and reactions known to those who have trodden the path to the Pathless. Though for the reasons mentioned above they have great practical value, they are evocative rather than truly descriptive. Negative statements, however, are quite sound and legitimate in themselves. They relate Nibbāna to the world of experience only by negations. The negating method of approach consists in a process of eliminating what is inapplicable to Nibbāna and incommensurate with it. It enables us to make much more definite and useful statements about the supramundane state of Nibbāna than by the use of abstract terms, the positive character of which can be only metaphorical. Negative statements are also the most appropriate and reverential way to speak of that which has been called 'the marvellous' (*acchariya*) and 'the extraordinary' (*abbhuta*).

Negative ways of expression have another important advantage. Statements like those defining Nibbāna as 'the destruction of greed, hatred and delusion' indicate the direction to be taken, and the work to be done to actually *reach* Nibbāna. And it is this which matters most. These words on the overcoming of greed, hatred and delusion set a clear and convincing task which can be taken up here and now. Further, they not only point to a way that is practicable and worthwhile for its own sake, but they also speak of the lofty goal itself which likewise can be experienced here and now, and not only in an unknown beyond. For it has been said:

If greed, hatred and delusion have been completely destroyed, insofar is Nibbāna visible here and now, not delayed, inviting of inspection, and directly experienceable by the wise.

Anguttara Nikāya, 3: 55

That visible Nibbāna has been lauded by those who attained to it as an unalloyed and inalienable happiness, as the highest solace, as the unspeakable relief of being freed from burden and bondage. A faint foretaste of it may be experienced in each act of joyful renunciation and in moments of serene detachment. To know oneself, if but temporarily and partially, to be free from the slavery of passions and the blindness of self-deception; to be master of oneself and to live and think in the light of knowledge, if but for a time and to a limited extent – these are truly not 'mere negative facts', but the most positive and elevating experiences for those who know more than the fleeting and deceptive happiness of the senses. 'There are two kinds of happiness, O monks: the happiness of the sense-pleasures and the happiness of renunciation. But the greater of them is the happiness of renunciation.' (Anguttara Nikāya, 2: 64)

Thus these seemingly negative words of the destruction of greed, hatred and delusion will convey to the thoughtful and energetic a stirring positive message: of a way that can here be trodden, of a goal that can here be reached, of a happiness that can here be experienced.

That aspect of a lofty happiness attainable here and now should, however, not be allowed to cover for us the fact that the attainment of Nibbāna is the end of rebirth, the cessation of becoming. But this end or cessation in no way involves the destruction or annihilation of anything substantial. What actually takes place is the ending of new origination owing to the stopping of its root-causes: ignorance and craving.

He who sees deeply and thoroughly the truth of suffering is 'no longer carried away by the unreal, and no longer shrinks back from the real'. He knows: 'It is suffering, indeed, that arises, it is suffering that ceases.' With a mind unswerving he strives after the deathless, the final cessation of suffering – Nibbāna.

The Holy Ones know it as bliss:
    the personality's cessation;

Repugnant to the worldly folk,
    but not to those who clearly see.

What others count as highest bliss,
    the Holy Ones regard as pain;

What those regard as only pain
is for the Holy Ones sheer bliss.

Sutta Nipāta, vv. 761–762

Notes

1. The extracts from both works have mainly been taken, with a few alterations, from Bhikkhu Ñāṇamoli's translation (see Note on Sources). Explanatory additions by this writer are in brackets, those by Bhikkhu Ñāṇamoli in parentheses.

2. Comy.: This is to show that, for Arahants, Nibbāna is established by their own experience.

3. Comy.: For others it is established by inference based on the words of the Master.

4. The paragraphs beginning with * are translated by the author of this essay; those without, by Bhikkhu Ñāṇamoli (taken from the notes to his translation of the *Visuddhimagga*).

5. These are some of the altogether 33 designations of Nibbāna, in Saṁyutta Nikāya, 43: 12–44.

6. This refers to Abhidhammic classifications in which Nibbāna is included, occurring, for instance, in the Dhammasaṅgaṇī.

7. These are the twenty kinds of individuality-belief (*sakkāya-diṭṭhi*).

8. See *The Discourse on the Snake Simile*, tr. by Nyanaponika Thera, (WHEEL No.47/48).

9. i.e. outside the aggregates taken singly.

10. i.e. outside the aggregates as a whole.

11. Pāli: *attanā'va attānaṁ sañjānāmi*. This refers to Vedantic conceptions. Quite similar formulations are found already in the Saṁhita, the pre-Buddhist Upanisads, and later in the Bhagavadgītā.

Shorter Essays

Seeing Things As They Are

If we contemplate even a minute sector of life's vast range, we are faced with a variety of living forms so tremendous that it defies all description. Yet three basic features can be discerned as common to everything that has animate existence, from the microbe to man, from the simplest sensations to the thoughts of a creative genius:

impermanence or change (*anicca*);
suffering or unsatisfactoriness (*dukkha*);
not-self or insubstantiality (*anattā*).

These three basic facts were first found and formulated over 2500 years ago by the Buddha, who was rightly called 'the Knower of the World' (*loka-vidū*). They are designated, in Buddhist terminology, the three characteristics (*ti-lakkhaṇa*) – the invariable marks or signs of everything that springs into being, the 'signata' stamped upon the very face of life itself.

Of the three, the first and third apply directly to inanimate existence as well as to the animate, for every concrete entity by its very nature undergoes change and is devoid of substance. The second feature, suffering, is of course only an experience of the animate. But the Buddha applies the characteristic of suffering to all conditioned things, in the sense that, for living beings, everything conditioned is a potential cause of experienced suffering and is at any rate incapable of giving lasting satisfaction. Thus the three are truly universal marks pertaining even to what is below or beyond our normal range of perception.

The Buddha teaches that life can be correctly understood only if these three basic facts are understood. And this understanding must take place, not only logically, but in confrontation with one's own experience. Insight-wisdom, which is the ultimate liberating factor in Buddhism, consists in just this experiential understanding of the three characteristics as applied to one's own bodily and mental processes, and deepened and matured in meditation.

To see things as they really are means to see them consistently in the light of the three characteristics. Not to see them in this way, or to deceive oneself about their reality and range of application, is the defining mark of ignorance, and ignorance is by itself a potent cause of suffering, knitting the net in which man is caught – the net of false hopes, of unrealistic and harmful desires, of delusive ideologies and of perverted values and aims.

Ignoring or distorting the three basic facts ultimately leads only to frustration, disappointment and despair. But if we learn to see through deceptive appearances, and discern the three characteristics, this will yield immense benefits, both in our daily life and in our spiritual striving. On the mundane level, the clear comprehension of impermanence, suffering and not-self will bring us a saner outlook on life. It will free us from unrealistic expectations, bestow a courageous acceptance of suffering and failure and protect us against the lure of deluded assumptions and beliefs. In our quest for the supramundane, comprehension of the three characteristics will be indispensable. The meditative experience of all phenomena as inseparable from the three marks will loosen, and finally cut, the bonds binding us to an existence falsely imagined to be lasting, pleasurable and substantive. With growing clarity, all things internal and external will be seen in their true nature: as constantly changing, as bound up with suffering and as unsubstantial, without an eternal soul or abiding essence. By seeing thus, detachment will grow, bringing greater freedom from egoistic clinging and culminating in Nibbāna, mind's final liberation from suffering.

Buddhism and the God-Idea

Quite contradictory views have been expressed in Western literature on the attitude of Buddhism toward the concept of God and gods. From a study of the discourses of the Buddha preserved in the Pāli Canon, it will be seen that the idea of a *personal deity*, a creator god conceived to be eternal and omnipotent, is incompatible with the Buddha's teachings. On the other hand, conceptions of an *impersonal godhead* of any description, such as world-soul, etc., are excluded by the Buddha's teaching on Anattā, no-self or unsubstantiality.

In Buddhist literature, the belief in a creator god (*issara-nimmāna-vāda*) is frequently mentioned and rejected, along with other causes wrongly adduced to explain the origin of the world; as, for instance, world-soul, time, nature, etc. God-belief, however, is not placed in the same category as those morally destructive wrong views which deny the kammic results of action, assume a fortuitous origin of man and nature or teach absolute determinism. These views are said to be altogether pernicious, having definite bad results due to their effect on ethical conduct.

Theism, however, is regarded as a kind of kamma-teaching in so far as it upholds the moral efficacy of actions. Hence, a theist who leads a moral life may, like anyone else doing so, expect a favourable rebirth. He may possibly even be reborn in a heavenly world that resembles his own conception of it, though it will not be of eternal duration as he may have expected. If, however, fanaticism induces him to persecute those who do not share his beliefs, this will have grave consequences for his future destiny. For fanatical attitudes, intolerance, and violence against others create unwholesome kamma leading to moral degeneration and to an unhappy rebirth.

Although belief in God does not exclude a favourable rebirth, it is a variety of eternalism, a false affirmation of permanence rooted in the craving for existence, and as such an obstacle to final deliverance.

Among the fetters (saṁyojana) that bind to existence, theism is particularly subject to those of personality-belief, attachment to rites and rituals and desire for fine-material existence or for a 'heaven of the sense sphere', as the case may be.

As an attempt at explaining the universe, its origin, and man's situation in his world, the God-idea was found entirely unconvincing by the Buddhist thinkers of old. Through the centuries, Buddhist philosophers have formulated detailed arguments refuting the doctrine of a creator god. It should be of interest to compare these with the ways in which Western philosophers have refuted the theological proofs of the existence of God.

But for an earnest believer, the God-idea is more than a mere device for explaining external facts like the origin of the world. For him it is an object of faith that can bestow a strong feeling of certainty, not only as to God's existence 'somewhere out there', but as to God's consoling presence and closeness to himself. This feeling of certainty requires close scrutiny. Such scrutiny will reveal that in most cases the God-idea is only the devotee's projection of his ideal – generally a noble one – and of his fervent wish and deeply felt need to believe. These projections are largely conditioned by external influences, such as childhood impressions, education, tradition and social environment. Charged with a strong emotional emphasis, brought to life by man's powerful capacity for image-formation, visualization and the creation of myth, they then come to be identified with the images and concepts of whatever religion the devotee follows. In the case of many of the most sincere believers, a searching analysis would show that their 'God-experience' has no more specific content than this.

Yet the range and significance of God-belief and God-experience are not fully exhausted by the preceding remarks. The lives and writings of the mystics of all great religions bear witness to religious experiences of great intensity, in which considerable changes are effected in the quality of consciousness. Profound absorption in prayer or meditation can bring about a deepening and widening, a brightening and intensifying of consciousness, accompanied by a transporting feeling of rapture and bliss. The contrast between these states and normal conscious awareness is so great that the mystic believes his experiences to be manifestations of the divine; and given the contrast, this assumption is quite understandable. Mystical experiences are also characterized by a marked reduction or temporary exclusion of the multiplicity of sense-perceptions and restless thoughts; and this relative unification of mind is then interpreted as a union or communion with the One God. All these deeply moving impressions and the first spontaneous interpretations the mystic subsequently identifies with his particular theology. It is interesting to note, however, that the attempts of most great Western mystics to relate their mystical experiences to the official dogmas of their respective churches often resulted in teachings which were looked upon askance by the orthodox, if not considered downright heretical.

The psychological facts underlying those religious experiences are accepted by the Buddhist and well-known to him; but he carefully distinguishes the experiences themselves from the theological interpretation imposed upon them. After rising from deep meditative absorption (jhāna), the Buddhist meditator is advised to view the physical and mental factors constituting his experience in the light of the three characteristics of all conditioned existence: impermanency, liability to suffering and absence of an abiding ego or eternal substance. This is done primarily in order to utilize the meditative purity and strength of consciousness for the highest purpose:

liberating insight. But this procedure also has a very important side effect which concerns us here: the meditator will not be overwhelmed by any uncontrolled emotions and thoughts evoked by his singular experience, and will thus be able to avoid interpretations of that experience not warranted by the facts.

Hence a Buddhist meditator, while benefiting by the refinement of consciousness he has achieved, will be able to see these meditative experiences for what they are; and he will further know that they are without any abiding substance which could be attributed to a deity manifesting itself to his mind. Therefore, the Buddhist's conclusion must be that the highest mystic states do not provide evidence for the existence of a personal God or impersonal godhead.

Buddhism has sometimes been called an atheistic teaching, either in an approving sense by freethinkers and rationalists, or in a derogatory sense by people of theistic persuasion. Only in one way can Buddhism be described as atheistic, namely in so far as it denies the existence of an eternal, omnipotent God or godhead who is the creator and ordainer of the world. The word 'atheism', however, like the word 'godless', frequently carries a number of disparaging overtones or implications, which in no way apply to the Buddha's teaching.

Those who use the word 'atheism' often associate it with a materialistic doctrine that knows nothing higher than this world of the senses and the slight happiness it can bestow. Buddhism is nothing of that sort. In this respect it agrees with the teachings of other religions, that true lasting happiness cannot be found in this world; nor, the Buddha adds, can it be found on any higher plane of existence, conceived as a heavenly or divine world, since all planes of existence are impermanent and thus incapable of giving lasting bliss. The spiritual values advocated by Buddhism are directed, not towards a new life in some higher world, but towards a state utterly transcending the world, namely, Nibbāna. In making this statement, however, we must point out that Buddhist spiritual values do not draw an absolute separation between the beyond and the here and now. They have firm roots in the world itself for they aim at the highest realization in this present existence. Along with such spiritual aspirations, Buddhism encourages earnest endeavour to make this world a better place to live in.

The materialistic philosophy of annihilationism (*uccheda-*

vāda) is emphatically rejected by the Buddha as a false doctrine. The doctrine of kamma is sufficient to prove that Buddhism does not teach annihilation after death. It accepts survival, not of an eternal soul, but of a mental process subject to renewed becoming; thus it teaches rebirth without transmigration. Again the Buddha's teaching is not a nihilism that gives suffering humanity no better hope than a final cold nothingness. On the contrary, it is a teaching of salvation (*niyyānika-dhamma*) or deliverance (*vimutti*) which attributes to man the faculty to realize by his own efforts the highest goal, Nibbāna, the ultimate cessation of suffering and the final eradication of greed, hate and delusion. Nibbāna is far from being the blank zero of annihilation; yet it also cannot be identified with any form of God-idea, as it is neither the origin nor the immanent ground or essence of the world.

Buddhism is not an enemy of religion as atheism is believed to be. Buddhism, indeed, is the enemy of none. A Buddhist will recognize and appreciate whatever ethical, spiritual and cultural values have been created by God-belief in its long and chequered history. We cannot, however, close our eyes to the fact that the God-concept has served too often as a cloak for man's will to power, and the reckless and cruel use of that power, thus adding considerably to the ample measure of misery in this world supposed to be an all-loving God's creation. For centuries free thought, free research and the expression of dissident views were obstructed and stifled in the name of service to God. And alas, these and other negative consequences are not yet entirely things of the past.

The word 'atheism' also carries the innuendo of an attitude countenancing moral laxity, or a belief that man-made ethics, having no divine sanction, rest on shaky foundations. For Buddhism, however, the basic moral law is inherent in life itself. It is a special case of the law of cause and effect, needing neither a divine law-giver nor depending upon the fluctuating human conceptions of socially conditioned minor moralities and conventions. For an increasing section of humanity, the belief in God is breaking down rapidly, as well as the accustomed motivations for moral conduct. This shows the risk of basing moral postulates on divine commandments, when their alleged source rapidly loses credence and authority. There is a need for an autonomous foundation for ethics, one that has deeper roots than a social contract and is capable of protecting the security of the individual and of human institutions. Buddhism offers such a foundation for ethics.

Buddhism does not deny that there are in the universe planes of existence and levels of consciousness which in some ways may be superior to our terrestrial world and to average human consciousness. To deny this would indeed be provincial in this age of space travel. Bertrand Russell rightly says: 'It is improbable that the universe contains nothing better than ourselves.'

Yet, according to Buddhist teachings, such higher planes of existence, like our familiar world, are subject to the law of impermanency and change. The inhabitants of such worlds may well be, in different degrees, more powerful than human beings, happier and longer-lived. Whether we call those superior beings gods, deities, devas or angels is of little importance, since it is improbable that they call themselves by any of those names. They are inhabitants of this universe, fellow-wanderers in this round of existence; and though more powerful, they need not be wiser than man. Further, it need not be denied that such worlds and such beings may have their lord and ruler. In all probability they do. But like any human ruler, a divine ruler too might be inclined to misjudge his own status and power, until a greater one comes along and points out to him his error, as our texts report of the Buddha.

These, however, are largely matters beyond the range and concern of average human experience. They have been mentioned here chiefly for the purpose of defining the Buddhist position, and not to serve as a topic of speculation and argument. Such involvements can only divert attention and effort from what ought to be our principal object: the overcoming of greed, hatred and delusion where they are found in the here and now.

An ancient verse ascribed to the Buddha in the *Questions of King Milinda* says:

Not far from here do you need to look!
Highest existence – what can it avail?
Here in this present aggregate,
In your own body overcome the world!

Devotion in Buddhism

The Buddha repeatedly discouraged any excessive veneration paid to him personally. He knew that an excess of purely emotional devotion can obstruct or disturb the development of a balanced character, and thus may become a serious obstacle to progress on the path to deliverance. The history of religion has since proved him right, as illustrated by the extravagancies of emotional mysticism in East and West.

The suttas relate the story of the monk, Vakkali, who full of devotion and love for the Buddha, was ever desirous to behold him bodily. To him the Buddha said: 'What shall it profit you to see this impure body? He who sees the Dhamma sees me.'

Shortly before the Buddha passed away, he said: 'If a monk or a nun, a devout man or a devout woman, lives in accordance with the Dhamma, is correct in his life, walks in conformity with the Dhamma – it is he who rightly honours, reverences, venerates, holds sacred and reveres the Perfect One (*tathāgata*) with the worthiest homage.'

A true and deep understanding of the Dhamma, together with conduct in conformity with that understanding – these are vastly superior to any external homage or mere emotional devotion. That is the instruction conveyed by these two teachings of the Master.

It would be a mistake, however, to conclude that the Buddha disparaged a reverential and devotional attitude of mind when it is the natural outflow of a true understanding and a deep admiration of what is great and noble. It would also be a grievous error to believe that the 'seeing of the Dhamma' (spoken of in the first saying) is identical with a mere intellectual appreciation and purely conceptual grasp of the doctrine. Such a one-sided abstract approach to the very concrete message of the Buddha all too often leads to intellectual smugness. In its barrenness it will certainly not be a substitute for the strong and enlivening impulse imparted by a deep-felt devotion to what is known as great, noble and exemplary. Devotion, being a facet and natural accompaniment of confidence (*saddhā*), is a necessary factor in the 'balance of faculties' (*indriya-samatā*) required for final deliverance. Confidence, in all its aspects, including the devotional, is needed to resolve any stagnation and other shortcomings resulting from a one-sided development of the intellectual faculties. Such development often tends to turn around in circles endlessly, without being able to effect a break-through. Here devotion, confidence, and faith – all aspects of the Pāli term *saddhā* – may be able to give quick and effective help.

Though the Buddha refused to be made the object of an emotional 'personality cult', he also knew that 'respect and homage paid to those who are worthy of it is a great blessing'. The Buddha made this statement in the very first stanza of one of his principal ethical injunctions, the Discourse on Blessings (*Mahā Mangala Sutta*).[1] Mentioning the value of a respectful, reverential attitude together with the blessings of 'avoiding fools and associating with the wise', the Buddha obviously regarded such an attitude as fundamental for individual and social progress and for the acquisition of any further higher benefits. One who is incapable of a reverential attitude will also be incapable of spiritual progress beyond the narrow limits of his present mental condition. One who is so blind as not to see or recognize anything higher and better than the little mud-pool of his petty self and environment will suffer for a long time from retarded growth. And one who, out of a demonstrative self-assertion, scorns a reverential attitude in himself and in others will remain imprisoned in his self-conceit – a most formidable bar to a true maturity of character and to spiritual growth. It is by recognizing and honouring someone or something higher that one honours and enhances one's own inner potentialities.

> When the high heart we magnify,
> And the sure vision celebrate,
> And worship greatness passing by,
> Ourselves are great.

Since respect, reverence and devotion are partial aspects of the Buddhist concept of confidence, one will now understand why confidence has been called the seed of all other beneficial qualities.

The nobler the object of reverence or devotion, the higher is the blessing bestowed by it. 'Those who have joyous confidence in the highest, the highest fruit will be theirs' (Anguttara, 4: 34). The supreme objects of a Buddhist's reverence and devotion are his Three Refuges, also called the Three Jewels or Ideals: the Buddha, his Teaching (Dhamma) and the Community of saintly monks and nuns (Sangha).[2] Here, too, the

Buddha is revered not as a personality of such and such a name, nor as a deity, but as the embodiment of Enlightenment. A text often recurring in the Buddhist scriptures says that a devout lay disciple 'has confidence, he believes in the Enlightenment of the Perfect One'. This confidence, however, is not the outcome of blind faith based on hearsay, but is derived from the devotee's reasoned conviction based on his own understanding of the Buddha Word, which speaks to him clearly with a voice of unmistakable Enlightenment. This derivation of his assurance is emphasized by the fact that, along with confidence, wisdom also is mentioned among the qualities of an ideal lay follower.

We may now ask: Is it not quite natural that feelings of love, gratitude, reverence and devotion seek expression through the entire man, through acts of body and speech as well as through his thoughts and unexpressed sentiments? Will one, for instance, hide one's feelings towards parents and other loved ones? Will one not rather express them by loving words and deeds? Will one not cherish their memory in suitable ways, as for instance, by preserving their pictures in one's home, by placing flowers on their graves, by recalling their noble qualities? In such a way, one who has become critical of the devotional aspects of religion may seek to understand the outward acts of homage customary in Buddhist lands when, with reverential gesture, flowers and incense are placed before a Buddha image and devotional texts are recited not as prayers but as meditation. Provided that such practice does not deteriorate into a thoughtless routine, a follower of the Dhamma will derive benefit if he takes up some form of a devotional practice, adapting it to his personal temperament and to the social customs of his environment.

Buddhism, however, does not in the least impose upon its followers a *demand* to observe any outward form of devotion or worship. This is entirely left to the choice of individuals whose emotional, devotional and intellectual needs are bound to differ greatly. No Buddhist should feel himself forced into an iron-cast mould, be it of a devotional or a rationalistic shape. As a follower of the middle way, he should, however, also avoid one-sided judgement of others, and try to appreciate that their individual needs and preferences may differ from his own.

More important and of greater validity than outward forms of devotion is the basic capacity for respect and reverence discussed at the beginning of this essay, and also the practice of meditations or contemplations of a devotional character. Many benefits accrue from these, and hence it was for good reasons that the Enlightened One strongly and repeatedly recommended the meditative recollection of the Buddha (*buddhānussati*), along with other devotional recollections.[3] Here again, the reference is to the embodied ideal; thus the Buddha, as a being freed from all traces of vanity and egotism, could venture to recommend to his disciples a meditation on the Buddha.

What, then, are the benefits of such devotional meditations? Their first benefit is *mental purification*. They have been called by the Buddha 'efficacious procedures for purifying a defiled mind' (Anguttara Nikāya, 3: 71). 'When a noble disciple contemplates upon the Enlightened One, at that time his mind is not enwrapped in lust, nor in hatred, nor in delusion. At such time his mind is rightly directed: it has got rid of lust, is aloof from it, is freed from it. Lust is here a name for the five sense desires. By cultivating this contemplation, many beings become purified' (Anguttara Nikāya, 6: 25).

If, by practising that devotional meditation, one endeavours to live, as it were, 'in the Master's presence' (*satthā sammukhī bhūta*), one will feel ashamed to do, speak or think anything unworthy; one will shrink back from evil; and as a positive reaction, one will feel inspired to high endeavour in emulation of the Master's great example.

Images, and not abstract concepts, are the language of the subconscious. If, therefore, the image of the Enlightened One is often created within one's mind as the embodiment of man perfected, it will penetrate deeply into the subconscious, and if sufficiently strong, will act as an automatic brake against evil impulses. In such a way the subconscious, normally so often the hidden enemy in gaining self-mastery, may become a powerful ally of such an endeavour. For the purpose of *educating the subconscious*, it will be helpful to use a Buddha image or picture as an aid in visualization. In that way concentration of mind may be attained fairly soon. For evoking and deeply absorbing some features of the Buddha's personality, his qualities should be contemplated, for instance in the way described in the *Visuddhimagga*.

The recollection of the Buddha, being productive of joy (*pīti*), is an effective way of *invigorating the mind*, of lifting it up from the states of listlessness, tension, fatigue and frustration, which occur during meditation as well as in ordinary life. The

Buddha himself advised: 'If (in the strenuous practice of meditation, for instance) in contemplation of the body, bodily
agitation, including sense desires, or mental lassitude or distraction should arise, then the meditator should turn his mind to
a gladdening, elevating subject' (Saṃyutta Nikāya, 47: 10).
And here the teachers of old recommend especially the recollection of the Buddha. When those hindrances to concentration
vanish under its influence, the meditator will be able to return to
his original meditation subject.

For a beginner especially, attempts at gaining concentration
are often frustrated by an uneasy self-consciousness; the meditator, as it were, squints back upon himself. He becomes
disturbingly aware of his body with its little discomforts, and of
his mind struggling against obstacles which only grow stronger
the more he struggles. This may happen when the subject of
meditation is one's own physical or mental processes, but it
may also occur with other subjects. In such a situation, it will be
profitable to follow the advice given earlier and to turn one's
attention from one's own personality to the inspiring visualization of the Buddha and the contemplation of his qualities. The
joyful interest thus produced may bring about that self-
forgetfulness which is such an important factor for gaining
concentration. Joy produces calm (*passaddhi*), calm leads to ease
(*sukha*), and ease to concentration (*samādhi*). Thus devotional
meditation can serve as a valuable *aid in attaining mental
concentration* which is the basis of liberating insight. This
function of devotional meditation cannot be better described
than in the words of the Master.

When a noble disciple contemplates upon the Enlightened
One, at that time his mind is not enwrapped in lust, nor in
hatred, nor in delusion. At such a time his mind is rightly
directed towards the Perfect One (Tathāgata). And with a
rightly directed mind the noble disciple gains enthusiasm for
the goal, enthusiasm for the Dhamma, gains the delight
derived from the Dhamma. In him thus delighted, joy arises;
to one who is joyful, body and mind become calm; calmed in
body and mind, he feels at ease; and if at ease, the mind finds
concentration. Such a one is called a noble disciple who
among a humanity gone wrong, has attained to what is right;
who among a humanity beset by troubles, dwells free of
troubles.

Anguttara Nikāya, 6: 10

Courageous Faith

Faith involves not merely a belief in the existence of a thing or in the truth of a creedal formula, but also confidence in the power of its object. Religious faith is the belief and confidence in the power of the Supreme Good, and Buddhist faith, in particular, the belief in the incomparable power of the Noble Eightfold Path, the confidence in its purifying and liberating efficacy.

Among those calling themselves 'believers' or 'religious people' or, in our case, Buddhists, there are still too few who have that kind of genuine faith in the actual power of the Good to transform and elevate the life of the individual and of society, to secure them against the resistance of the evil in themselves and in the world outside. Too few dare to entrust themselves to the powerful current of the Good, too many secretly believe, in spite of a vague sort of 'faith', that the power of the evil in themselves and the world is stronger – too strong to be contended with. Many politicians everywhere in the world seem to believe the same, particularly those who call themselves 'realists', obviously implying that only the evil is 'real'. They think that of necessity they have to submit to its greater power. If they are not willing to put it to a test, it is no wonder that they cannot achieve much good.

To be sure, in face of the great forces of evil and stupidity, this kind of genuine faith in the Good requires a certain amount of courage. But no progress of any kind is possible without courage. Progress means to overcome the natural inertia of present unsatisfactory conditions in the individual and in society. It certainly requires courage to take the first step in breaking through that resistance of the natural inertia and the self-preserving tendency of things and minds. But just that courage is the preliminary condition of success.

The ancient teachers of the Buddhist doctrine were well aware that courage is an essential feature of true faith. They therefore compared faith to a strong and courageous hero who plunges ahead into the turbulent waters of a stream to lead safely across the weaker people who timidly stop at the shore, or, excitedly and in vain, run up and down the bank engaged in useless arguments about the proper place to cross. This simile can be applied to the social as well as to the inner life. In the case of social life, the 'weaker people' are those who are willing to follow and support a leader but who cannot make a start by themselves. In the case of the inner life, the 'weaker people' are those qualities necessary for spiritual progress which are either undeveloped or isolated from their supplementary virtues.

Two factors of inner progress which supplement, support and balance each other are intellect (*paññā*) and faith (*saddhā*). If intellect remains without the confidence, devotion and zeal of faith, it will stop short at a mere theoretical understanding and intellectual appreciation of teachings meant to be lived and not only thought or talked about. In the words of our simile: intellect, if not helped by the hero of faith, will merely 'run up and down the bank of the stream', an activity with a very busy and important appearance but with few actual results. Intellect separated from faith will lack the firm belief in its own power to be the guide on the path of life. Without this inner conviction it will hesitate to follow in earnest its own conclusions and commands; it will lack the courage to make an actual start on the task of 'crossing over'. Faith as a supplementary quality, supported by the vigour and endurance of energy (*viriya*), will give wings to the intellect, enabling it to rise above the barrenness of unapplied knowledge and the futile wordy wars of conceptual thought. In exchange, intellect will give to faith discriminative judgement and reliable guidance. It will prevent faith from becoming exhausted, from wasting its energies by ineffective emotional effusions and misdirected efforts. Therefore, faith and intellect should always be harmonized. With right mindfulness keeping them balanced, the two together will prove to be ideal companions, able to meet by their combined efforts any dangers and difficulties on the road to liberation.

Why End Suffering?

The Buddha declares that he teaches the Dhamma for the sole purpose of leading beings to freedom from suffering. If, moved by that teaching, we resolve to make an end of suffering, it is of prime importance that we understand the problem of suffering clearly in its true width and depth. If our grasp of the problem is too glaringly incomplete, our endeavours to eliminate it will also be incomplete, incapable of garnering the strength needed to yield fully satisfactory results.

When asked 'Why end suffering?', the obvious answer is that

one wishes to end suffering because it is the natural innermost urge of one's being to be free from affliction. However, in aspiring to the extinction of suffering, we should think not only of our own affliction, but also of the pain and sorrow we inflict upon others as long as we have not reached the perfect harmlessness of a passion-free heart and the clear vision of a liberated mind. If we regularly recollect the fact that, on our way through saṁsāric existence, we inevitably add to the suffering of others too, we shall feel an increased urgency in our resolve to enter earnestly the path leading to our own liberation.

The suffering we may inflict upon our fellow-beings includes first those cases where other beings become passive objects of our harmful actions. Our greed robs, impoverishes, deprives and detracts, soils and violates. Our hate kills and destroys, hurts and rouses fear. The turbid waters of our interfering ignorance flood and devastate the neighbour's peaceful shores; our misjudgements lead him astray and leave him in calamity.

Then there is a second and even more detrimental way our defilements may cause harm for others. Our evil or impure actions often provoke in others a harmful response that entangles them still more in the meshes of their defilements. Our own greed increases the competitive greed of others; our own lust rouses in others lustful desires which might have slumbered had we not awakened them. Our own hate and anger provoke hostility in return, starting thus the endless round of mutual revenge. Our prejudices become infectious. By our own illusions we deceive others who, by believing them, lend them increased weight and influence. Our wrong judgements, false values and erroneous views, sometimes only casually expressed, are taken up and expanded by others into extensive systems of deceptive and perverted notions working untold harm on peoples' minds. In all these cases a good part of the responsibility will be ours. How careful we must be in what we speak and write!

A third way we may cause suffering to others is due to the limited and varying lifetime of our emotions. Our own love towards a certain person may die a natural death, while the person whom we loved still loves us, and thus suffers under our neglect. Or, in reverse: while the other's love for us has died, our own still lives and constantly urges him, encroaches upon his need for freedom, disturbs his peace and tears at his heart, causing him sorrow because he cannot help us. These are quite common situations in human relationships, and their consequences are often tragic. We feel their poignancy particularly strongly because no moral guilt seems to be involved, only the stern impassive law of impermanence impressing its painful stamp upon this scene of life. Yet here too a moral principle applies, though it is a matter of definition whether we use the word 'guilt'. Understood rightly, the situation presents a case of lust, attachment or craving causing pain through lack of fulfilment. Looking at the case in this light, how clear will become the second noble truth: 'Craving is the origin of suffering.' And so too that seeming paradox: 'From what is dear to us, suffering arises.' When deeply contemplating that little specimen of life's suffering as presented here, we shall feel indeed: 'Truly, this alone is enough to turn away from all forms of existence, to become disenchanted with them, to become detached from them!'

We still have not exhausted all the ways our own imperfections may draw others into the whirlpool of suffering. But it may suffice here to add a fourth and last point. Our own passions and ignorance, whether they involve another directly or only as an observer, may contribute to his harm by destroying his trust in man, his belief in high ideals and his will to contribute to the fund of goodness in the world. Our own imperfections may thus induce him to become egocentric out of disappointment, a cynic or a misanthrope out of personal or impersonal resentment. Owing to our own imperfections, the forces of Good will again have been weakened not only in us, but in others too.

There are many who will reply to the Buddhist doctrine of suffering by saying: 'We are well aware that happiness and beauty, joy and pleasure, have to be paid for by a certain amount of suffering. But we are willing to pay the price without grumbling, even the last price, death; and we think it is worth the price, and that it adds zest to our enjoyment.' Before those who speak thus, we may place the facts indicated above, and ask them: 'Are you aware that the price you are speaking of is paid not only by your own suffering, but also by the suffering of others? Do you think that it is right and fair for you to make *others* pay for your happiness? Will you still find "added zest" if you look at your happiness from that angle?' And our partner – provided he is honest and noble-minded (and only then would it be worthwhile to speak to him) will pensively say: 'I did not think of that. It is true, I must not make others pay for my shortcomings. If I consider it unfair and ignoble to do so in my everyday dealings, should it not likewise be so in relation to these higher problems of life?' We may then be sure that we have planted the seed in his mind and conscience which will sprout in due time.

We return now to our initial line of thought. We have seen how our actions may affect others through many channels, how our shortcomings may drag others into suffering, entanglement and guilt. Thus our constantly accumulating responsibility for much of the suffering and unhappiness in the world should be an additional and powerful incentive for us to become holy and whole for the sake of others, too.

Certainly our own wholeness and health will not cure others, at least not directly and not in all cases. Our own harmlessness will only rarely keep others from doing harm. But by winning to spiritual health, we shall diminish at least by one the sources of infection in the world and our own harmlessness will lessen the fuel nourishing the fires of hate which ravage this earth.

By remaining conscious of the suffering we cause and the suffering we might prevent, we add two powerful motives to those already urging us to enter the liberating path: the challenging sense of manly responsibility, and the fullness of motherly love and compassion. These complementary ideals of duty and love, which we may call the male and the female principles, will help to keep us unswervingly on the path. Love and compassion towards those who might become the victims of our own imperfections will urge us to fulfil our duty towards them in the only way possible: by fulfilling our duty towards ourselves.

The above lines of thought are tersely expressed by a saying of the Buddha that is much too little known:

> By protecting oneself, one protects others; by protecting others, one protects oneself
>
> Saṁyutta Nikāya, 47: 19

In the light of the observations made above, these simple yet profound words of the Master will become still more translucent, charged with a magical power stirring the very depth of our being. By contemplating how our own defiled actions can have detrimental effects upon others, we shall still better understand that both statements in this passage are complementary: by guarding ourselves we are doing our best to protect others; wishing to protect others against the suffering we ourselves can cause, we shall do our utmost to guard ourselves.

Therefore, for our own sake and for the sake of our fellow-beings, we have to be watchful of every step we take. Only by a high degree of mindfulness shall we succeed. Thus it is said in the same discourse that the method of practising that twofold protection is the firm establishing of mindfulness (satipaṭṭhāna), which here too proves to be 'the sole way' (ekāyano maggo):

'I shall protect myself', thus the establishing of mindfulness has to be cultivated. 'I shall protect others', thus the establishing of mindfulness has to be cultivated.

The same idea and method is expressed in a passage of the Buddha's 'Advice to Rāhula' (Majjhima Nikāya 61):

After reflecting again and again, actions by deed, word and thought should be done. . . . Before doing such actions by deed, word and thought, while doing them and after doing them, one should reflect thus: 'Does this action lead to the harm of myself, to the harm of others, to the harm of both?' After reflecting again and again, one should purify one's actions by deed, word and thought. Thus, O Rāhula, should you train yourself.

Again it is said:

Thus, O monks, should you train yourselves: Considering one's own welfare, this is sufficient to strive untiringly. Considering the welfare of others, this is sufficient to strive untiringly. Considering the welfare of both, this is sufficient to strive untiringly.

Saṁyutta Nikāya, 12: 22

These three sayings of the Master will illuminate each other. By reminding us of the right motives of our quest, and supplying us with the right methods for accomplishing our task, they will be infallible guides in treading the path.

Kamma and its Fruit

I

Most writings on the doctrine of kamma emphasize the strict lawfulness governing kammic actions, ensuring a close correspondence between our deeds and their fruits. While this emphasis is perfectly in place, there is another side to the working of kamma – a side rarely noted, but so important that it deserves to be stressed and discussed as an explicit theme in itself. This is the modifiability of kamma, the fact that the lawfulness which governs kamma does not operate with mechanical rigidity but allows for a considerably wide range of modifications in the ripening of the fruit.

If kammic action were always to bear fruits of invariably the same magnitude, and if modification or annulment of kamma-result were excluded, liberation from the saṁsāric cycle of suffering would be impossible; for an inexhaustable past would ever throw up new obstructive results of unwholesome kamma. Hence the Buddha said:

> If one says that 'in whatever way a person performs a kammic action, in that very same way he will experience the result' – in that case there will be no (possibility of a) religious life[4] and no opportunity would appear for the complete ending of suffering.
>
> But if one says that 'a person who performs a kammic action (with a result) that is variably experienceable, will reap its results accordingly' – in that case there will be (a possibility of) a religious life and an opportunity for making a complete end of suffering.

> Anguttara Nikāya, 3: 110

Like any physical event, the mental process constituting a kammic action never exists in isolation but in a field, and thus its efficacy in producing a result depends not only on its own potential, but also upon the variable factors of its field, which can modify it in numerous ways. We see, for example, that a particular kamma, either good or bad, may sometimes have its result strengthened by supportive kamma, weakened by counteractive kamma, or even annulled by destructive kamma. The occurrence of the result can also be delayed if the conjunction of outer circumstances required for its ripening is not complete; and that delay may again give a chance for counteractive or destructive kamma to operate.

It is, however, not only these extraneous conditions which can cause modification. The ripening also reflects the kamma's 'internal field' or internal conditions – that is, the total qualitive structure of the mind from which the action issues. To one rich in moral or spiritual qualities, a single offence may not entail the weighty results the same offence will have for one who is poor in such protective virtues. Also, analogously to human law, a first-offender's punishment will be milder than that of a reconvicted criminal.

Of this type of modified reaction the Buddha speaks in the continuation of the discourse quoted above:

'Now take the case when a minor evil deed has been committed by a certain person and it takes him to hell. But if the same minor offence is committed by another person, its results might be experienced during his lifetime and not even the least (residue of a reaction) will appear (in the future), not to speak about a major (reaction).

'Now what is the kind of person whom a minor offence takes to hell? It is one who has not cultivated (restraint of) the body, not cultivated virtue and thought, nor has he developed any wisdom; he is narrow-minded, of low character and even for trifling things he suffers. It is such a person whom even a minor offence may take to hell.

'And what is the person by whom the result of the same small offence will be experienced in his lifetime, without the least (future residue)? He is one who has cultivated (restraint of) the body, who has cultivated virtue and thought and who has developed wisdom; he is not limited (by vices), is a great character and he lives unbounded (by evil).[5] It is such a person who experiences the result of the same small offence during his lifetime, without the least future residue.

'Now suppose a man throws a lump of salt into a small cup of water. What do you think, monks: would that small quantity of water in the cup become salty and undrinkable through that lump of salt?' – 'It would, Lord.' – 'And why so?' – 'The water in the cup is so little that a lump of salt can make it salty and undrinkable.'

'But suppose, monks, that lump of salt is thrown into the

river Ganges. Would it make the river Ganges salty and undrinkable?' – 'Certainly not, Lord.' – 'And why not?' – 'Great, Lord, is the mass of water in the Ganges. It will not become salty and undrinkable by a lump of salt.'

'Further, O monks, suppose a person has to go to jail for a matter of a halfpenny or a penny or a hundred pence. And another man does not have to go to jail on that account.

'Now, what is the kind of person that has to go to jail for a matter of a halfpenny, a penny or a hundred pence? It is one who is poor, without means or property. But he who is rich, a man of means and property, does not have to go to jail for such a matter.'[6]

Anguttara Nikāya, 3: 110

Hence we may say that it is an individual's accumulation of good or evil kamma and also his dominating character traits, good or evil, which affect the kammic result. They determine the greater or lesser weight of the result and may even spell the difference between whether or not it occurs at all.

But even this does not exhaust the existing possibilities of modifications in the weight of kammic reaction. A glance into the life histories of people we know may well show us a person of good and blameless character, living in secure circumstances; yet a single mistake, perhaps even a minor one, suffices to ruin his entire life – his reputation, his career, and his happiness – and it may also lead to a serious deterioration of his character. This seemingly disproportionate crisis might have been due to a chain-reaction of aggravating circumstances beyond his control, to be ascribed to a powerful counteractive kamma of his past. But the chain of bad results may have been precipitated by the person's own action – decisively triggered by his initial mistake and reinforced by subsequent carelessness, indecision or wrong decisions, which, of course, are unskilled kamma in themselves. This is a case when even a predominately good character cannot prevent the ripening of bad kamma or soften the full force of the results. The good qualities and deeds of that person will certainly not remain ineffective; but their future outcome might well be weakened by any presently arisen negative character changes or actions, which might form a bad counteractive kamma.

Consider too the converse situation: A person deserving to be called a thoroughly bad character may, on a rare occasion, act

245

on an impulse of generosity and kindness. This action may turn out to have unexpectedly wide and favourable repercussions on his life. It might bring about a decisive improvement in his external circumstances, soften his character, and even initiate a thorough 'change of heart'.

How complex, indeed, are situations in human life, even when they appear deceptively simple! This is so because the situations and their outcome mirror the still greater complexity of the mind, their inexhaustible source. The Buddha himself has said: 'The mind's complexity surpasses even the countless varieties of the animal kingdom' (Saṁyutta Nikāya, 12: 100). For any single individual, the mind is a stream of ever-changing mental processes driven by the currents and cross-currents of kamma accumulated in countless past existences. But this complexity, already great, is increased still very much more by the fact that each individual life-stream is interwoven with many other individual life-streams through the interaction of their respective kammas. So intricate is the net of kammic conditioning that the Buddha declared kamma-result to be one of four 'unthinkables' (acinteyya) and warned against treating it as a subject of speculation. But though the detailed workings of kamma escape our intellection, the practically important message is clear: the fact that kammic results are modifiable frees us from the bane of determinism and its ethical corollary, fatalism, and keeps the road to liberation constantly open before us.

The potential 'openness' of a given situation, however, also has a negative side, the element of risk and danger: a wrong response to the situation might open a downward path. It is our own response which removes the ambiguity of the situation, for better or worse. This reveals the kamma doctrine of the Buddha as a teaching of moral and spiritual responsibility for oneself and others. It is truly a 'human teaching' because it corresponds to and reflects man's wide range of choices, a range much wider than that of an animal. Any individual's moral choice may be severely limited by the varying load of greed, hatred and delusion and their results which he carries around; yet every time he stops to make a decision or a choice, he is potentially free to throw off that load, at least temporarily. At this precarious and precious moment of choice he has the opportunity to rise above all the menacing complexities and pressures of his unfathomable kammic past. Indeed, in one short moment he can transcend aeons of kammic bondage. It is through right mindfulness that man can firmly grasp that fleeting moment, and it is mindfulness again that enables him to use it for making wise choices.

II

Every kammic action, as soon as it is performed, first of all affects the doer of the deed himself. This holds with as much truth for bodily and verbal deeds directed towards others as it does for volitional thoughts that do not find outward expression. To some extent we can control our own response to our actions, but we cannot control the way others respond to them. Their response may turn out to be quite different from what we expect or desire. A good deed of ours might be met with ingratitude, a kind word may find a cold or even hostile reception. But though these good deeds and kind words will then be lost to the recipient, to his own disadvantage, they will not be lost to the doer. The good thoughts that inspired them will ennoble his mind, even more so if he responds to the negative reception with forgiveness and forbearance rather than anger and resentment.

Again, an act or word meant to harm or hurt another, may not provoke him to a hostile reaction but only meet with self-possessed calmness. Then this 'unaccepted present will fall back to the giver', as the Buddha once told a brahmin who had abused him. The bad deeds and words, and the thoughts motivating them, may fail to harm the other, but they will not fail to have a damaging effect on the character of the doer; and it will affect him even worse if he reacts to the unexpected response by rage or a feeling of resentful frustration. Hence the Buddha says that beings are the responsible owners of their kamma, which is their inalienable property. They are the only legitimate heirs of their actions, inheriting their legacy of good or bad fruits.

It will be a wholesome practice to remind oneself often of the fact that one's deeds, words, and thoughts first of all act upon and alter one's own mind. Reflecting thus will give a strong impetus to true self-respect which is preserved by protecting oneself against everything mean and evil. To do so will also open a new, practical understanding of a profound saying of the Buddha:

In this fathom-long body with its perceptions and thoughts there is the world, the origin of the world, the ending of the world and the path to the ending of the world.

Anguttara Nikāya, 4: 45

III

The 'world' of which the Buddha speaks is comprised in this aggregate of body-and-mind. For it is only by the activity of our physical and mental sense faculties that a world can be experienced and known at all. The sights, sounds, smells, tastes and bodily impressions which we perceive, and our various mental functions, conscious and unconscious – this is the world in which we live. And this world of ours has its origin in that very aggregate of physical and mental processes that produces the kammic act of craving for the six physical and mental sense objects.

'If, Ānanda, there were no kamma ripening in the sphere of the senses, would there appear any sense sphere existence?' – 'Surely not, O Lord.'

Anguttara Nikāya, 3: 76

Thus kamma is the womb from which we spring (kamma-yoni), the true creator of the world and of ourselves as the experiencers of the world. And through our kammic actions in deed, word and thought, we unceasingly engage in building and re-building *this* world and worlds beyond. Even our good actions, as long as they are still under the influence of craving, conceit and ignorance, contribute to the creation and preservation of this world of suffering. The Wheel of Life is like a treadmill set in perpetual motion by kamma, chiefly by its three unwholesome roots – greed, hatred and delusion. The 'end of the world' cannot be reached by walking on a treadmill; this only creates the illusion of progress. It is only by stopping that vain effort that the end can be reached.

It is 'through the elimination of greed, hatred and delusion that the concatenation of kamma comes to an end' (Anguttara Nikāya, 10: 174). And this again can happen nowhere else than in the same aggregate of body-and-mind where suffering and its causes originate. It is the hopeful message of the third noble truth that we *can* step out of the weary round of vain effort and misery. If, despite our knowledge of the possibility of release, we keep walking on the treadmill of life, that is because of an age-old addiction hard to break, the deeply rooted habit of clinging to the notions of 'I', 'mine', and 'self'. But here again there is the hopeful message in the fourth noble truth with its eightfold path, the therapy that can cure the addiction and gradually lead us to the final cessation of suffering. And all that is required for the therapy is again found in our own body and mind.

The treatment proper starts with correctly understanding the true nature of kamma and thereby our situation in the world. This understanding will provide a strong motivation for ensuring a prevalence of good kamma in one's life. And as it deepens by seeing the human condition still more clearly, this same understanding will become the spur for breaking the chains of kammic bondage. It will impel one to strive diligently along the path, and to dedicate all one's actions and their fruits to the greatest end of action – the final liberation of oneself and all sentient beings.

Contemplation of Feelings

'To feel is everything!' – so exclaimed a German poet, and exuberant though these words may be, they do point to the key role that feeling plays in human life. Whether deliberately or not, most people pass their days and nights in an avid endeavour to increase pleasant feelings and to avoid unpleasant ones. All human ambitions and strivings are geared to that purpose. From the simple amusements of the common man to the power urge of the mighty and the creative activity of the great artist, what is basically wanted is to enjoy pleasure, to gain satisfaction and to obtain happiness. Pleasant feelings come in many forms, and the longing to experience them in all their variety and intensity gives rise to courses of action and ways of life as equally numerous and diverse. To satisfy 'the pleasure principle' many heroic deeds have been performed, and many more that were unheroic. The modern world, particularly, has seen the craving for physical comfort, emotional gratification and sensual enjoyment expand at a geometric rate. In every major country thousands of industries and services have sprung up, employing millions of workers, harnessing all the magic of technology first to excite, and then to satisfy, the desire for pleasure and convenience. By providing questionable escape routes, these same purveyors of emotional and sensual titillation also try to allay the worry, boredom, frustration and discontent so rampant in this present 'age of anxiety'.

From this brief survey one may now appreciate the significance of the Buddha's terse saying that 'all things converge on feelings'. The central position of feeling in human life also makes it clear why the Buddha included feelings as a separate category among the five constituent aggregates of personality (pañcakkhandhā) and as a separate mode of contemplation in the four foundations of mindfulness (satipaṭṭhāna).

In the precise pinpointing of mental states undertaken in Buddhist psychology, feeling (vedanā) is understood as the bare sensation experienced as pleasant, unpleasant (painful) or neutral (indifferent). It is distinguished from emotion, a more complex phenomenon which arises from the basic feeling, but adds to it various overlays of an evaluative, volitional and cognitive character. Feeling, in the Buddhist sense, is the second of the five aggregates constituting what is conventionally called 'a person'. The specific factors operative in emotion belong to the aggregate of mental formations (sankhāra-kkhandha), the fourth aggregate. All the four mental aggregates arise inseparably in all states of consciousness: feeling, perception, mental formations and consciousness. Because feeling is associated with emotional factors, the two tend to be confused, but on close analysis they are seen to be distinct.

Feeling arises whenever there is the meeting of three factors —sense-organ, object and consciousness. The meeting of these three is called in Buddhist psychology sense-impression, contact or impact (phassa). Sense-impression is a mental, not a physical, event. It is sixfold, as being conditioned either by one of the five physical senses or by the mind. This sixfold sense-impression is the chief condition for the corresponding six kinds of feeling born of contact through the five physical senses and of mind-contact. In the formula of dependent origination (paṭicca-samuppāda), this relationship is expressed by the link: 'Sense-impression conditions feeling' (phassa-paccayā vedanā). When emotions follow, they do so in accordance with the next link of dependent origination: 'Feeling conditions craving' (vedanā-paccayā taṇhā).

The feeling that arises from contact with visual forms,

sounds, odours and tastes is always a neutral feeling. Pleasant or unpleasant feelings do not always follow in relation to these four sense perceptions; but when they *do* follow, they then mark an additional stage of the perceptual process, subsequent to the neutral feeling which is the first response. But bodily impressions such as touch or pressure can cause either pleasant or unpleasant feelings. Mental impressions can cause gladness, sadness or neutral indifferent feeling.

Feeling is one of those mental factors (*cetasika*) common to all types of consciousness. In other words, every conscious experience has a feeling-tone, pleasant, painful or neutral, the latter being also a distinct quality in its own right. The subsequent emotional, practical, moral or spiritual values attached to any particular feeling are determined by the associated mental factors belonging to the aggregate of mental formations. It is the quality of those other mental functions that makes the co-nascent feeling either good or bad, noble or low, kammic or non-kammic, mundane or supramundane.

Since feeling, in its primary state, simply registers the impact of the object, in itself it is quite devoid of any emotional bias. Only when volitional evaluations are admitted will there appear emotions such as desire and love, aversion and hate, anxiety and fear, as well as distorting views. But these admixtures need not arise, as the emotions are not inseparable parts of the respective feelings. In fact, many of the weaker impressions we receive during the day stop at the mere registering of a very faint and brief feeling, without any further emotional reaction. This shows that it is psychologically possible to stop at the bare feeling and that this can be done intentionally with the help of mindfulness and self-restraint, even in cases when the stimulus to convert feelings into emotions is strong. Through actual experience it can thus be confirmed that the ever-revolving round of dependent origination can be stopped at the stage of feeling, and that there is no inherent necessity for feeling to be followed by craving. Here we encounter feeling as a key factor on the path of liberation and can see why, in the Buddhist tradition, the *contemplation of feeling* has always been highly regarded as an effective aid on the path.

The contemplation of feeling is one of the four foundations of mindfulness (*satipaṭṭhāna*). As such it may be undertaken in the framework of that meditative practice aiming at the growth of insight (*vipassanā*). It is, however, essential that this contemplation should also be remembered and applied in daily life whenever feelings are prone to turn into unwholesome emotions. Of course, one should not intentionally try to *produce* in oneself certain feelings just for the sake of practice; they should rather be taken up for mindful observation only when they naturally occur. There will be many such occasions, provided the mind is alert and calm enough to notice the feelings clearly at their primary stage.

In the contemplation of feelings, there should first be a mindful awareness of the feelings when they arise. One should clearly distinguish them as pleasant, unpleasant (painful) or neutral. There is no such thing as 'mixed feelings'.

Mindfulness should be maintained throughout the short duration of a specific feeling, down to its cessation. If the vanishing point of feelings is repeatedly seen with increasing clarity, it will become much easier to forestall the emotions, thoughts and volitions which normally follow them so rapidly and so often become habitually associated with them. Pleasant feeling is habitually linked with enjoyment and desire; unpleasant feeling with aversion; neutral feeling with boredom and confusion, and also serving as a background for wrong views. But when bare attention is directed towards the arising and vanishing of feelings, these polluting additives will be held at bay. If they do arise, they will be immediately recognized as soon as they appear, and that recognition may often be sufficient to stop them from growing stronger by unopposed continuance.

If feelings are seen blowing up and bursting like bubbles, their linkage with craving and aversion will be weakened more and more until it is finally broken. As attachments to likes and dislikes are reduced by this practice, an inner space will open up for the growth of the finer emotions and virtues: for loving-kindness and compassion, for contentment, patience and forbearance.

In this contemplation it is of particular importance to dissociate the feelings from even the faintest thoughts of 'I' and 'mine'. There should be no ego-reference to oneself as subject: 'I feel (and, therefore, I am).' Nor should there be any thought of being the owner of the feelings: 'I have pleasant feelings. How happy I am!' With the thought, 'I want to have more of them' craving arises. Or when thinking, 'I have pains. How unhappy I am!', and wishing to get rid of the pains, aversion arises.

Avoiding these wrong and unrealistic views, one should be aware of the feelings as a conditioned and transient process. Mindfulness should be kept alert, focused on the bare fact that there is just the mental function of such and such a feeling; and this awareness should serve no other purpose than that of knowledge and mindfulness, as stated in the Satipaṭṭhāna Sutta. As long as one habitually relates the feelings to a person who 'has' them, and does so even during meditation, there cannot be any progress in contemplation.

To be aware of the feelings without any ego-reference will also help to distinguish them clearly from the physical stimuli arousing them, as well as from the subsequent mental reactions to them. Thereby the meditator will be able to keep his attention focused on the feelings alone, without straying into other areas. This is the purport of the phrase 'he contemplates feelings in feelings' as stated in the Satipaṭṭhāna Sutta. At this stage of the practice, the meditator will become more familiar with the 'insight-knowledge of discerning mentality and materiality' (nāma-rūpa-pariccheda).

Further progress, however, will require persistency in the mindful observation of the arising and passing away of every instant of feeling whenever it occurs. This will lead to a deepening experience of impermanence (anicca), one of the main gates to final liberation. When, in insight meditation, the vanishing moment of feelings becomes more strongly marked, the impermanent nature of the feelings will impress itself deeply on the meditator's mind. This experience, gained also from other mental and bodily processes, will gradually mature into the 'insight-knowledge of dissolution' (bhaṅga-ñāṇa). On reaching this stage, the meditator will find himself well on the road to further progress.

It is within the practice of insight meditation that the contemplation of feelings can unfold its full strength as an efficient tool for breaking the chain of suffering at its weakest link. But considerable benefits can also be derived from this contemplation by those who, in their daily life, can only devote a little quiet reflection to their feelings and emotions. Even if they do this retrospectively, they will soon find that feelings and emotions are 'separable'. This reflective and retrospective contemplation will help them to a fuller awareness of feelings and emotions when they actually occur, and this again can save them from being carried away by the emotional cross-currents of elation and dejection. The mind will then gradually reach a higher level of firmness and equipoise, just by that simple procedure of examining and reviewing one's feelings and emotions.

This, however, should not, and need not, be made a constant practice. It should be taken up on suitable occasions for a limited period of time until one has become familiar with the mechanism of feelings followed by emotions. Such an understanding of the process will result in an increasing control over one's emotional reactions, a control gained in a natural, spontaneous way. One need not fear that focusing the mind on feelings and emotions in the manner described will lead to a cold aloofness or an emotional withdrawal. On the contrary, mind and heart will become more open to all those finer emotions like friendship, human sympathy and forbearance. It will not exclude warm human relationships, nor the enjoyment of beauty in art and nature. But it will remove from them the fever of clinging, so that these experiences will give a deeper satisfaction than is possible when the mind is overrun by tempestuous emotions.

A life lived in this way may well mature in the wish to use the contemplation of feelings for its highest purpose: mind's final liberation from suffering.

Protection Through Right Mindfulness

Once the Buddha told his monks the following story:

'There was once a pair of jugglers who performed their acrobatic feats on a bamboo pole. One day the master said to his apprentice: "Now get on my shoulders and climb up the bamboo pole." When the apprentice had done so, the master said: "Now protect me well and I shall protect you! By protecting and watching each other in that way, we shall be able to show our skill, make a good profit and safely get down from the bamboo pole." But the apprentice said: "Not so, master! You, O master, should protect yourself, and I too shall protect myself. Thus self-protected and self-guarded we shall safely do our feats."

'This is the right way', said the Blessed One and spoke further as follows:

'It is just as the apprentice said: "I shall protect myself" – in that way the foundations of mindfulness (*satipaṭṭhāna*) should be practised. "I shall protect others" – in that way the foundations of mindfulness should be practised. Protecting oneself, one protects others; protecting others, one protects oneself.

'And how does one, in protecting oneself, protect others? By the repeated and frequent practice of meditation.

'And how does one, in protecting others, protect oneself? By patience and forbearance, by a non-violent and harmless life, by loving-kindness and compassion.'

Saṁyutta Nikāya, 47: 19

This sutta belongs to the considerable number of important and eminently practical teachings of the Buddha which are still hidden like buried treasure, unknown and unused. Yet this text has an important message for us, and the fact that it is stamped with the royal seal of Satipaṭṭhāna gives it an additional claim to our attention.

The sutta deals with the relations between ourselves and our fellow beings, between individual and society. It sums up in a succinct way the Buddhist attitude to the problems of individual and social ethics, of egoism and altruism. The gist of it is contained in those two concise sentences:

Protecting oneself, one protects others.
Protecting others, one protects oneself.

These two sentences supplement each other and should not be taken or quoted separately.

Nowadays, when social service is so greatly stressed, people may be tempted to support their ideas by quoting only the second sentence. But any such one-sided quotation would misrepresent the Buddha's standpoint. It has to be remembered that in our story the Buddha expressly approved the words of the apprentice, that one has first to watch carefully one's own steps if one wishes to protect others from harm. He who himself is sunk in the mud cannot help others out of it. In that sense, self-protection forms the indispensable basis for the protection and help given to others. But self-protection is not selfish protection. It is self-control, ethical and spiritual self-development.

There are some great truths which are so comprehensive and

profound that they seem to have an ever-expanding range of significance that grows with one's own range of understanding and practising them. Such truths are applicable on various levels of understanding, and are valid in various contexts of our life. After having reached the first or the second level, one will be surprised that again and again new vistas open themselves to our understanding, illumined by that same truth. This also holds for the great twin truths of our text which we shall consider now in some detail.

'Protecting oneself, one protects others' – the truth of this statement begins at a very simple and practical level. This first material level of the truth is so self-evident that we need say no more than a few words about it. It is obvious that the protection of our own health will go far in protecting the health of others in our environment, especially where contagious diseases are concerned. Caution and circumspection in all our doings and movements will protect others from the harm that may come to them through our carelessness and negligence. By careful driving, abstention from alcohol, self-restraint in situations that might lead to violence – in all these and many other ways we shall protect others by protecting ourselves.

THE ETHICAL LEVEL

We come now to the ethical level of that truth. Moral self-protection will safeguard others, individuals and society, against our own unrestrained passions and selfish impulses. If we permit the 'three roots' of evil – greed, hate and delusion – to take a firm hold in our hearts, then their outgrowths will spread far and wide like a jungle creeper, suffocating much healthy and noble growth all around. But if we protect ourselves against these three roots, our fellow beings too will be safe. They will be safe from our reckless greed for possessions and power, from our unrestrained lust and sensuality, from our envy and jealousy; safe from the disruptive consequences of our hate and enmity which may be destructive or even murderous; safe from the outbursts of our anger and from the resulting atmosphere of antagonism and quarrelsomeness which may make life unbearable for them.

The harmful effects our greed and hate have upon others are not limited to the times when they become passive objects or victims of our hate, or when their possessions become the object of our greed. Both greed and hate have an infectious power which vastly multiplies their evil effects. If we ourselves think of nothing else than to crave and to grasp, to acquire and possess, to hold and to cling, then we may rouse or strengthen these possessive instincts in others. Our bad conduct may become the standard of behaviour for those around us – for our children, our friends and our colleagues. Our own conduct may induce others to join us in the common satisfaction of rapacious desires; or we may arouse in them feelings of resentment and competitiveness. If we are full of sensuality, we may also kindle the fire of lust in them. Our own hate may provoke them to hate and vengeance. We may also ally ourselves with others or instigate them to common acts of hate and enmity. Greed and hate are, indeed, like contagious diseases. If we protect ourselves against these evil infections we shall, to some extent at least, also protect others.

PROTECTION THROUGH WISDOM

As to the third root of evil, delusion or ignorance, we know very well how much harm may be done to others through the stupidity, thoughtlessness, prejudices, illusions and delusions of a single person.

Without wisdom and knowledge, attempts to protect oneself and others will usually fail. One will see the danger only when it is too late; one will not make provision for the future; one will not know the right and effective means of protection and help. Therefore, self-protection through wisdom and knowledge is of the greatest importance. By acquiring true wisdom and knowledge, we shall protect others from the harmful consequences of our own ignorance, prejudices, infectious fanaticism and delusions. History shows us that great and destructive mass delusions have often been kindled by a single individual or a small number of people. Self-protection through wisdom and knowledge will protect others from the pernicious effect of such influences.

We have briefly indicated how our own private life may have a strong impact on the lives of others. If we leave unresolved the actual or potential sources of social evil within ourselves, our external social activity will be either futile or markedly incomplete. Therefore, if we are moved by a spirit of social responsibility, we must not shirk the hard task of moral and spiritual self-development. Preoccupation with social activities must not be made an excuse or escape from the first duty, to tidy up one's own house first. On the other hand, he who earnestly devotes himself to moral self-improvement and spiritual self-development will be a strong and active force for good in the world, even if he does not engage in any external social service. His silent example alone will give help and encouragement to many, by showing that the ideals of a selfless and harmless life can actually be lived and are not only topics of sermons.

THE MEDITATIVE LEVEL

We proceed now to the next higher level in the interpretation of our text. It is expressed in the following words of the sutta: 'And how does one, by protecting oneself, protect others? By the repeated and frequent practice of meditation.' Moral self-protection will lack stability as long as it remains a rigid discipline enforced after a struggle of motives and against conflicting habits of thought and behaviour. Passionate desires and egotistic tendencies may grow in intensity if one tries to silence them by sheer force of will. Even if one temporarily succeeds in suppressing passionate or egotistic impulses, the unresolved inner conflict will impede one's moral and spiritual progress and warp one's character. Furthermore, inner disharmony caused by an enforced suppression of impulses will seek an outlet in external behaviour. It may make the individual irritable, resentful, domineering and aggressive towards others. Thus harm may come to oneself as well as to others by a wrong method of self-protection. Only when moral self-protection has become a *spontaneous* function, when it comes as naturally as the protective closing of the eyelid against dust – only then will our moral stature provide real protection and safety for ourselves and others. This naturalness of moral conduct does not come to us as a gift from heaven. It has to be acquired by repeated practice and cultivation. Therefore our sutta says that it is by repeated practice that self-protection becomes strong enough to protect others too.

But if that repeated practice of the good takes place only on the practical, emotional and intellectual levels, its roots will not be firm and deep enough. Such repeated practice must also extend to the level of meditative cultivation. By meditation, the practical, emotional and intellectual motives of moral and spiritual self-protection will become our personal property which cannot easily be lost again. Therefore our sutta speaks here of *bhāvanā*, the meditative development of the mind in its widest sense. This is the highest form of protection which our world can bestow. He who has developed his mind by meditation lives in peace with himself and the world. From him no harm or violence will issue. The peace and purity which he radiates will have an inspiring, uplifting power and will be a blessing to the world. He will be a positive factor in society, even if he lives in seclusion and silence. When understanding for, and recognition of, the social value of a meditative life ceases in a nation, it will be one of the first symptoms of spiritual deterioration.

PROTECTION OF OTHERS

We have now to consider the second part of the Buddha's utterance, a necessary complement to the first: 'Protecting others one protects oneself. And how? By patience and forbearance, by a non-violent and harmless life, by loving-kindness and compassion.'[7] He whose relation to his fellow-beings is governed by these principles will protect himself better than he could with physical strength or with any mighty weapon. He who is patient and forbearing will avoid conflicts and quarrels, and will make friends of those for whom he has shown a patient understanding. He who does not resort to force or coercion will, under normal conditions, rarely become an object of violence himself as he provokes no violence from others. And if he should encounter violence, he will bring it to an early end as he will not perpetuate hostility through vengeance. He who has love and compassion for all beings, and is free of enmity, will conquer the ill-will of others and disarm the violent and brutal. A compassionate heart is the refuge of the whole world.

We shall now better understand how those two complementary sentences of our text harmonize. Self-protection is the indispensable basis. But true self-protection is possible only if it does not conflict with the protection of others; for one who seeks self-protection at the expense of others will defile as well as endanger himself. On the other hand, protection of others must not conflict with the four principles of patience, non-violence, loving-kindness and compassion; it also must not interfere with their free spiritual development as it does in the case of various totalitarian doctrines. Thus in the Buddhist conception of self-protection all selfishness is excluded, and in the protection of others violence and interference have no place.

Self-protection and protection of others correspond to the great twin virtues of Buddhism, wisdom and compassion. Right self-protection is the expression of wisdom, right protection of others the expression of compassion. Wisdom and compassion, being the primary elements of Bodhi or Enlightenment, have found their highest perfection in the Fully Enlightened One, the Buddha. The insistence on their harmonious development is a characteristic feature of the entire Dhamma. We meet them in the four sublime states (*brahma-vihāra*), where equanimity corresponds to wisdom and self-protection, while loving-kindness, compassion and sympathetic joy correspond to compassion and the protection of others.

These two great principles of self-protection and protection of others are of equal importance to both individual and social ethics and bring the ends of both into harmony. Their beneficial impact, however, does not stop at the ethical level, but leads the individual upwards to the higher realization of the Dhamma, while at the same time providing a firm foundation for the welfare of society.

It is the writer's belief that the understanding of those two great principles of self-protection and protection of others, as manifesting the twin virtues of wisdom and compassion, are of vital importance to Buddhist education, for young and old alike. They are the cornerstones of character building and deserve a central place in the present world-wide endeavour for a Buddhist revival.

'I shall protect others' – thus should we establish our mindfulness, and guided by it devote ourselves to the practice of meditation, for the sake of our own liberation.

'I shall protect others' – thus should we establish our mindfulness, and guided by it regulate our conduct by patience, harmlessness, loving-kindness and compassion, for the welfare and happiness of many.

Notes

1. See *Life's Highest Blessings*, Dr. R. L. Soni, WHEEL No. 254/256.
2. See 'The Three Refuges', Bhikkhu Ñāṇamoli (BODHI LEAVES No. A5).
3. See *The Path of Purification (Visuddhimagga)*, Chapter VII.
4. Comy.: a religious life led for eradication of kamma.
5. According to the commentary, this refers to the Arahat, with regard to offences he may have committed either in this life before attaining Arahatship or in former existences. In his case, he is not bound by the limiting forces of greed, hatred and delusion.
6. The application of these two similes to kamma and its fruit, given in full in the original text, corresponds to the second and third paragraphs of this quote.
7. In Pāli: *khantiyā avihiṃsāya mettatāya anuddatāya.*

Glossary

Abhidhamma: the 'higher doctrine'; a strictly systematic philosophical treatment of the Buddha's teachings, presented in the third division of the Pāli Canon, the *Abhidhamma Piṭaka*.

Āhāra: nutriment both physical and mental:

Akusala: bad, unwholesome; a morally faulty state of mind having unfavourable karmic results.

Anāgāmi: 'a non-returner'; one who has realized the third of the four fruits of liberation and will attain final deliverance after being reborn in a higher world without ever returning to the human plane. (See *sotāpanna*, *sakadāgāmi*, Arahat.)

Ānāpānasati: the practice of mindfulness of breathing.

Anattā: egolessness, not-self or insubstantiality; the non-existence of an abiding self or substance. One of the three characteristics of all conditioned existence, the other two being *anicca* and *dukkha*.

Anicca: impermanence or change of all conditioned phenomena.

Aññā: the highest knowledge or gnosis attained by an Arahat.

Anusaya: the three 'underlying tendencies' – to lust, resistance (or aversion) and ignorance.

Appamaññā: the four boundless states – loving-kindness, compassion, sympathetic joy and equanimity. Same as *Brahma-vihara*.

Arahat, Arahant: 'the Liberated One'; one who has realized the fourth and final fruit of liberation, by which he has destroyed all mental defilements and attained release from the round of rebirths.

Ariya: noble, a noble one. The term refers collectively to the eight types of noble beings: those who have entered upon the four supramundane paths to liberation and those who have realized the four corresponding 'fruits' or completion stages of those paths. (See *sotāpanna*, *sakadāgāmi*, *anāgāmi*, Arahat.)

Bhāvanā: meditation, development of the mind, particularly towards tranquillity (*samatha*) and insight (*vipassanā*).

Bhikkhu: a Buddhist monk.

Bodhisatta (Sanskrit: Bodhisattva): a Buddha-to-be, one who is capable of attaining Buddhahood, particularly Siddhattha Gotama prior to his own Enlightenment.

Bojjhanga: the seven factors of enlightenment – mindfulness, investigation, energy, rapture, tranquillity, concentration and equanimity.

Brahma-vihāra: the four 'Sublime States' or Divine Abodes, being the meditations on loving-kindness (*mettā*), compassion (*karuṇā*), sympathetic joy (*muditā*) and equanimity (*upekkhā*).

Buddhānussati: the meditative recollection of the Buddha.

Cittānupassanā: the contemplation of (the state of) mind.

Dāna: giving.

Dhamma: There are numerous connotations of this term. Broadly speaking it means the ultimate truth of things and the Buddha's teaching as disclosing this truth; in a more restricted sense it means all phenomena and mind-objects or mental contents.

Diṭṭhi: views, especially wrong views and theories. The primary wrong views rejected by the Buddha are the eternalist view (*sassata-diṭṭhi*) and the annihilationist view (*uccheda-diṭṭhi*).

Dosa: hate, comprising all degrees of antipathy from the weakest dislike to the strongest fury.

Dukkha: suffering, both in the narrower sense of experienced pain and sorrow and the comprehensive sense of the unsatis-factoriness of all conditioned existence.

Indriya: spiritual faculties, here applied to the five faculties of faith (*saddhā*), energy (*viriya*), mindfulness (*sati*), concentration or calm (*samādhi*) and wisdom (*paññā*).

Jhāna: meditative absorption, usually divided into four or eight stages of increasing concentration.

Kamma: lit. 'action' (in Buddhism, never the 'result of action'). Wholesome and unwholesome volition, considered as produc-tive of rebirth and as generating favourable and unfavourable results according to a universal impersonal moral law.

Karuṇā: compassion. One of the four *Brahma-vihāra*.

Kilesa: mental defilements, chiefly greed, hate and delusion.

Kusala: good, wholesome; a morally faultless state of mind having favourable kammic-results.

Lobha: greed.

Mahāyāna: 'the Great Vehicle (or Career)'. Collective name for those later schools of Buddhism which advocate the Bodhisatta ideal.

Manasikāra: attention.

  Yoniso manasikāra: wise attention.

  Ayoniso manasikāra: unwise attention.

Māra: the Evil One; the personification of the forces antagonistic to enlightenment.

Mettā: loving-kindness. One of the four *Brahma-vihāra*.

Muditā: sympathetic joy. One of the four *Brahma-vihāra*.

Mūla: root or source. There are three roots of the unwholesome: greed, hatred and delusion; and there are three roots of the wholesome: non-greed, non-hatred and non-delusion.

Nibbāna (Sanskrit: *Nirvāṇa*): the ultimate goal in Theravāda Buddhism – the cessation of suffering, the Unconditioned, liberation from the round of birth and death.

Nīvaraṇa: the five mental hindrances: sense-desire, ill-will, sloth and torpor, agitation and worry and doubtful wavering.

Pañcakkhandhā: the 'five aggregates' into which the Buddha analyzes the individual personality: body, feelings, perceptions, volitions (mental formations) and consciousness.

Paññā: wisdom, understanding of the true nature of things. One of the five spiritual faculties.

Papañca: the multiplicity, or diffuseness, of inner and outer phenomena.

Pāramī: 'perfections'; the virtues and faculties required for the attainment of Buddhahood.

Paṭicca-samuppāda: dependent origination; the principle of conditionality which, in its primary formulation, accounts for the structure of conditions maintaining the round of rebirths.

Phassa: sense-impression, contact; the contact of consciousness with its objects occurring through the six senses (including the mind).

Rāga: lust.

Saddhā: faith, confidence. One of the five spiritual faculties.

Sakadāgāmi: 'a once-returner'; one who has realized the second of the four fruits of liberation and will attain final deliverance after returning only once more to the human world. (See *sotāpanna, anāgāmi,* Arahat.)

Samādhi: concentration of mind; calmness of mind. One of the five spiritual faculties.

Samatha: tranquillity; one of the two primary types of Buddhist meditation, the other being the development of insight (*vipassanā*).

Sampajañña: clear comprehension, developed in conjunction with the practice of mindfulness.

Saṁsāra: the beginningless round of rebirths.

Saṁyojana: the 'fetters' of mind binding to the round of rebirths.

Saṅgha: in the ordinary sense, the community of monks and nuns; in a higher sense, the community of noble ones (see *Ariya*). In this second sense, the Saṅgha is the third of the Three Jewels and the Three Refuges.

Sati: mindfulness. One of the five spiritual faculties.

> *Satipaṭṭhāna*: 'the foundations of mindfulness'; the meditative practice of right mindfulness, consisting in the mindful contemplation of body, feelings, states of mind and mind-objects or mental contents.

Sīla: virtue; morality.

Sotāpanna: 'a stream-enterer'; one who has realized the first of the four fruits of liberation and is assured of attaining final deliverance after seven more births at most. (See *sakadāgāmi*, *anāgāmi*, Arahat.)

Sutta: a discourse of the Buddha or of one of his eminent disciples.

Taṇhā: craving, threefold as sensual craving, craving for existence and craving for annihilation or non-existence.

Theravāda: lit. 'the Doctrine of the Elders'; the more conservative of the two main Buddhist traditions, in contrast to the more liberal Mahāyāna Buddhism. Based on the Pāli Canon, the Theravāda is prevalent today in Sri Lanka, Burma, Thailand and elsewhere in Southest Asia.

Triple Gem: the Buddha, the Dhamma and the Saṅgha.

Upekkhā: equanimity. One of the four *Brahma-vihāra*.

Vedanā: feeling, the affective quality of experience usually analyzed into pleasant, painful and neutral feeling.

Vipallāsa: the four great illusions or distortions of reality, i.e. wrongly taking the impermanent to be permanent, what is truly suffering to be happiness, what is void of a self to be a self and what is impure to be beautiful.

Vipassanā: insight into the true nature of phenomena as impermanent, suffering and not-self.

> *Vipassanā-bhāvanā*: the type of meditation which leads to this insight.

Virāga: dispassion.

Viriya: energy, vigour, strength of will. One of the five spiritual faculties.

A Bibliography of Nyanaponika Thera's Publications in English

Abhidhamma Studies. Researches in Buddhist Psychology, (Colombo: 1949; revised and enlarged edition, BPS Kandy, 1965.)

Advice to Rahula, Four Discourses of the Buddha, edited with Introduction, (BPS WHEEL No. 33, Kandy, 1961, 1974.)

Anattā and Nibbāna, Egolessness and Deliverance, (BPS WHEEL No. 22, Kandy, 1959, 1971.)

Anguttara Nikāya. An Anthology. (BPS Part I WHEEL No. 155/158, 1970; Part II WHEEL No. 208/210, 1975; Part III WHEEL No. 238/240, 1976; Kandy.)

Buddhism and the God-Idea, Selected texts, edited with Introduction, (BPS WHEEL No. 47, Kandy, 1962, 1970.)

The City of the Mind and Other Writings ('Courageous Faith', 'Why End Suffering?'), (BPS WHEEL No. 205, Kandy, 1974.)

Contemplation of Feeling, The Discourse-Grouping on the Feelings, (BPS WHEEL No. 303/304, Kandy, 1983.)

Devotion in Buddhism (WHEEL BPS No. 18, Kandy, 1960, 1972.)

The Discourse on the Snake Simile (Majjh. 22), Translated wth Introduction and Notes, (BPS WHEEL No. 48/49, Kandy, 1962, 1974.)

The Five Mental Hindrances and their Conquest, (Colombo: 1946) (in 'The Buddhist,' YMBA); (Colombo: 1947) (Bauddha Sahitya Sabha); revised and enlarged edition, (BPS WHEEL No. 26, Kandy, 1961, 1973.)

The Four Nutriments of Life, Selected Texts, translated with Introduction, (BPS WHEEL No. 105/106, Kandy, 1967.)

The Four Sublime States (Brahmavihāra), (Colombo: 1940); revised edition, (BPS WHEEL No. 6, Kandy, 1958, 1960, 1972.)

The Heart of Buddhist Meditation (Satipaṭṭhāna), (Colombo: 1954, 1956); revised and enlarged edition, (London: Rider & Co., 1962, 1969, 1972.)

266

The Life of Sāriputta, From the Pāli Texts, (BPS WHEEL No. 90/92, Kandy, 1966.)

The Power of Mindfulness, (BPS WHEEL No. 121/122, Kandy, 1968, 1971, 1976); (Santa Cruz (USA), 1972.)

'Protection through Satipaṭṭhāna', (BPS BODHI LEAVES No. B34, Kandy, 1967.)

The Roots of Good and Evil. An Anthology, with Introduction and Commentary, (BPS WHEEL No. 251/253, Kandy, 1977.)

The Simile of the Cloth; The Discourse on Effacement, Translated with Introduction and Notes, (BPS WHEEL No. 61/62, Kandy, 1962, 1974.)

The Threefold Refuge, (Colombo: 1949) ('Servants of the Buddha'); (BPS WHEEL no. 76, Kandy, 1965.)

The Worn-out Skin. Contemplations on the Uraga Sutta of the Sutta Nipāta, (BPS WHEEL No. 241/242, Kandy, 1977.)

All publications marked BPS are available from: Buddhist Publication Society, P.O. Box 61, Kandy, Sri Lanka.